ROBERT PENN WARREN:

THE DARK AND BLOODY GROUND

ROBERT
PENN
WARREN

THE DARK AND BLOODY GROUND

BY LEONARD CASPER

GREENWOOD PRESS, PUBLISHERS
NEW YORK

Reprinted in 1969 by Greenwood Press
A division of Congressional Information Service, Inc.
88 Post Road West, Westport, Connecticut 06881

Library of Congress catalog card number 71-90479
ISBN 0-8371-2131-0

Printed in the United States of America

10 9 8 7 6 5 4 3 2

For Linda

FOREWORD

In the preface to his *Selected Essays,* Robert Penn Warren
writes of "the variety and internecine vindictiveness of voices"
characteristic of the present age of criticism. With their variety he has no quarrel. He recognizes that the New Critics
themselves have never represented a "massive and systematic
orthodoxy, " that each perspective is partial only, and that any
view made responsible by intelligent scruple deserves respect.
However, vindictiveness that threatens legitimate variety is
another matter. Warren has noted the similarity between those
absolutists whose literary preconceptions are ultimatums
obliging unanimity and that "certain breed of professional de-
fender-of-the-good, who makes a career of holding the right
thoughts and admiring his own moral navel. "[1] Such critics are
no less than subtypes of the American Pharisee, archimage for
so many of Warren's characters.

If the reasonableness of Warren's own opinions also tempers most of his public remarks on others', it is probably not that he feels more indebted than Faulkner to his detractors, but rather that he knows too well the difficulties involved in searching for identity, as writer or man, and in reporting that search and its running image of self.

The unpreparedness of some readers has only confirmed his philosophy that neither popular nor critical opinion is half so important as self-knowledge. Nicholas Joost quotes him as saying, "Writing a best seller was gratifying . . . a writer writes to be read, but if he is a writer with any claim to seriousness he writes to be read on his own terms."[2] Although popularity lately has come running, with the list of prizes, Literary Guild contracts, and Pulitzer awards still growing, fuller recognition from comprehending minds dallies on the way.

That Warren was so long ignored by literary historians was sometimes an accident. To critics like Joseph Warren Beach and Alfred Kazin, writing at the end of the thirties, he was still an apprentice; for John W. Aldridge's *After the War Generation* (1951) he was too old to be a newcomer. At other times neglect has been the result of persistent shortsightedness. Understandably in *Writers in Crisis* (1942) Maxwell Geismar considered Warren a subspecies Southerner, to whom any criticism of Faulkner and Wolfe also applied. But in *Rebels and Ancestors* (1953) he reduced Warren further to equality of unimportance with Hamilton Basso. And reviewing *Band of Angels* for the *Nation* in 1955, he declared: "Mr. Warren has never been a primary fiction writer: that is to say, either a writer whose primary source is life experience, or a writer whose work is of major importance. His talent is literary and derivative. . . . He is a formalist and conceptualist—the perfect example of the dry mind. . . ." George Snell, in *The Shapers of American Fiction* (1947), concurs with Geismar; Alexander Cowie's *Rise of the American Novel* (1948) fails even to recognize Warren's existence. By contrast, Edward Wagenknecht allows Warren some small place at the end of his *Cavalcade* (1951), despite an alleged lack of unity in *All the King's Men* and a "tendency toward anticlimax" in *World Enough and Time* because it ends not at the gallows but with "a series of wild adventures among the Indians"![3]

More just amounts of attention are paid Warren by Frederick J. Hoffman, Ray B. West, Jr., and William Van O'Connor in their series of midcentury inventories. Hoffman writes that Warren's novels "suffer from an embarrassment of riches"[4] which nevertheless construct the world-trap to which man delivers himself inextricably by failure to find his own true motives. West says that the better short stories testify to the mystery of man's transiency and "his uncertain relationship with nature."[5] O'Connor relies on Warren for examples of Coleridgean brilliance and clarity in contemporary criticism. In the same series, however, surveying fifty years of poetry, Louise Bogan mentions Warren only as author, with John Crowe Ransom, of "sophisticated Southern balladry"[6] and excludes him altogether from the appended anthology. Such oversight is all the more inexplicable since as early as 1939, in *Modern Poetry and the Tradition,* Cleanth Brooks's close analyses already had shown adequate cause for considering Warren equal to Ransom in understatement and the ironic discountenancing of sentimentality. At that moment of equilibrium, one poet's career stood at mid-point, the other was concluded.

If mention in Miss Bogan's mid-century assessment is less than a celebration, the lengthy inquest conducted by W. M. Frohock's *The Novel of Violence in America* is an undeserved honor. Committed to finding correspondences with some procrustean proto-novel, Frohock is prevented from seeing Warren's long and thorough defense of choice as a native human condition. Warren's is not the Manichean concept of "choice," a dilemma in disguise which always victimizes one's self or another, but rather a true choice within the limits of human understanding. Something more of the artist in the round is apprehended in Bradbury's *The Fugitives* (1958), an objective account of many of Warren's writings, though handicapped by certain omissions and an overplaying of the game of "influences." Compensating for years of critical underreading by others, Bradbury can certify almost instinctively which words in two lines of Warren's poetry were fathered by Tate, which by Ransom, and which by Eliot, progenitor of them all!

Perhaps a more adequate expiation for the sins of omission in others has been the regard paid Warren's work in various published symposia. Unfortunately, in the earliest of these, *A Southern Vanguard* (1947), William Van O'Connor doubted that Warren could ever develop a more than naturalistic vision of life or divine higher than sociological solutions to human riddles. In Nicholas Joost's contribution to *Fifty Years of the American Novel: 1900-1950,* the confusion between the philosophy of Warren and that of his characters is continued so that the supposed naturalism of the first novels is mitigated only to the extent of later becoming "a mingling of Manicheism and Calvinism, " a despairing acknowledgment not of a corrupting universe but of man's incorrigible nature. The one error Joost laboriously avoids, the failure to discriminate between determinism and a faith in causality however dimly its uttermost reaches are traced, is committed throughout Harry Modean Campbell's essay in *Southern Renascence* (1953). Insufficiently appreciating Warren's ironic view of the infirmities of written history, he sees the historian-narrator's function in *World Enough and Time* only as a corrective to Beaumont's melodrama and as a thin disguise for the author himself. Charles Anderson's study of the interplay of violence and order, in the same volume, is a closer reading of Warren. Anderson suggests how polarized forces, proud anarchy and naïve traditionalism, can be reconciled where utopian aspirations are qualified by long suffering and practice. The value of formalist inquiry is also evidenced in much of the Carnegie Institute symposium (1957) on *All the King's Men.* The unprofitable orientation given these essays by A. Fred Sochatoff's initial equating of Willie Stark with Huey P. Long, and by Erwin Steinberg's pleading for a Willie uncharacteristically uncomplex, is rectified particularly by William Schutte's "The Dramatic Versions of the Willie Stark Story. " (Schutte however mistakenly assigns the motion-picture script to Warren.)

Whatever major errors are perceptible in such literary histories or symposia seldom originate there but rather are vestiges of long-lived uncritical habits which Warren himself, and others, have tried to re-educate and reform. These habits persist as well in the monthlies and quarterlies, sometimes even at the dead center of words meant to flatter his reputation. It is not only the merchant-critic or the man of spleen whose oversights outnumber his insights.

There is a handicap as well as a blessing in having been a Fugitive and a Southerner. Despite vehement denials all around, Ransom, Tate, and Warren are often presumed to be mirror images of each other, as are Capote, Wolfe, Faulkner, Carson McCullers, and a dozen others. A half-truth about Agrarian theory becomes a blueprint for a career still in full swing. (John Aldridge's *In Search of Heresy*, 1956, addresses itself with Falstaffian vigor to Warren's "parochial view," a straw man left by others on the battlefield.) One consequence has been the constant need for critics to rediscover Warren after each cycle of being satisfied with a stereotype for substitute. In 1936, Morton Zabel commended him for having achieved in *Thirty-six Poems* an identity equal to and separate from other Fugitives and for having therefore escaped "premature forcing of the intellectual manner." In 1944, Horace Gregory felt that with his *Selected Poems* Warren had finally stepped out of the shadow of the thirties' crippling propensity for group movements; and in 1958, George P. Garrett, reviewing *Promises*, patronizingly applauded Warren, poet of the True South, for finally reaching maturity! This critical lag, created by the inability to keep Warren long in timely individual focus, has its own consequence. He is required to renew at intervals his reminder that he is not primarily a writer of historical romances. Few readers long remember that the Tobacco War occurred during Warren's infancy, and that he and this century were in their thirties together.

Part of the additional penalty for being a Southerner is that Warren can expect to be called disillusioned ("morbid" was the favorite word in early reviews), primitivistic (John L. Stewart), a Puritan-Calvinist (Kelvin), provincial, Gothic, and apologetic (McCormick), and of course a determinist with naturalistic tendencies. Newton Stallknecht, in the 1950 *Folio* symposium on *All the King's Men*, decided that Warren was a "Christian *nihilist*." By sheer weight alone such critics have done much to negate the attempts of Southard, Nemerov, and Brantley to analyze the religious accent in Warren's work.

The fact that over a dozen of his critics have been Southern-born or former faculty members from Louisiana State Uni-

versity (Heilman, O'Connor) or students of his students (Brantley, Forgotson) has almost offset any advantage gained from
their familiarity with the availability of local culture as symbol
for everyman's crucible. Any suspicion of a "closed shop" con-
ference would only confirm the long-standing charge of provincialism and special interest. Ironically, Warren has sometimes been read with nearly as little perception by John Crowe
Ransom, Francis Fergusson, and Parker Tyler as by mid-
westerner John McCormick who, as late as *Brother to Dragons*
(1953), which implicates all humanity in its warnings of hubris,
could insist, "The Southern writer then only says to the out-
lander, suffer with us if you can, but only we really know how
to suffer."[7]

Another version of classification without differentiation is the
habit of so many reviewers of attempting explication of a book
by Warren not by reviewing the author's unique context first,
the direction that his prior thoughts have taken, but by incomplete comparisons with some more removed and irrelevant
portion of literary history. Because no adequate analysis is
made of the "original" function of a method or persuasion, the
question of *present* function in Warren is rarely permitted to
arise. The critic is satisfied with name-dropping and often,
by innuendo, a charge of imitation. Warren's work presumably
derives from Eliot, MacLeish, MacNeice, Faulkner, Spender,
Melville, St. Augustine, Santayana, Shakespeare, John Web-
ster, Milton, Dostoevsky, De Maupassant, Yeats, Aeschylus,
Graham Greene, Anatole France, D. H. Lawrence, Carlyle,
Bernanos, Kenneth Burke, Duns Scotus, Emily Dickinson,
Seneca. Not all readers have been as perceptive as Dudley
Fitts, writing of Warren's *Selected Poems* in 1944: "even in
responding to his influences Mr. Warren shows his strength.
He does not 'write like' Marvell; he becomes Marvell in our
time, as Yeats became Swift, as Eliot became Andrewes."
Perhaps only Pound, for resorting to calligraphy, has ever
been accused of greater learning. The most that is proved is
what has never been denied: that Warren does not repudiate
past knowledge but rather commemorates it by his contributions. More fruitful than the practice of specious and momentary analogy would be the sort of extended exploration of the
terms of a comparison made by Heilman, tracing the Hamlet

thread through *World Enough and Time,* or by the joint effort
of Thale, Gross, and Ruoff, in 1957, to describe certain Conradian functions in *All the King's Men:* the transformation of
narrator as spectator into narrator as participant, the sacrifice of initial idealism in Willie and Kurtz to the abiding codes
of their worlds, the "just lie" of Burden to his mother and of
Marlow to Kurtz's intended. Such examinations of resemblances have succeeded to the degree that they have provided
transport to literature, that is, worked from context to text.

Criticism by exclusion, by classification and uninformed
association, by underdeveloped comparison—to these retreats
from literature must be added the kind of inhibition enforced
by measuring literary value according to adherence to public
fact rather than to imaged truth. The sort of oversimplified
social interpretation of literature that economic distractions
in the thirties and privileged war years prescribed made possible the immediate misreading from which *All the King's Men*
suffered in the mid-forties. Though aware that, without reservation, Warren denied Stark's being a fictive disguise for Long,
and though forced to admit that no Anne Stanton had inhabited
the governor's life and that Long's investigator was quite unlike Burden, Hamilton Basso righteously argued that "once a
writer begins to write about these Hueys-who-aren't-Hueys,
the real Huey jumps up and clings to his back like the old man
of the sea . . ."[8] (or is fastened there by crusaders in search
of a cause?). The words have been prophetic. Despite Warren's
detailed "genetic explanation" of his theme and characters in
1953, facile identification of "The Boss" and "The Kingfish"
has continued in such articles as Rubin's "All the King's Meanings" (1954) and Sillars' "A Study in Populism" (1957).

To such obduracy is surely due, in some part, Warren's
continued experimentation with dramatic versions of *All the
King's Men*; his extension of Adam Stanton's role through the
figure of Jerry Beaumont, meretricious avenger of dishonored
womanhood, as further evidence that idealism self-deceived
can be even more dangerous, because sacrosanct and therefore unsuspected, than Executive pragmatism; his published
self-explications and aliterary protestations, such as the is-
suance of *Segregation* (1956), one of whose services was to
corroborate the theme in *Band of Angels* (1955), already threat-

ened by misunderstanding. Perhaps the semiopacity of reviewers is responsible, too, for consolidation of the New Critical view that, by deportment and dimension, literature tries to
prevent its experience from being vicarious only, inasmuch as
a poem or novel must live, first and afterward, always with
itself, just as a man must live with the utmost self-knowledge
permitted him. Even misplaced critical praise merely ratifies
Warren's personal philosophy that passage to identity, to even
temporary truth of self and of others, is treacherous and perplexing. That his belief in the need for such redefinition has
been found puzzling by critics as separate in time and sympathy as F. O. Matthiessen (1944) and Robert Lowell (1953)
is evidence enough for the existence of that need.

Abroad, the reputation of Robert Penn Warren has prospered
steadily, largely through translation of *All the King's Men* into
Italian, Scandinavian, French, and German. In 1958, even
while the "final" stage version of *Willie Stark: His Rise and
Fall* was being prepared for production in Dallas' Margo Jones
Theater, the Piccolo Teatro di Milano was waiting to borrow
the recent transcription for the French stage. The earlier
twenty-four-scene adaptation of the novel (first produced by
Erwin Piscator, in 1947, at New York's New School for Social
Research) had already played, in German, at the Ruhr-Fest-
spiele, and an Italian version had been contracted for to be
directed in Rome. What image of truth would be retained from
such readings and performances was another, and immeasurable, matter. In the past, European critics, like their American counterparts, have attenuated perception as often as they
have tried to extend it.

J. Létargeez, a Belgian scholar, observing Warren's prefatory warning that *Night Rider* "is not, in any strict sense, a
historical novel" (the French version goes farther: *"ce roman
aspire à être poésie, et non pas histoire")*, accepts Warren
as creator of a "stylized world." Yet Létargeez' sole interest,
the tracing of correspondences between the fiction of *Night
Rider* and the facts of the Tobacco War, implies that Warren
is to be approved to the degree that he was a just chronicler.
Michel Mohrt, in his introduction to the French translation of
All the King's Men, makes a suggestive contrast between Faulkner's "mythology of sin" and Warren's "mythology of redemp-

tion." However, through a series of elaborate distortions (sometimes based on such misinformation as the alleged use of federal troops in the Tobacco War) Warren's "hero-rebels" are interpreted as "champions of forever-lost causes" because of their "wild idealism that comes from being born in the great despair of the South"! The outlaws' martyrdom, in accord with "the Christian dogma of the reversibility of merits, " redeems "the arrogant, the politicos, " according to Mohrt. Less ingeniously, in Great Britain Irving Kristol has inclined to consider *Brother to Dragons* relevant only to an America, "incorrigibly Manichean and inwardly destructive, " where innocence and experience are still separable and antagonistic. Were this nation mature, presumably it would hold no ideals left unmodified and therefore could not suffer disillusionment. Kristol's attitude is too sophisticated to be cynical, but Warren's is neither. *Night Rider* has been called by Angus Wilson a sure portrait of the twentieth-century hollow man, the Koestlerian rebel committed to action on doctrinaire pretexts, but later Wilson forgets that the hollowness is characteristic of Munn and blames Warren for making him anonymous and unknowable.

Ironically, now that England's publication of Warren's novels is almost simultaneous with America's, imperfection due to haste is sometimes added to that due to distance. English reviewers have acquainted themselves with Warren's work just in time to lament signs of an abrupt decline in *The Cave* (1959). The *Times Literary Supplement* speaks of crude satire and the substitution of sexual motivation for "analyses properly rooted in social life and habit. " *The Observer* is concerned over this middle-aged mixture of apathy and pornography. Neither sees how all the major characters except Ike, who insists on utter loneliness, grope through desire for a reality beyond desire; explore the cave of one another, sometimes to escape the responsibilities of self through the violence of the act, sometimes to encounter a larger identity through the exchange of love. The gentlest unpremeditated touch, between husband and wife, lovers, child and parent, friends, betrays and thereby rescues the smaller self of ego. The erotic lunge is only blind counterpart to this quiet, knowing laying on of hands. And because he recognizes the naturalness of need's answering need,

Warren less than ever before has to usurp the story's role as
its own storyteller. The idiom used is the unschooled commonplace of a Tennessee town, but the gesture of hands speaks
adequately for all the inarticulate. Moreover, by dramatizing
the communal definition of self, the theme of *The Cave* need
not be established consciously in an *exemplum* or be confirmed
in any suddenly cleared, syllogistically ordered, self-consult-
ing mind. The novel's meaning is everywhere implicit in planes
of analogous dilemma and action, as well as in vast symbolic
correspondences. The same foreign readers who could not
appreciate the appropriateness of melodrama and ornate speech
in *World Enough and Time* now puzzle over the porous coarse-
ness of *The Cave*.

Nevertheless, the test of extraneous authority; effacement of
individual features through absorption into culture prototypes
and caricatures; dispersion of meaning through the reader's
assumption of the writer's role; failure to register irony and
consequent overidentification of author and character—none
of these errors in judgment is native to literature in translation
or in foreign context. At least two Americans have felt the
necessity of indicting catchword critics: Robert Heilman in
"Melpomene as Wallflower" and F. Cudworth Flint in "Mr.
Warren and the Reviewers." The most effective countercriti-
cism, however, has been the periodic appearance of seminal
articles, conspicuous "experiments in reading." By sheer
force of viewpoint these must survive, and not because they
are definitive or dogmatic. The possibilities of understanding
have been enlarged by the work of Norton R. Girault on prenatal imagery and symbols of rebirth functioning in *All the
King's Men*, Eric Bentley on the theme of self-knowledge in
the early novels, Robert Heilman on the recovery of tragedy
in *All the King's Men* and the interplay of multileveled action
and comment in *World Enough and Time*, Sam Hynes on the
persistence of withdrawal-return motifs in ranging narrative
forms, W. P. Southard on Warren's "religious poems" and
Howard Nemerov on the metaphysical structure and texture
of "Love's Parable."

This present study is offered more as verification and extension of such critics than as reprimand of any others. The

status of Warren criticism invites caution; the best opinions are now as always a calculated risk. Surely Warren, in the preface to his *Selected Essays,* is right to expect that electronic computers will never replace the necessary uneasiness of human decisions, literary or otherwise. Aware that conclusions often differ because of variations in reading, I have attempted through "narrative briefs, " interpretative (though I hope not arbitrary or distorted) résumés of the novels, to present the evidence on which the logic of my criticism is based, in a form complementary to exposition otherwise used. They are not offered in competition with Warren's own story-telling; but, since readings are especially variable where devices of implication are subtle and diversified, such briefs may serve to substantiate and justify larger conclusions later. They are the coordinates of my map of Warren. It is precisely because other maps can and will be drawn that this one is made public.

To avoid extra complication, Warren's works have been treated chronologically only within genres, although their relationship in time as well as in theme and method is established by cross-reference and review. Although at some later date undoubtedly his dramas will have a station of their own along the line of his development, at present it is more practical to associate them with the novels and narrative poems of which they are the stage versions, however modified. The checklist of Warren's work corrects Robert Stallman's trial list of Warren's poetry criticisms (1947), multiplies the genres, and extends the data to the present.

In the preparation of this critical account, the oppressiveness of personal limits has been lightened by many hands. Robert Penn Warren generously made available manuscripts and minute information, and his occasional criticism of his own writing has set an example in objectivity. It is with the permission of Mr. Warren and of Ralph Ellison that the uncut transcript of their conversations at the American Academy in Rome is quoted.

Work on the original of this book was encouraged and advised by Frederick J. Hoffman, and the present version has benefited from the judgment of Albert Erskine. The kindness of others, particularly those who offered acting scripts of Warren's plays, made possible whatever thoroughness is discoverable in these pages. I am indebted to Kerker Quinn of the University of Illinois and Wesley Swanson of the Illini Theatre Guild for *Proud Flesh*, A and B versions; William M. Schutte and the Department of Drama at Carnegie Institute of Technology for the script of *All the King's Men;* the William Morris Agency, for *Willie Stark: His Rise and Fall,* and Aaron Frankel for the acting script of the same play, with his directions intact. Research would have been impossible without assistance from the library staffs at the University of Wisconsin, Stanford University, Cornell University, Harvard University, and Boston College. To all these who have shown personal interest, my gratitude is due.

Portions of this study, in modified form, have appeared in the following periodicals by whose permission they are reprinted here: "The Founding Fathers, " *Western Review,* XXII (Autumn, 1957), 69-71; "Golden Eye, Unwinking: the Poetry of Robert Penn Warren, " *Perspective,* X (Winter, 1959), 201-8; "Mirror for Mobs: the Willie Stark Stories, " *Drama Critique,* II (November, 1959), 120-24; "Miscegenation as Symbol: *Band of Angels,* " *Audience,* VI (Autumn, 1959), 66-74. Criticism of twentieth-century avant gardism is adapted, with permission, from my article in the forthcoming *Dictionary of Poetry and Poetics,* edited by A. Preminger, F. J. Warnke, and O. B. Hardison, Jr., for the Philosophical Library.

Leonard Casper

Boston College
Chestnut Hill, Massachusetts

CONTENTS

PART I

POINT OF DEPARTURE

1

A SYMPOSIUM OF VOICES

Violence in the world of Robert Penn Warren's fiction is token for the individual's laboring emergence from and through his circumstances, the struggle of each man for self-consciousness. All life becomes a striving to be born. Man fears inconsequence, fears too much resemblance to others, as if to conform were to be deformed. His delivery is never without its midnight contortions, recoiling from the demands of nearly allegorical prenatal names: Fort, Bond, Burden, Stark, Starr.

Gradually, however, through time's slow attrition, he reaches the understanding that his fullest definition can be achieved only through submission to the knowledge of his imperfections as human and as himself. He cannot be what he would without admitting what he was. The hope that is geography deceives: man in his quest to realize himself cannot leave behind the person that he was, like a cache of old clothes. Nor is there

lasting sanctuary in that image of green innocence which he
tries to recapture from childhood. Nor does concealment of
identity in the crowd, surrender to the beck of leaders in exchange for security from the fret of responsibility, relieve
him of the need to find his own share of truth. Even his wife
cannot pierce his essential isolation. Man's is the hard, the
lonely, the devious and enduring way; worse, man is his own
adversary. Those characters who claim to have been reborn
and consequently to have found release are the ones who invite suspicion, seeming to be outside the living process.

Willie Stark, more than a monument to his own image, is
fully alive and therefore tortured. So are Perse Munn and young
Jerry Beaumont, self-flagellated with their iron-claw justice;
and Amantha Starr, in whose veins whole histories run. For
these, life is not simple locomotion but convulsion, the jar-
ring of particles in search of sanction and conciliation. But
from that dialectic motion, a "logic of experience" sometimes manages direction and a certain destination. Warren's
work, seeming to retrace relentlessly the same track of experience, nevertheless advances, in a way that can be cali-
brated, toward a fuller comprehension of itself. His growth
as writer parallels the crabbed and tacking movement, the
drift-and-compensation of his characters toward self-knowledge.

No contemporary American has more justifiable claim to
the title of man of letters. Major novelist, poet, critic, influential dramatist, and short story writer: these various strat-
egies, especially as they coalesce, are his resource for mediating between the groundling and the box seat. However, the
double-jointed, wisecracking intellectualism of a Jack Burden
is more than the price paid by the author to be admitted to two
publics, the best of two possible worlds. It represents the
sometimes hostile divisions in the modern mind. But perhaps
because as writer Warren has seen the necessity of conflict
and has experienced the constant accommodation of opposites
through formal ordering, he makes credible the mutual redemption of seeming incompatibles: world and idea, reality
and idealism, innocence and guilt. Moreover, Warren's nimble
vision has succeeded in discovering the more fortunate face
of the man most lowly fallen. For this reason all his humor

is not grim, though horseplay is rare. There is a delight in life, even in the darkness, something like childhood's "joy of fear." He cannot help answering the tootle of the passing riverboat horn which might speak his name; the glint of an unblued rifle sight, the smell of morning, catch his sense and stretch his mind, as if each day the author felt a little closer to home.

In the most outright statement of his position, "Knowledge and the Image of Man," an address delivered at Columbia University in 1954, Warren said of man:

In the pain of isolation he may achieve the courage and clarity of mind to envisage the tragic pathos of life, and once he realizes that the tragic experience is universal and a corollary of man's place in nature, he may return to a communion with man and nature. . . . Man eats of the fruit of the Tree of Knowledge, and falls. But if he takes another bite, he may get at least a sort of redemption.

The individual is the object of all this attention; but not as the Romantics conceived him, in full-winged flight toward perfection. The sin of the Enlightenment, earlier, had been its *denial* of sin. Warren compels acceptance of an older image, man with a sense of guilt proper to his nature and unpurgeable by the substitute delusions of psychiatry. Moreover, men are made accomplices in each other's guilt. (For example, the degrading Nazi image of man was made possible, he suggests, not by one leader's corrupted ego alone but by the needs of depraved millions; its horror conceivably contaminated even some of those who fought against it, using it to excuse their own brutalities.[1]) But as Cass Mastern discovers, conscience-stricken as any Warren character, this harsh fellowship is itself preparation for the propagation of a society of friends unknown to each other and the ultimate community of the freshly canonized.

The work of Warren dramatizes the American experience seen as the proportioning of self to society and traceable historically through the philosophies of Jonathan Edwards, Thomas Jefferson, Ralph Waldo Emerson, Charles Peirce, and John Dewey. Warren, however, abstains from the consensus of the "other-directed" societies of the twentieth century by refusing the individual the consolation of delegating to others authority for defining himself. The inadequacy of the Western dream, that compulsion to salvage innocence through restless migration and repeated beginnings, is a major recurring theme in Warren's novels and poetry. The continental spaciousness of the New World, the vastness of its free land, reinforced the image of man's unlimited capabilities already fullblown in the minds of pioneers as part of their rejection of Europe's closed societies and burrowing nationalism. Equality of economic opportunity on the frontier shaped American democracy while the silver cords of kings were being cut in Europe. But if the presence of free land is the fountainhead of republican forms and the crucible of civilization, what happens when that free land runs out? Which dies first, democracy or the supposition that it depends on bounties of open territory? Even Frederick Jackson Turner was disturbed by such a question and, according to Henry Nash Smith, retreated in the end to a blind faith not in the plenitude of natural resources but in the assumed wisdom of human majorities, rural or urban, propertied or landless.[2] The alternative view, which America itself chose, was the "theory of social stages" with its corollary of unlimited progress. Because a once agricultural civilization was superseded by an industrial civilization, the latter was presumed to be an improvement. The change of culture hero from rugged outlaw to ruthless tycoon was at least attempted. The newest horizon became a stretch of skyscrapers, pursued vertically in elevators (although their psalmist, Hart Crane, sometimes was embarrassed by his own beliefs and in *The Bridge* let Edgar Allan Poe hang garroted from a subway handstrap).

Warren's typically personal view rejects the state worship and general dehumanization which he associates with giantism in industry and pyramided cities. Yet his special agrarianism cannot abide either that naïve optimism, kin to the frontier dream of perpetually renewed innocence, which sprang from Jeffersonian neglect of man's dark ancestry.

These broad themes emerge with all the conviction that fullness of style at once intense and delicate can provide. They have been grounded by Warren in everyday particulars of a South which lends itself to metaphor and metaphysical expansion, as William Faulkner and Caroline Gordon have also demonstrated. Perhaps any particular, resurrected from the death of daily stupefaction, becomes universal. But the South in Warren's novels—those arsenic green fields of Kentucky, Tennessee, Louisiana—in a special way offers meaning to violence. This South, not at its worst, still takes pride in its "piety, " its feeling for kin and clan as well as its sense of tradition as a repository of values, a scheme of common sanctions and imperatives shaping present action.

The advantage of "piety" is that its disciples feel less solitary in an otherwise comfortless world that seems to reject man's importance and sometimes his very presence. At best, those wholly rejected, like Hemingway heroes whom experience no longer can surprise, succeed by strenuous effort in obtaining some recognition from the life that antagonizes them or even threatens mutilation. Others, weary of having to justify their existence, pretend to be blessed by being Outsiders. But even they demand recognition of their otherness from the world. The lyrics of such "bardic children" sound like cries of the demanding unborn, fearful of the world's premature death. Of those who dare to be themselves though not disengaged, two things are required: that they heft the full burden of their birthright, the sins as well as the splendors of their fathers, and that the self-respect earned through this act of "piety" not become cause for pride, the beginning of spiritual sloth.

The South has known firsthand the misery of rejection. Among people whose memories traditionally are long, the abuses of the Reconstruction period are recent, their effects still present. A war was lost, but not the cause which for the great majority of Confederate soldiers was the only cause: the right of self-determination. In defeat the need for asserting whatever was distinctive and valuable in Southern thought became increasingly important. Separation from the North during and after the war only helped to define what was enduringly Southern. Those years were too hotly fierce to be denied, and the memory of their reality has prevented any easy accommodation later to more abstract entities: government by statistics, or a ready-made corporation mentality, through which people are wholly possessed by their possessions.

The occupied states felt that they had been defeated by their dearest virtues: indifference to organization and distaste for urban industry. They could not agree that, because centralization of authority and the beginnings of mass production had made the North victorious, this marked a better way of life.

They had special cause, therefore, to beware the pragmatic reduction of human values. (Warren speaks of "the philosophy of the ad-man, the morality of the Kinsey report, and the gospel of the bitch-goddess."[3])

At least an active portion of the South has resisted attempts to convert the population wholesale into another North (the quarrel between the Vanderbilt Agrarians and the New Planners of North Carolina still persists). Instead, the South has sometimes argued that if its virtues were once its misfortune, now its misfortune may be its virtue. Military defeat still lies outside the national experience. Consequently, the country may be deluded into thinking itself immune to forces of history or at least may be tempted to continue its idolatry of material means and its arguments from success. A greater wisdom might be derived from the Southern experience of vulnerability.

The excruciating self-consciousness and willful complexity of the South, its ferment of tensions, its acceptance of complicity (even its rejection of the Negro often seems motivated less by denial of guilt than by fear of retribution)—these provide Warren with handy symbols for the fate of the modern self, subsectioned by Freud and indexed in depth by Jung. The malices of society are used to dramatize the inward twist of shadows in any man, anywhere. Despite exacting research, Warren has refused to restrict the identity of any character to that of Luke Lea or Huey Long or even Jereboam Beauchamp of Kentucky. The value of his characters is that they are composites and therefore can present a kind of truth not available from the proxies of history.

For the same reason, *Segregation*, Warren's report on conversations with "the voices in my blood," is subtitled *The Inner Conflict in the South*. It is not a poll. But perhaps it penetrates the actual status of events more deeply by not trying to represent in any simple fashion the complex course of thought of a whole region. A multitude of diverse individual opinions is put on record, but even the darkest of them is not cause for despair. Even allowing some room for permanent dissent and nonconformity, there is a basic resemblance among the less extreme differences which may reconcile them.

Without its bitterness being justified, the automatic hatred for all Negroes felt by the boy visiting the replica of Fort Nashborough is made more understandable with the realization that he has identified himself with those first settlers who, having defined themselves through violence in the face of extermination, must have felt heroic and distinct. (Similarly, Brown's brutal act of massacre in Conrad's *Lord Jim* is interpreted by Warren, in his Columbia address, as an attempt on Brown's part to assert himself as other than brute and, even by this awful outbreak of retribution, to affirm "the human need for moral vindication.") The boy's error is commonplace. It is a refusal to grant others the right to self-definition which one assigns to himself. Where democracy does not mean leveling or the interchangeability of persons in the manner of manufactured parts, only each man's history can discover what his personal definition will be, within the circumference of possibility inscribed by human nature itself. (The mistake of Jerry Calhoun, in *At Heaven's Gate*, for example, is to emulate the circle of subservients around millionaire Murdock because he thinks he wants recognition as an equal, that is, interchangeable identity. Since this is not equivalent to equal recognition of personal identity, Calhoun like many another Warren character fails himself the more he tries to be someone else. One sees here at least a faint reflection of the Southern principle of equality but separation, requiring mutual respect for differences. The same presumption made possible defense of reserved states' rights in a free confederation. In *Segregation* Warren implies that the South has erred not in maintaining this principle but in usurping the right to define the nature of its members' individual differences.)

The South above all, from its history of fearing abstraction, fearing death by being half known, should be able to appreciate this same fear in its Negroes. When Warren asked one Negro if segregation differed from the exclusions which any man "must always face at some point," the answer was "Yes . . . when your fate is in your face."[4] The Negroes' predicament thus becomes the epitome of the human predicament. Or as Warren himself expresses it, "I don't think the problem is to learn to live with the Negroes. . . . It is to learn to live with ourselves."[5] The fundamental conflict is personal before it is social; it is interior and universal. In other states, other nations, where Pharisees busy themselves confessing the sins of their brothers, the divisions nevertheless exist and the causes are the same. There is no relief from the responsibility of self-discovery. In the South at present it is the Negro who becomes the scapegoat of that "deep intellectual rub, a moral rub, anger at the irremediable self-division, a deep exacerbation at some failure to find identity."

Fortunately, it is this very rub, this resistance, which proves the possibility of change because it is a requirement of change. Movement through inertia is not the same as growth, since growth fulfills a pattern of challenge and response, often uproarious. One man told Warren that "segregation has test steel into the Negro race" which subsequently has not only endured but indeed has flourished. The same circumstances offer the South a chance to achieve its own moral identity by recognizing that of its Negroes. Its example then may rescue the nation from its present suicidal "rhythm between complacency and panic."

Warren has spoken of the cultural shock endured by the "closed and static society" of the South during the mass intrusion of industrialism after World War I. In addition, the experience of writers returning from overseas had to be assimilated, sometimes violently. But, above all, old racial tensions were aggravated by the growing self-consciousness among Negroes, insisting they were more than squatters on the horizon. The resultant imbalance between Southern loyalties and pieties created a social-moral crisis which Warren has compared with the changes awakened by the Italian Renaissance or by Elizabethan England. Warren considers the South today the region of cultural ferment that New England was before the Civil War.[6] In its tremors and trepidations, in its recall of conscience, one can divine the end of a whole nation's naïveté. The age of innocence has been outgrown.

Because of the availability of the Southern experience as symbol, Warren has used it to test his personal vision: the dialectic course of man's compulsion to be known. In this sense he is a Southern writer, rather than by a stroke of birth. It has offered authentic parables of action as counterpart to the rigors of soul-searching: the tobacco wars of Kentucky, modern Tennessee's bank-managed land grab, assassination of a red-neck political strongman, the stabbing of a frontier land reformer for having dishonored a woman, the ax-slaying of a slave by Jefferson's nephews, defilement of blood and human bondage during the Civil War. Warren's graphic documentation of Jim Bowie, lace-shirt patriot and friend of pirates, could describe as well a Hamish Bond or Colonel Fort:

But in a darker, more brutal world than the drawing rooms of New Orleans, men had seen the gray eyes in the handsome ruddy face go suddenly narrow, had seen the head draw back in the fighting stance with the left foot soft-catting forward, had seen the strong thumb, sprigged with red hair, set flat along the side of the heavy blade, ready for slash to either side or the upthrust to the guts.[7]

Or, had there been no Jereboam Beauchamp, Jerry Beaumont could have been made in the image of Sam Houston of the Tennessee wilderness. Of Houston Warren has written, "He was an actor in the deepest sense—the sense that makes a man see himself in history."[8] Under the touch of imagination, fiction and history become one flesh.

Each of Warren's characters is minutely prepared in place and time. But his novels, even regarded individually, are not only physically but also philosophically exciting. Action and idea have been recruited to reinforce each other. Such robust narratives would be incongruous, of course, as carriers of a tidy doctrine. The still developing canon of thought evident when these novels are illuminated by Warren's poetry and criticism is the result of the gradual redemption of action by idea, and of one literary form as a mode of experience by another.

A vision with such dimensions requires great capacity for discovering a sufficient variety of plausible human references to warrant its existence. Otherwise the new myth will be no more adequate than the old. A portion of Robert Penn Warren's peculiar endowment is the fact of his birth in a border state. Although Kentucky stayed loyal to Lincoln during the Civil War, Warren's favorite grandfather was an ex-Confederate officer. Similarly, while he was gathering Southern views on segregation, he was often treated with suspicion, not only because he had lived so long in the North but because of his Tennessee license and accent.[9] Under such conditions a man might feel estranged from all society. But Warren's adaptiveness has rewarded him instead with a multiplicity of perspectives which, taken with his versatility in the forms of art, constitutes a formidable talent.

His history as a writer can be traced through the interplay of these forms and perspectives and their occasional tendency to contradict or stifle one another in the struggle for emergence of one vision indivisible. However, the struggle would not have been so meaningful had it occurred in utter isolation. Warren has long believed that man is obliged to discover himself *in* the world. Even the necessary, constant act of trying to distinguish himself from the other elements of that world is impossible without an intimate comprehension of the "texture of relations" that complements the individual. Warren's voice has been one in a symposium of voices.

2

THE NEW CRITICISM

Student members of the new Fugitive writing group at Vanderbilt University had been allowed to use the typewriter in one of the faculty quarters for purposes of readying their manuscripts. It was at this machine that Allen Tate was seated one day early in 1923 when he noticed the approach of a tall, thin sophomore who walked with a sliding shuffle, "as if his bones didn't belong to one another." In a soft whisper the stranger asked to see a poem of Tate's, then in return showed one of his own, about the purple lilies of Hell. This young man was "Red," Robert Penn Warren, whom Tate was later to call "the most gifted person I have ever known."[1]

Soon afterward, Warren, Tate, and another Fugitive started rooming together on the top floor of the university's theological building in a room whose dingy plaster walls Warren decorated with Waste Land murals. Although the *Fugitive* magazine began

13

publishing Warren's verse in the summer of that same year, he did not officially become a member of the writing group until February, 1924. The delay indicates not lack of interest on Warren's part—a freshman chemistry course and the influence of both Donald Davidson and John Crowe Ransom had already dissuaded him from the study of science—but rather the casual manner of Fugitive membership in general.

James Frank, a Nashville business man, and his brother-in-law, Dr. Sidney Mttron Hirsch, had provided a meeting-place in the city where Vanderbilt students and faculty could read their own poetry or discuss philosophical and philological matters. Later Hirsch suggested that they begin a magazine and that it be called the *Fugitive,* after the image of the poet as wandering outcast, "the man who carries the secret wisdom around the world," in Tate's later phrase.

Although Vanderbilt did not encourage creative writing and at first officially frowned upon the *Fugitive,* the fellowship of interest which the self-styled outcasts felt survived the suspension of their magazine in December, 1925, when they discovered that editing was interfering with their dispersing interests. During this final year, Warren was coexecutive editor with Ransom, who was already helping Tate compound the formalist esthetic that would result in a New Criticism.

Young Warren had come from the tobacco lands of Todd County, Kentucky, via Clarksville, Tennessee. But after graduation in 1925, he became another Southerner-at-large, first as a teaching fellow at Berkeley and Yale, then as a Rhodes scholar in the quadrangles of Oxford. "Repatriated," he taught his way through the early years of depression in Memphis classrooms and at Vanderbilt, writing when he could, still mostly poetry. Later at Louisiana State University with Charles Pipkin and Cleanth Brooks, two other Vanderbilt alumni, he helped found the *Southern Review* where the manifestoes of rebel critics, disguised in dignity, first appeared. When wartime shortages of paper and funds suspended this magazine in 1942, Warren transferred to Minnesota and afterward to the drama faculty of Yale. Finally in 1956, he relinquished his classes for the sake of writing. He had already produced five novels, three volumes of poetry, a book of short stories, one biography, several anthologies and textbooks, as well as various critical essays and reviews.

Those thirty years of writing and teaching constitute Warren's exceptional contribution to the symposium of ex-Fugitive voices which, despite significant differences,[2] have spoken of a profound common interest in the condition of modern culture: the fractioning of man by scientism, the pragmatic reduction of literature to the rank of social documentation and therefore the need to define an art work through separation from all utility, the importance of restoring paradox to the human imagination and religion to the impoverished secular soul. Together they have helped sustain a renascence richer and farther reaching than those heralded by more clamorous avant garde groups.

In the twentieth century when denial or fragmentation of individual value by "other-directed" societies threatens, avant gardes are usually not riders of the first wave in man's undifferentiated surge forward, but rather those moving in crosscurrents to mass culture. During the first World War, the threat of self-destruction by technologically superior peoples revolted idealists once certain of the inexorable advancement of man. Through their art both the wartime Dadaists and the postwar surrealists illustrated the new psychic geography in which dreams were disguises for will, and in which will dominated ethical imperatives. Belief in the newly revealed night mind and the "collective unconscious" explained disillusioned survivors to themselves, those bitterly self-styled "unique eunuchs" who had to justify their existence and cleanse themselves of conspiracy in the holocaust. From Bergson, Freud, and Einstein they derived the primacy of relativism and disorder in life, so that they declared journalistic whatever was comprehensible. With Kierkegaard they accepted the world's absurdity as proof of God's otherness. The Italian futurists had already denied any usable past; the German expressionists distorted lines and surface areas in order to dramatize inner states of feeling. Increasingly, textural density, in a desperate attempt to fix the instant as fact despite cinematic flux, blurred distinctions between prose and poetry.

In the fifties, the new disillusioned have been those who watched Greenwich Village grow doctrinaire and decline. By

rejecting the role of the naïf, assumed in the "liberal" excitement of depression and a second war, many writers have been
led to greater disengagement from any cause whatsoever (except existential rapture) than even the 1918 expatriates. San
Francisco's "hipsters," desperately different, argue their existence through jazz idiom, as the Dadaists did, in search of a
self to express. The world's guilt overwhelms them more than
it has Warren, Tate, and Ransom. Antagonistic to Organization
Men without becoming disorganized, proud aliens in a world
that asks the atomic weight of art, like Eliot the three chief
Fugitives have demanded restoration of kinship and communion, an end to automatic writing and submission to gratuitous
experience. Yet for years they too have dangled limbs too close
to the common trap and have sought detachment from the *uses*
of poetry.

Several of the New Critics have remarked enviously the social and personal equilibrium of the Middle Ages, when each
man presumably was instructed in his divinely appointed portion of labor and served with humility under the obdurate shadow of final judgment. The "dance of death" organized their day
as well as their art, with its various disguises reminders of
the worm inside the skull, beneath the skin. Sackcloth was
man's other flesh; Gothic scrollwork, God's strange lean witness. But the faithful felt the promise of a heavenly communion which would more than compensate for suffering.

Modern man, by converting sin with psychiatric help into a
major but wholly corporal illness, has also betrayed his sense
of goodness to the cult of health. In times of descriptive morality, which rejects those restrictions that traditionally provided form and final purpose, each man must justify his own
existence or believe that his motives are momentary. Personal relativism, the pride of the romantics, has proved too
great a burden for the average ex-individual, no longer capable
of hourly decision. Despite having managed after centuries to
stand free of paternalistic kings and deities, prodigal man has
surrendered each new responsibility to machinery and to the
machine-state.

The inordinate pride in human reason and primitive goodness that was forerunner to personal relativism (and to the
greed of laissez faire; and to renunciation of fraternity by

the Reign of Terror) has its present-day equivalent. Scientific knowledge is in the average eye the only form of knowledge; to the new romantic, "progress" is the modern "god-term."

In the twentieth century the preferred alternative to problematic relativism as a test for truth has long been logical positivism, the flat dismissal of questions that are not "genuine" because not verifiable by sense experience. In preparing their *Principia Mathematica* (1910), Alfred North Whitehead and Bertrand Russell decided that certain recurring logical contradictions are entirely the result of illegitimate ambiguities in language. Under the stimulation of this discovery Rudolph Carnap's "Vienna school" of logical positivism suggested that philosophy employ the exacting methods of science for semantic investigation and control and thereby provide science with the invulnerable logic of carefully considered language. Even before this school gained recognition during the thirties, it had vehemently rejected metaphysics for being lyrical rather than representational in character. In Britain, metaphysicians were called "misplaced poets." In America the way was prepared for logical positivism by the tradition of pragmatism developed by Peirce, James, and Dewey, although the American tendency has been less formalistic and poetry seldom has been treated as a primitive and failing attempt at reproducing scientific statements of fact. [3]

Literature, indeed, has served to measure the actual accomplishment of science-oriented societies during the great unbroken years of war and threat of war. Interpreting its verdicts, Nathan A. Scott, Jr., has proposed metaphysical loneliness as the by-product of our times, the deepest fact of contemporary man's self-knowledge. The threefold image of man's estrangement and dereliction is exemplified, internationally, by Kafka's "cosmic exile" (absolute alienation), Ignazio Silone's community outlaw (relational), and D. H. Lawrence's victim of egocentrism (ontological). Fiction has assumed the task of presenting the dissonant philosophical character of its times—the dislocations and excommunications suffered by substituting a mechanistic view of behavior for a once tragic acceptance of life as purgatorial opportunity; a sense, among traditionless peoples, of the irreducible mystery of being and the dilemmas of freedom, made fearful by strange new contemplations of the

irrational; the cheerless finitude of individual man shrunken
among self-invoked visions of everlasting inventiveness; the
yearning after possibilities of humaneness in an age of slaughter.[4] Yet fiction's view of the inadequacies of science has been
most clear, ironically, to critics trained by the systematic
cautions of science.

While Whitehead and Russell were requesting the adaptation
of language for scientific service, another Englishman, T. E.
Hulme, through conversations with a coterie of his own coun-
trymen and certain expatriates from America, was also chal-
lenging the vagueness of a literature still recovering from
the influence of romantic thought and speech and from the concept of man as an "infinite reservoir of possibilities." Like
the positivists, he encouraged rejuvenescence of meaning in
words by summoning up the sense qualities of physical objects. The first result of this demand for concentration on
things-in-themselves through language equivalents (what Eliot
later called objective correlatives) was that, with the assistance of Ezra Pound and others, the school of imagist writers
was presented with a cornerstone. The imagist strategy was
to avoid extended intellectual comment by fixing an object as
it might be perceived if torn from time. The resultant poem
was often incisive but also detached, minute, naïve, and immo-
bilized. By the time of the posthumous publication of Hulme's
Speculations in 1924, the movement was already beginning to
lose its vanguard of prophets to the influence of the symbolists
and seventeenth-century metaphysical poets, largely because
of the apostasy of T. S. Eliot.

Although Eliot valued the imagists' recovery of the sense
world, he refused to deny the world beyond the realm of human
senses. Isolation of things-in-themselves was more proper to
controlled experiments in a laboratory than to poetry as a mode
of truth. In literature the sense image was to be only a point
of departure. He reintroduced controlled association of ideas,
resonant ambiguities whose very complicity conveyed theme,
synesthetic overlapping of responses, tolerance of extrarational
faculties, and the mutual qualification of idea and action.

As early as 1917, Eliot had already rejected the scientific
method as a way of life. With "Tradition and the Individual
Talent" he proposed an alternative to the short-term views of

personal relativism and logical positivism. The continuity of
such bodies of faith as the Christian tradition, he felt, provides
the lost intellect with a sense of home, even if at the price of
willed submission and suspension of doubt. The individual willing to serve esthetic and religious disciplines discovers that
he has achieved a degree of personal importance because tradition is so responsive that even the past can be partly modified
by present action. Submission, therefore, is not thorough; after
surrender there is restoration. But for literature the process
means making poetry an escape from personal emotion. By
not substituting the unreality of isolated objects for the unreality of isolated individuals, Eliot refined Hulme's attack
on romanticism.

The prevalence of the romantic attitude in literary criticism
made imperative a new approach, free of any predilection for
gossip, distraction through anecdotal history, and uninformed
impressionism. While the romantics hovered half-seen among
the peripheries of experience, those quasi-critics were equally
distant from the truth of fiction who employed doctrinaire paraphrases to fight their political, religious, or economic battles. [5]
Forgotten were the very formal matters—point of view, scale,
irony, deployment of symbols, thematic progressions—required
for any interpretation of subject. To comprehend the work of
art in its fullness became the esthetic motive of the New Critics, just as so many of them sought, through tradition, to rediscover man in *his* fullness.

Not all of the young critics, however, were so cautious about
what they rendered unto science as were Eliot and the Fugitive
group. I. A. Richards, who with *The Meaning of Meaning* (1923)
had been one of the first to make of language a philosophy, imported psychological methods into literary study with his *Principles of Literary Criticism* (1924). Poetry, he argued, cannot
be separated from science on the grounds that one is contemplative and the other practical. He insisted on the utilitarian
importance of poetry, at least as a storehouse of accessible
values or for its influence on the general improvement of response. Art cannot be a mere object of contemplation, for the
simple reason that the esthetic nature of man cannot be separated from his moral or intellectual nature. Literature appeals to all of the faculties—to the unified sensibility. On what

basis, then, can poetry be distinguished from science? The answer was that generality and vagueness of reference are the marrow of poetry! In *Science and Poetry* (1926) Richards predicted that the poetic view eventually would be neutralized by the scientific attitude and disappear, just as its predecessor, the magic view, already had. The pseudo statements of fiction gradually would be replaced by the certitudes of scientific discoveries. It was not until the mid-thirties, after Richards had experienced Coleridge on imagination and Mencius on the mind, that his esthetic changed habit sufficiently to be found presentable to the company of New Critics.

Views such as those of the earlier Richards, raising science like a monstrance over human heads, dismayed Allen Tate and John Crowe Ransom. Despite all the devices for controlling nature that science was placing at the disposal of mankind, men were not relieved even though liberated from the custody of religion and myth. In fact, mankind's new facility in the physical world only widened the area of moral responsibility. What man took into his own hands he could not ignore.

In essay after essay Tate defended self-determination (what Eliot had named the autotelic principle) in a work of art: "the poem is its own knower." The splendor of poetry was its inutility. Years later, in 1941, when John Crowe Ransom was already making his separate peace, Tate still rejected semanticist Charles Morris who, having cautioned that the pragmatic aspect was only one face of truth, had become Ransom's most nearly ideal critic. Tate's *On the Limits of Poetry* (1948) renewed the stormy attack on John Dewey and justified his temper as the proper defense of minority-held opinion against the "positivistic religion."

What has sustained Tate's seeming irascibility is the fear that scientism might give dangerous false comfort to man's agony of will and ache for power, as romanticism previously did. Like Eliot, Tate contrasts the scientist's oversimplified view of man with the complex body of unquestioned assumptions that underlay moral and rational reckoning during the Middle Ages. Also similar to Eliot's has been Tate's conviction that his religious nature is crucial to man and to literary purpose. Tate's defense of the private imagination often reads like a defense of the private soul. In a 1952 symposium of several former contributors to the Agrarian volume, *I'll Take My Stand* (1930), Tate wrote that he saw more clearly what must have been in his mind earlier: the impossibility of the humane life outside "the order of a unified Christendom."[6] By 1956, his astringent humor had been turned even against those who used the narcissistic view of literature as an excuse for "perfecting an apparatus for 'explicating' poems (not a bad thing to do), in a kind of prelapsarian innocence of the permanently larger ends of criticism."[7]

This same concern over the problem of restoring morality to a day-by-day world caused John Crowe Ransom, son and grandson of theologians, to write *God without Thunder* (1930) while at Vanderbilt. According to Ransom, myths are attempts to account for the fullness of nature in supernatural terms. Because such accounts are dependent on imaginative reconstruction, where ordinary sense cannot counsel with absolute confidence, a feeling of humility is quickened in the imaginer. Science, on the other hand, because it specializes in physical inquiry and so restricts the problems it can solve, is unjustifiably proud of its achievements. It chooses to ignore how many of its own basic principles—causation, substance, and the like—are matters of faith, "official fictions." Because it deals with only small compartments of experience, science actually is more abstract than metaphysics, which stretches out for the fullest comprehension of which the human spirit is capable. Eliot's "unified sensibility," Ransom suggested, might be contingent on the restoration of God the Father to the triune godhead of which Christ, for all his attractiveness as brother and lover of mankind, is only one manifestation. To salvage his soul, man must learn again to be God-fearing as well as God-loving. The most creative act of any society would be to sanction a religious myth in whose terms it could function. Ransom advised renewing the fundamentalist's submission to an unremittingly stern Old Testament divinity.

The relevance of these views to the formation of esthetic theory became clear by 1938 when *The World's Body* established a fundamental resemblance between art and religion on the basis of their being objects of sensibility and love, beyond possession or use. Ransom testified to the superiority of implicit communion to explicit communication.

However, by 1941, Ransom was willing to concede, in *The New Criticism*, that science had advanced sufficiently in self-analysis to deserve re-evaluation. I. A. Richards, for example, had ceased to talk of art as if it were a mode of passion (Ransom's own interpretation was that the forms of art are means of mediation and restraint, not release) and from Coleridge had learned that emotions in themselves are fictions. John Dewey's views in *Art as Experience* could be accommodated to the New Critics' understanding of poetry as the tension between structure and texture, requiring variety within uniformity, and reflecting the law of the actual world everywhere. Poetry makes knowledge accessible as revelation, divination of some universal system participating in both matter and spirit, but its contemplation in the realm of timeless actuality, the ultimate nature of things, is an end in itself.

The esthetic of Cleanth Brooks, another of the Vanderbilt school and several times collaborator with Robert Penn Warren, has become more severe and uncompromising with utilitarianism as Ransom's has mellowed. In Brooks's strict separation of dramatic truth from philosophical truth, advocated in *The Well-Wrought Urn* (1947), there is a return to the distinction once made by T. S. Eliot between poetic assent and philosophical truth. A work of art has a life and *persona* of its own which can be discovered only on its own terms, its emotional and intellectual organization. In this way literature is relieved of service as mere footnote to social history. The very value of fiction, according to the New Critics, lies in its fullness of expression, its awareness of the restless and multitudinous relations whose presentation is dependent on those same "impurities" of irony, ambiguity, and paradox that scientific discourse abhors because supposedly they disturb the clarity of simple, immediately useful facts.

Because Brooks was a Rhodes scholar at Oxford while *I'll Take My Stand* was being prepared, he did not contribute to it. Yet he had felt even then along with others that "Agrarianism" was not the best name for the contemplative life, informed by religion, that represented the Southern aspiration championed by the Vanderbilt group.[8] Moreover, despite strict applications of formalist disciplines in his own criticism, the epilogue to *Literary Criticism: A Short History* (1957), on which he collaborated with William K. Wimsatt, Jr., clearly accepts Christianity rather than Platonism or Gnosticism as the context in which their own preferred literary theory is most credible. While this maintains the sovereignty of literature, it does permit, as does the more recent Tate, an alliance between esthetic and religious motives. Far from being a recantation of earlier ideology, the new alignment suggests the still current intention of holding literature so remote from scientific discourse that the humanities and the human soul, to use Brooks's coupling, can be preserved.

3

THE NEW AGRARIANISM

The same bone-deep impulse to defend the humanities and the human soul against the world's drift to physicalism made these literary critics occasional critics of society as well. In 1926, after the *Fugitive* magazine had already suspended publication and its contributors were dispersing, Allen Tate and John Crowe Ransom proposed that they find further means for expressing what they felt about the place of Southern culture as an obstacle to that drift. Within a few years the new Agrarianism was heard, loud and importunate, throughout the land.

The sentiments it propagated were at least as old as French physiocracy's devotion to the soil, in the version imported by Jeffersonian democracy. That the heritage had continued unbroken up to 1860 was due largely to the presence of a Southern population only half as large as the North's in an area

twice the North's size. The importance of subsistence farming was affirmed after the Civil War by necessity and by the
bitter identification of manufacturing with the North's military
triumph. Then for nearly ten decades after 1870, the spread
of railroads, industrial monopoly, and agricultural landlordism
was resisted by a growing Populist movement, composed of
farmers' protective associations, benefit societies, and agricultural unions. Originally its members had hoped to improve
the general culture, but more and more they found themselves
involved in economic issues and development of class consciousness.

Although Populism was more successful in the Midwest, it
did manage to elect reform governors in the Carolinas and
Georgia in 1890 and to provoke Senate investigations of the
cotton crisis in 1894. By 1896, Populism was so strong that
the Democratic party almost lost its footing in the South. However, in the end, white supremacy became the obscuring issue. Every vote for the Populist ticket, which was supported
by the Alliance of Colored Farmers, one million strong, was
advertised as a proxy for the Republican party and as an invitation to Negroes to take office.

Subsequently the hold of Populism diminished rapidly, although the farmers' union movement was to rekindle ten years
later in the Black Patch tobacco wars of Kentucky, and agrarian reform was to set the pattern forty years later for Huey
Long's "Share the Wealth" program. In the interim it became
politically expedient to suppress the bloc of accumulating non-
caste votes. Southerners themselves chose to ignore the fact
that even in the Old South a large and important rural middle class had existed, in addition to slaveholders and "poor
whites." Slaveholding families had constituted only one third
of the antebellum white population, and 60 per cent of these
had owned less than five slaves. Rather than face the implications of such facts, even agricultural communities now chose
to believe the legend of the Old South's landed aristocracy and
plantation system. With that legend went the sense of a more
glorious loss, of a victimization so exquisite as to justify con-
tinuation of social underprivilege to former chattels.[1]

It was in fact from this very legend that the Fugitives agreed
they were fleeing. With firm politeness their June, 1923, edi-

torial refused Harriet Monroe's suggestion that they write of
the "soft silken reminiscent life of the Old South, " after the
fashion of Du Bose Heyward and Hervey Allen. Nashville not
only lay outside the cotton belt, but also had little industry to
trouble it. The Fugitives themselves were campus intellectuals who wanted to be considered cosmopolitan, not provincial. Yet as Tate has suggested, perhaps as Southerners they
possessed a quickened sense of the expense of postwar eras
in the coin of human confusion. In addition, many of the Fugitives had been Rhodes scholars or had otherwise resided in
England, where social conditions were awakening the Distrib-
utist movement; Hilaire Belloc and G. K. Chesterton, along
with other British intellectuals, had already seen the importance of restoring to each citizen some stake in society,
through redistribution of arable lands.

A crisis came during the widespread farm failures of the
1920's. Certainly the first issues of the *Fugitive*, with poetry
signed "Henry Feat002ertop, " "Roger Prim, " and "Robin Galli-
vant, " seemed remote from the question of whether or not
industrialism in the South should be encouraged to expand. Yet
as poets increasingly aware of the need for resistance to the
splintering of their own sensibilities, they had also to be conscious of the possible risk to themselves if the society of which
they were inescapably a part were shattered. The result was
that John Crowe Ransom, the leading Fugitive, undertook to
debate publicly with Stringfellow Barr from Virginia, who represented the view that industry should be encouraged to cross
into the South; and several of the other ex-Fugitives, now Agrarians, jointly published *I'll Take My Stand* (1930).

Warren, Tate, and Andrew Lytle favored calling the volume
A Tract against Communism, a title more appropriate than
the chosen one to the actual outlook of those essayists anxious
to recall man to the realization that economic motive is not
his most distinguishing property. Nevertheless, although only
four Fugitives were numbered among the Agrarians, the newer
rebels retained something of the old defensive attitude of those
original "outcasts, " and the hint of Dixie provincialism per-
sisted.

Although the introductory statement of principles, drafted
by Ransom, did not commit each of the separate authors to the

stand of the others, yet they all clearly saw as their common target industrial brutalization of man. By dedicating itself to the discovery of labor-saving methods and machinery, science had assumed that labor could not be a happy function of human life but was practiced only for the pleasure of its rewards. Worse, by giving man the illusion of controlling nature, science deprived him of his religious respect for the mysterious and contingent; nor could the arts thrive where there was this general decay of sensibility. A culture close to the imponderables of nature, however, would renew feelings of responsibility and humility.

Ransom sought a favorable comparison between Southern and European cultures in their temperate pursuit of material wealth, permitting sufficient leisure for the free life of the mind. At work or at rest, however, man was informed of his precarious position in the universe. Donald Davidson's appeal for a community that would not isolate the artist, man of sensitivity, was balanced by Lyle Lanier's reproach of John Dewey's collective emphasis (and the heresy of progress toward always undetermined goals). Tate's own version of the limits of possible human development offered religion's reminder of evil's daily attrition and casualties from error.

Compared with the scope of these convictions, Robert Penn Warren's contribution, "The Briar Patch," might seem a minor comment. Nevertheless, its importance to Agrarian theory becomes more evident with the realization that in 1930 two thirds of the Southern population was rural and one third of the land in the deep South was farmed by Negroes. In Warren's own canon, the essay early established his eagerness to bring abstract theory to terms with facts historically deployed, and his conviction—extrapolated nearly thirty years later in *Segregation*-that the doom and hope of Southern white and Negro are inextricable.

Mainly, "The Briar Patch" was an attack on industrialism for reducing Northern Negroes to a status worse than slavery, and on the North in general for depriving the Negro of the trust and confidence of other Southerners and for prying him loose, thereby, from the land or small town where "by temperament and capacity" he still was most at home. Warren predicted that, unless Southern rural life was reconstituted around agri-

cultural communities for all men, the Negro would continue
to run off to an abstract life in Northern factory cities. (In
one sense, Warren's views have remained constant between
"The Briar Patch" and *Segregation*. He has always urged each
man to be himself, rather than try to pass as someone else.
But in "The Briar Patch," presuming like other Southerners
to define the identity of all Negroes, Warren fashioned an image
for emulation that allowed no choice or change. This contradiction, this expectation of conformity, Warren does not repeat in
Segregation. He clearly recommends that each man, without
qualification, be allowed to explore and report on the unique
nature of his own potential.)

The Agrarians had agreed that the volume would emphasize
Southern opinion west of the Appalachians, with only a rare
guest comment from the Atlantic states. To the number of
readers alienated by this decision, others were added when it
was discovered that yeomen farmers were being eulogized. As
Donald Davidson explained later, "It was not a rhapsody on
Pickett's Charge or the Old Plantation."[2] Tate's biography of
Jefferson Davis and Frank Owsley's *State Rights in the Confederacy* had already been too candid in their criticism of the
South. The authors were accused of disloyalty, and when they
contributed to the volume of Agrarian essays, repudiation of
the combined views mounted.

On a secondhand hearing of Agrarian arguments, the average Southerner, perhaps already overinvested in ideas of the
Leviathan state and the parade of material progress, did not
take kindly to the volume. Probably he was wondering why the
Agrarians were not in the fields following a bull-tongue plow,
instead of talking in parlors (in *The Web and the Rock*, Thomas
Wolfe refers to them as "lily-handed intellectuals"). Or he
simply failed to understand the religious motive which was
foremost with many of the Agrarians but which did not find
clarification in their own minds until years later. The fact
that *I'll Take My Stand* received its most serious consideration
in the North would seem ironic had not the Agrarians in their
statement of principles welcomed being accounted members
of a national movement.

Some Southerners, however, did recognize that the issues
being raised were timely and just (a few months before the

book's publication there had been severe rioting around the
mills of North Carolina and Tennessee; that same year the
stock exchange had collapsed from overcapitalization). *I'll
Take My Stand* provoked the printing of other books, such as
Culture in the South (1935), edited by W. T. Couch, who, though
personally convinced that the Agrarian representation of both
farming and industry was exaggerated, allowed arguments of
every complexion. Some deplored what Southern agriculture
had come to mean: preoccupation with staples that could not
be eaten, child and woman labor, and nearly two million tenant
farmers. These looked to railroads and Northern aid for rescue. Others argued that such conditions proved the need for
small-scale subsistence farming on land privately owned. And
there were reminders that Southern arts and handicrafts could
not be mass-produced; if the surrounding society became industrial, such arts would be isolated and become perishable.

In *Who Owns America? A New Declaration of Independence*
(1936), jointly edited by Herbert Agar and Allen Tate, the kindred views of Agrarians and British Distributists, a movement led by Hilaire Belloc, found common expression. All the
writers shared a consuming respect for individual rights and
responsibilities; and, although most of them directed their
efforts against corporate interests and toward economic de-
centralization and free tariffs, several (Belloc and Cleanth
Brooks) scrutinized the materialist threat to man's religious
nature, the foundation of his culture.

Robert Penn Warren's contribution to this volume, "Literature as a Symptom, " explained how powerful and coherent cultures of the past helped shape their literatures, while modern
man has to invent his deepest assumptions before proceeding
to his art. Yet the artist in any age has the responsibility of
transcending his own personality by finding some portal for
traffic with his community. The modern citizen-artist has two
choices: he may associate himself with either regionalism or
the proletarian movement. The latter, valuing a class abstraction above the individual, reduces literature to propaganda in
the name of its own dogmas and saints. Regionalism, on the
contrary, holds hands with its past and has a stake in real
property, land, and its local inhabitants.

Although the Agrarians, by nature a loose confederacy, abandoned Vanderbilt, and a few abandoned the South altogether, their interest in social issues survived and was provided public forum throughout the thirties by the *Southern Review* and the *American Review*.

Of the Fugitive originals, Allen Tate has proved the most durable spokesman on these issues. In *Reactionary Essays* (1936) he described the weakness of the Old South. Its "peasantry, " the Negroes, w?re not free, nor could they identify themselves with their landlords, but they were liberated from one system only to become enslaved by finance capitalism. Southern Protestantism, a "non-agrarian and trading religion, " bore its share of blame for not protecting what could have been one of those great free-peasant soils in which cultures find their roots. *Reason in Madness* (1941) honored Jeffersonian society, in which the owning and working of land was considered not so much a livelihood as a means of exercising man's moral nature. *On the Limits of Poetry* (1948) claimed that America, by rejecting the regional consciousness of the classical Christian world that valued imagination and limited acquisitiveness, had penalized herself with a new provincialism that saw utopia in material welfare and legal justice. Finally, in the reappraisal of Agrarianism conducted by *Shenandoah* magazine in 1952, Tate joined others in declaring that their emphasis earlier should have been more firmly religious than economic.

In the same symposium, John Crowe Ransom observed neutrally that no section of America will ever again see an identifiable agrarian society. Aside from his statements in *I'll Take My Stand,* he had long since abandoned scouting for such a society. *God without Thunder,* published the year of the Agrarian tracts, generally ignored occupation in recommending reconstruction of the religious nature of man. His later books and the *Kenyon Review* itself have authorized an esthetic concern indifferent to the influences of material environment.

An identical pattern of disengagement is visible in the issues of the *Southern Review*. From its initiation in 1935 to the summer of 1940, with Charles Pipkin in charge, assisted by Cleanth Brooks and Robert Penn Warren, articles published were predominantly socioeconomic or political in nature. After the three men became coeditors in 1940, the core of the magazine turned almost completely literary and remained so during the last year of publication, with Brooks and Warren as editors (Pipkin died in 1941).

The recurrence of this withdrawal pattern in Warren, Ransom, and Tate indicates the position of Agrarianism within the comprehensive measure of their philosophies. As writers they encountered problems of art, in the attempted statement and solution of which they inevitably found and explored related problems in the world of Hoover Republicanism and the New Deal. The fullness of an agrarian condition, as counterforce to the mining of human resources by industry, could not be accomplished by them alone, especially because they acknowledged their amateur standing in the area of economic opinion. Therefore, confirmed in their knowledge that art must remain undefiled by scientism, they returned to the writing and criticizing of poetry and fiction, where they were most at home.

Only rarely has Warren allowed himself the luxury of direct comment on the effects of America's political economy. In 1939, some time after Donald Davidson had complained that Roosevelt's policies were only comforting human casualties, not changing the way of life that was their cause, Warren was more moderately expressing sympathy with the objectives of the New Deal, though its basic philosophy seemed in need of clarification: ". . . I believe that unless ownership and control can be more widely diffused American democracy is a goner."[3]

More recently, in his Columbia University address, while reaffirming his regard for the aims of the New Deal, Warren has admitted one reservation, one "heartburning"—the condescension and leveling, the "Common Man-ism" that the New Deal sometimes promoted, rather than helping each man stretch up to his highest manhood.

Other than these outcries of the individual voice against collectivism, Warren has reserved whatever remnant of Southern Agrarianism lingers for momentary appraisal in the portraits of "commentators," those outside the ruck and moil, in his novels—Willie Proudfit, who, tired of blind butchery or prairie buffalo, leaves the West and returns to the hard, godly farm labor of his ancestors; or Wilkie Barron's father, whose green memories of Old Virginia cannot make the "midnight pulse" of Jerry Beaumont pause—or in Warren's quiet admiration for his own father, manifest in "Blackberry Winter" and "When the

Light Gets Green, "or in his "Kentucky Mountain" poems. There
is little in his fiction of the undramatized preaching of primitive
virtue that an indulgent Faulkner allows Ike McCaslin in "The
Bear, " nor are his symbols usually so transparent as Eula in
The Hamlet, the "fertility goddess" of Frenchman's Bend.

The tendency among Agrarians to permit the dissociation of
esthetic and social concerns undoubtedly made possible those
exacting methods of literary concentration identified with the
New Criticism that they were then intent on developing. However, it went far to discredit the seriousness of the Agrarians'
social motives, which, once subordinated, rapidly threatened
to become submerged. And in Warren's case the critic's habit
of detached contemplation has harassed the novelist's need
for dramatic construction. The narrative movement of *World
Enough and Time,* for example, is toward a revelation pro-
hibited from being tested in the completeness of action. Jerry
Beaumont is beheaded almost at the very moment of his understanding that the poles of life, word and flesh, must meet at
some common equator toward which they yearn. He dies too
soon to experience their reconciliation or to learn how it would
be possible.

Nevertheless, Warren's respect for physical presence has
redeemed his work, rescuing it from pure idea or abstract
doctrine. Like Jack Burden, startled to a pause by the silver
tatter of water tossed by a distant, unknown woman before the
moving window of his train, Warren's traveling eye is taken
by the instantaneous image, immediately assigned some hieratic role. Characteristically, the homing-pigeon minds of his
grown men never quite return all the way but cannot forget
either mother on the stairs, the stringiness of grandpa's thighs,
the baying of dogs in the evening, the land that is not background but rather inseparable grain of the human bodies gradually settling into it.

In "Causerie, " poet Allen Tate mourned Warren's skepticism
toward miracles.[4] But in a sense dramatic writers cannot afford miracles. Myth must be volunteered to explain even the
inscrutable. Greater faith has been ventured by Warren on
vigilant exertion, at the daily job of earning his share of insights, and on the caution of self-correction. This is his risk,
and part of his achievement.

PART II

THE IMAGINATIVE JOURNEY

4

APPROACH TO LITERATURE

In 1939, having already published *Thirty-six Poems* and *Night Rider*, Robert Penn Warren, then an instructor at Louisiana State University and editor of the *Southern Review*, valiantly refused to think of these various labors as rivals for his attention. Instead he endorsed teaching for requiring the writer daily to attempt clarification of literary questions. Nearly ten years later at Minnesota, while admitting that universities have their comic aspects and the defects of any institution, he still felt that the academic process produces "truly profound and humanistic people who serve as a sort of buffer against the jittery, fashionable kind of thing."[1] The problems of academic life are acknowledged in only two of his short stories, "The Life and Work of Professor Roy Millen" and "The Unvexed Isles, " as well as in student Bohemian portions of *At Heaven's Gate*. Nevertheless, it is the counterpointing of scholarly and

colloquial elements that establishes the dominant structure of
Brother to Dragons, the *Ballad of Billie Potts,* and *At Heaven's
Gate,* while the union of these same elements in the tangled
idiom of Jack Burden determines the texture of *All the King's
Men.* Moreover, the critical textbooks prepared by Warren,
clearly devices for mediating between literature and the middling imperfect intellect, are proof of his scholastic apostle-
ship.

The mission of the Agrarians was to reconstruct man in his
fullest image; the New Criticism searched for a corresponding
wholeness in art. This was the community of interest that kept
intact those fugitives from Southern poverty who propagated
their beliefs through Northern colleges. This was the resource
of scruple that kept Warren's daily attendance on literature
disciplined.

In 1936 with two other members of the Louisiana faculty,
Cleanth Brooks and John Purser, Warren had edited *An Approach to Literature,* which brought the new revolution to the
barricades by defining fiction as ideas dramatized, committed
to action within the art frame, and by restoring to poetry,
through the inlaying of attitudes and felt force, its function to
communicate more than denatured ideas. Although the anthology
takes for granted that esthetic experience is best defined by the
act of reading the selections offered, clearly that experience is
not mechanical accumulation of historical fact, the finger-
pointing of sociological sermons, or the pigeonholing of a work
in some ready-made genre. Literature is rescued from the
useful arts. No longer is it valued as a container for canned
propaganda, for ideas that can be judged before experienced.
Meanings do not exist except as theme is tempered by a con-
fluence of formal relations. Being seized by the experience is
all; seizing it, nothing. What one does or fails to do as a result
of his reading is irrelevant to literary values.

The same careful redirecting of intrusive nonliterary traffic
back to main thoroughfares is evident in the second edition of
An Approach to Literature (1939), even where additional selections have been introduced that warrant Agrarian comment.
For example, its explanation of how Robert Louis Stevenson's
"Pulvis et Umbra" discovers that man's enduring moral sense
and inclination to dignity will survive even the scientific view

of an abstract, mechanical cosmos might have become a manifesto in defense of the humanities. However, the remarks are
justifiable as necessary explication of the problem treated by
Stevenson.

Similar validation may be offered comments attached to
Hardy's story, "The Three Strangers" (the simplicity and
humanity of the English villagers in this story are made comparable with agrarian life in the Tennessee mountains); or
Arnold's "Culture and Anarchy" (the authors concur with his
abhorrence of machines but propose no revolt); or Shakespeare's *Antony and Cleopatra* (because the Roman world,
lacking the ripeness of immemorial custom, lacked also orderly ambition, Antony had no worthy project to serve).

Brooks and Warren, who, as editors of the *Southern Review*
in those same years, were occasionally printing their friends'
Agrarian tracts, could have drawn striking comparisons with
the condition of modern man, using such literature as corrobo-
rative documents. Yet their hand shows not here but elsewhere,
in minor ways and then perhaps without deliberation. Their pursuit of a "code" of conduct throughout the crannies of "Frankie
and Johnnie" betrays an Agrarian overenthusiasm for spying
traditions behind every blink and gesture. And their critical
lingering over Pompey, whose subordinate presence in *Antony
and Cleopatra* hardly merits such attention, can be explained
only by the attractiveness they find in any character who clings
to "an ideal beyond mere practical success, " as Pompey does
when he refuses to murder the triumvirs in his power. It is
not difficult to imagine how such earmarks served as controls
for classroom discussion. What is remarkable, however, is
their infrequency.

Selections substituted in the 1952 edition of *An Approach to
Literature* must have offered a more serious temptation to be
didactic. William Carlos Williams' "The Use of Force" makes
possible a gloss on how violence, even in a good cause, may
unmask the evil in man's dark nature, his delight in cruelty.
A story by Hemingway becomes the occasion for an attempted
definition of his stoic code, primitive proxy for a lost tradition. Another, by Eudora Welty, seems to satisfy the editors'
predilection for expiation performed after the manner of the
Ancient Mariner—or of modern man, guilt-stricken and, al-

though not completely adequate to the business of obtaining
forgiveness, still humanized by a remnant moral sense. In
Katherine Anne Porter's "Noon Wine," "the difficult definition
of guilt and innocence" becomes visible when a man's soul is
flayed alive, proof that the more available an experience, the
greater its value.

It is even possible that *Murder in the Cathedral* was included
in the 1952 edition for dramatizing through caustic self-ques-
tioning the ambiguity of man's divided motives in a manner
symbolic of contemporary sensibility, much as *Hedda Gabler*
is domesticated with the observation that Ibsen's play is a
parody, tragic scale no longer being possible in a world that
has forfeited its "sense of mission."

Still, the preponderance of critical notes warns that what
appears to be descriptive of the modern scene is not *ipso facto*
prescriptive. The truth of fiction has a timeless value, beyond
usefulness. Apprehension of such truth is an end in itself. On
that presumption the editors can speak of the social criticism
in Arthur Miller's *All My Sons* as endorsing neither revolution
nor even revulsion. Any use to which literature may be put to
prepare a "better citizenry" is always parenthetical. Distinction is still made between poetic assent and philosophical belief resulting in changed behavior.

Substantially, this approach remained unchanged in both the
1938 and 1950 editions of Brooks and Warren's *Understanding
Poetry,* although the later edition did find it necessary to explain that, because most critics mistook literary history as
an end in itself, the editors temporarily had overexalted concentration on the internal coil and fret of structure. History
that illuminates the anatomy of art is allowable, but the work
of art itself does not re-enter history and is not to be judged
as if it did. The absence of lesson-drawing in the notes to *Understanding Poetry* demonstrates the editors' ability to follow
their own advice—that the reader's participation in the experience of the poem is more important than participation of the
poem in his.

Understanding Fiction (1943) did not find editorializing so
easy to avoid. Although Brooks and Warren insist that concepts
in fiction need not be agreeable but only worthy of serious exploration, in several of their own interpretations preference

for a particular world view appears. Caroline Gordon's "Old
Red" becomes the occasion for a lengthy gloss on the value of
fishing as an art involving the whole man harmoniously. Fishing remote from pleasureless abstract activities engaged in
for gain becomes a symbol for the contemplative life, a symbol
for the art of fiction itself.

From the *Southern Review* they reprinted "The Face" by
Louis Moreau, a story of outcasts and homesickness which they
translated metaphorically into that cosmic loneliness all men
feel, having committed some "crime" which makes their past
world irrecoverable (paralleling the original sin motif employed
in Warren's *Eleven Poems on the Same Theme*, 1942). This
interpretation is reinforced by their reading of Kafka's "Penal
Colony": that no man finds his true "homeland" in the natural
world of time. Yet they admire the isolated individualism of
Emily, in Faulkner's "A Rose for Emily, " because like Hemingway's heroes she makes life come to her on her own terms.
To her community she is both scapegoat and idol because of
her refusal to conform. The Hemingway code itself is found
valuable not as a sufficient end, but as a stopgap measure allowing man means to collect breath and self-respect, and time
to reassert his next-to-godliness. In accordance with the Jeffersonian ethic, forms and codes function to preserve the individual during the season of his fulfillment. The more self-
reliant he is, the less necessary they become.

Such examples, although in the minority, do show a pattern
of appeal and by their implicit use of ideas in fiction modify
the "purity" of Warren's literary approach. If a definition of
esthetic experience is to be formulated through study of these
texts, their notes included, such experience would seem forced
to acknowledge the progressive momentum that contemplation
of a world vision, through fiction, generates. The notes are
either an intrusion and betrayal, or recognition of a legitimate
pull beyond literature in itself.

Similarly, the *Modern Rhetoric* of Brooks and Warren, though
designed for less advanced or less specialized writers, finds
opportunities to direct attention toward the editors' characteristic interests, in the process of illustrating the kinds of discourse and the function of their respective techniques. The
ethical reproach to pragmatic tests for salesmanship is in-

troduced in the 1949 edition and elaborated in 1958. Furthermore, in both volumes the readings seem carefully chosen
protests against the amorality and professional self-interest
of scientism. Christian Gauss's "The Threat of Science" has
its counterpart later in C. S. Lewis' "The Abolition of Man."
By position, each serves to refute or qualify preceding remarks
by scientists on their role in society. The skepticism of John
H. Troll in "The Thinking of Men and Machines" is similar to
Warren's own prefatory remarks (about the absence of a "complete criticism") in his *Selected Essays:* "Who would punch the
cards? Somebody has to punch them, if you have such a machine, and the hand that punches the cards rules the world."
Both editions reprint Carl Becker's Socratic undercutting of
Communist ideology; and both relate "The Hickman Story, "
of a Negro's ordeal among Northern Pharisees. Some of the
earlier special interests are not repeated: an attack on John
Dewey's verbal incoherence as a sign of failing intellectual
discipline; Aldous Huxley's satire on the naïve romanticism
of Wordsworth, confusing cultivated gardens with man's natural
state; and repeated reference to the text itself as a "tissue" of
analyses and a "tissue" of examples, illustrating the insep-
arability of form and substance. Apparently the revised edition
considers this concept adequately established and both Dewey
and Wordsworth no longer dangerous. Despite such apparent
relaxation, the readings in *Modern Rhetoric* are far from random examples. A consistent philosophical attitude makes them,
implicitly, converse with one another.

Even a running survey of the book reviews and critical articles that Robert Penn Warren wrote without collaboration establishes that the broader view of esthetic experience is the one
at which he gradually arrived, as he learned the nature of
criticism through its practice. His first reviews in the *New
Republic,* written while he was a graduate student at Yale and
Oxford during the late twenties, show the influence of Fugitive
conversations. Warren praises Hawthorne's devotion to the
Puritan sense of sin in the face of his contemporaries' vul-
garization of its tragic possibilities. Traditionless Sherwood
Anderson, on the other hand, is charged with inflicting his
personal shortcomings on his characters, who shrivel into
enigmatics, creatures of simple impulse and capricious oc-

casion. James Joyce is said to have rejected the world because he understood it; Anderson because he was at a loss to understand even himself. The Jeffersonian image of man is more acceptable to Warren who, reviewing a biography of the Virginian, commends the libertarian for never having abandoned his belief in the natural aristocracy of the intellect and the contractual concept of society, with their corollaries, inalienable personal and states' rights. Jefferson's political program turned westward for renewal of the old East and, feeling that North and South had followed different principles of development, did not want to force either to become like the other through overcentralization of government.

Such partiality for discussing content, often detached from formal matters, was intensified by Warren's return from England to teach in the South, at Vanderbilt and Louisiana State. Discussing several books on the Reconstruction period, he speaks of the failure of the "Second American Revolution" under pressure from bayonet and Northern dollar. However, to protect himself from charges of being a professional Southerner, in "Not Local Color" he instructs fellow critics not to change their standards when judging writers from their own home state. As illustrations he contrasts the genuine regional detail, inseparable from character, in three Faulkner novels with the mediocre novelists' choice of decorative local color and the blurred motivation of fatalism. Yet that same year, 1932, "A Note on Three Southern Poets" marks Warren's reconsideration of poetic intention rather than execution. Donald Davidson is pictured engaged in an "adventure of self-definition" through a search among ruins for some sane continuity of values; Ransom's use of irony, according to Warren, grows out of his feeling for the artist askew in a misshapen society; and Tate is described busily redefining morality and its status in the present age. These three, still resident in the South, are presented as examples of poets sustained by their region. In contrast, the increasingly abstract quality of John Gould Fletcher's poetry is related to his self-exile as artist and citizen from his native South, resource of his earlier strength.

Although treatment of this sort traces the main movements of author's minds, only in Fletcher's case is the effect of the poet's attitude on his poem adequately shown. That the work of the loyalist Southerners was already rich and varied in 1932 is an assertion lacking evidence. Yet in 1939 it was Lionel Trilling's use of this same approach in *Matthew Arnold*—praising the artist for his antipathies rather than assessing his actual contributions—that annoyed Warren. Trilling had failed to see that Arnold, by detaching himself from his age because its industrialism reduced men to abstraction, succeeded only in writing poetry equally abstract, a poetry of idea unredeemed by the senses.

The change to a more vigorous and genuinely formal method of criticism that this review indicates can be accounted for by the fact that by 1939 Warren had already coedited *An Approach to Literature* and *Understanding Poetry*. Furthermore, the *Kenyon Review* had been created as a special agency for the New Criticism, and it was here that Warren's reviews began to appear. At a time when fashionable liberals could find no storage space for Faulkner's books in their salvage of usable fiction, Warren was discussing thematic repetition in *The Hamlet* and confirming the interpretation of George Marion O'Donnell (another Vanderbilt graduate) that the central conflict in Faulkner's work is between humanistic traditionalism and naturalistic industrialism.

After becoming advisory editor of the *Kenyon Review* in 1942, Warren rebuked Van Wyck Brooks for acting as if formalist talk was vulgar. The New Critics' position was that the more literature is enriched by rational commentary, the more fully, paradoxically, the reader can be absorbed by its illusions.

Warren's last review for fifteen years, in the *Nation*, illustrates the New Critical principle of complexity by contrasting Faulkner's novels with one whose characters are motivated by environment alone. Faulkner's concern with illustrating the conflict of Southern values transcends regional history only inasmuch as it provides "the forms in which the pyschological and ethical issues are dramatized."

Even in such reviews, engaged with individual works, one can feel the critic drawn to the formulation of general statements, and the growth of coherent realms of emphasis. These, however, are better (because more elaborately) traced in the history of Warren's articles. The division of allegiance in Robert Penn Warren's critical articles is strikingly marked

by differences in the editorial policies of those two magazines
where the major portions of his work appeared: the *American
Review* and the *Kenyon Review*.

In the first issue of the *American Review*, in 1933, editor
Seward Collins pledged his magazine to the cause of those he
called "Radicals of the Right." He intended to carry on the
work of the *Bookman*, whose policy had been set by conserva-
tive moralists Irving Babbitt and Paul Elmer More; to nurture
available traditional philosophers, neo-scholastics of the "Aris-
totelico-thomistic" variety; and to promote in America the
ideas of Belloc's and Chesterton's British Distributists. Organized as a median to the extremes of communism and finance
capitalism, the Distributists favored a monarchy to preserve
established order and to protect individual rights (egalitarian
societies, they said, were proven failures, and there were too
few dependable aristocrats). A principal right of each citizen
would be his share of the redistributed land of the realm. Collins himself, in several editorials, praised the concept of con-
stitutional monarchies to inhibit communism, and, although
he admitted that his opinion might be premature, he volunteered Mussolini and Hitler as examples of benevolent strong-
men!

Nevertheless, the *American Review* itself courted a variety
of persuasions, several of which labeled Fascism latter-day
imperialism or non-Marxist collectivism. Finally, however,
the *Review* was forced to discontinue because as late as 1937
it was still publishing the unpopular pro-Franco articles of
Douglas Jerrold and others like Ross J. S. Hoffman's "The To-
talitarian Regimes." Although Hoffman classified both Nazism
and communism as party dictatorships, Italian fascism was
declared safe because Mussolini, by not interfering with the
Vatican, had proved himself to be in the same main line of advancement as Aristotle, St. Thomas, and Machiavelli!

Guilt by association lingered over the names of other contributors, particularly those modern critics who advocated
a strict (but self-imposed) regimen of traditional order in literature, religion, or political organizations. In 1946 certain
readers, trying to make of Willie Stark in *All the King's Men*
the dictator whom they could assassinate vicariously without
the expense of understanding, found that Warren resisted iden-

tification of Stark with Huey Long, remembered the *American Review,* and cried fascism. Evidently they were not familiar with his articles.

In 1933, a year after flaying John Gould Fletcher for exiling himself from his native soil and audience, Warren in the *American Review* dubbed another Southerner, Sidney Lanier, "The Blind Poet" because his process of "etherealization, " supposed to sublimate the world of sensations, ignored the senses from the outset. It was Lanier's reverence for science that conditioned him to abstractions. Ironically, he "failed to perceive that the science he adored was the handmaid of the industrial system he detested, " just as he objected to the domination of society by trade even while he applauded the nationalism that permitted it. A romantic in his theories of personality and progress, Lanier could appreciate only doctrinaire works of art.

This social-political assumption that human potential is perverted by overcentralized government, heavy industrialization, commercial domination, and the romantic theory of progress is antithetical to both fascism and communism. Such ideologies depend on chauvinistic or racial propaganda, total control by a central agency, glorified trade syndicates or the industrial proletariat, or the romance of dialectical progress toward a classless society. On the contrary, such assumptions are the province of Jeffersonian democracy modified by an Agrarian fear of the scientific bias and skepticism of unlimited progress.

Although at the time of this article Warren was still three years away from *An Approach to Literature,* in his criticism of T. S. Stribling just before leaving his instructorship at Vanderbilt he had managed to achieve a temporary balance between social and esthetic concerns. By recording facts but never values, Stribling, according to Warren, inevitably distorts the facts also. He pictures the lowborn Southerner as a congenital brute rather than as the result of postbellum "commerical liberalism. " Although one may suspect that the Lanier and Stribling articles were written to rehearse certain nonliterary notions, still their ideas are duly assimilated in the discussion of total form.

Nevertheless, Warren's next article, "John Crowe Ransom: A Study in Irony, " in the *Virginia Quarterly Review* (1935) describes ideas as important in themselves instead of merely contributing to the fullest meaning of poetry. Although the article is eventually a tribute to Ransom's poetic method, its approach is roundabout, proceeding slowly through restatement of the prose of *God without Thunder*. So that it might recover through poetry its former sensitivity, a decadent world is pricked with ironic wit by Ransom. Gradually he has ceased to confuse the true agrarian impulse with the simplicities of bucolic life.

Warren's "A Note on the Hamlet of Thomas Wolfe, " which appeared a few months later, is stricter in its loyalty to literary demands. The charge lodged against Wolfe, as previously against Lanier, is romanticism, the naïve exploitation of disordered experience. As autobiography, where nothing is irrelevant however insignificant, Wolfe's work could be excused, but, since his characterization of Gant and his own lyric mystique tend to objectify his life in terms of fable, his novels must be judged as such. Because often the moving force in these novels is a furious, unformed sense of hidden destiny, the narrative cannot be sustained. Warren is clearly disappointed not by the themes involved—old Gant, vigorous symbol of the fatherland of human origin to whom the disillusioned son seeks constantly to return, has a particularly strong attraction for him—but by Wolfe's inability to transform those abstract themes into literature.

Perhaps because at this time Warren was at work on textbooks, his study of Southern writers showed increasing interest in the formulation of general principles. After a brief omnibus review in an early issue of the *Southern Review*(1936), Warren proceeds to contrast regional and proletarian writers so successfully that, retitled "Literature as a Symptom, " the review was used in *Who Owns America?* later that same year. Proletarian writers are dismissed because their major objective is the propagation of certain ideas abstracted from recognizable person and place, and their orientation is toward a shapeless future. Regionalists, on the other hand, in touch with the realities of time and locale, are more likely to see the origin of literature in human conduct.

Allegiance to characteristic truth of place became the principle by which Brooks and Warren defended literature, after

a few months, from a certain Mrs. Gerould's advice that Southern writers forget "degenerate realism" and stoop to sentimentality by writing of urban life where civilization prospers.
The reply made is that violence has as significant a part in
modern as in Elizabethan literature, and that the antithesis of
an agrarian society is not urbanism but industrialism. Later
that same year Warren repeated this position in "Some Don'ts
for Literary Regionalists, " making society responsible for
the literature it produces but saying nothing of the responsibilities of literature to that society.

In 1937, a year before publication of *Understanding Poetry,*
Brooks and Warren anticipated the conscientiousness of their
approach with "The Reading of Modern Poetry" in the *American
Review;* and, contributing to a 1939 symposium in the *Partisan
Review,* Warren wrote that, although he had often been in sympathy with the social protests of the thirties, he felt it unfor-
tunate that "a lot of writers seem to have felt that if the protest was all right the writing would automatically be all right."

Warren's full acceptance of his formalist stewardship, leaving social comment to others, is indicated by the fact that since
1937 all but one of his critical articles have appeared in *Kenyon
Review, Sewanee Review,* or the *Southern Review.* The exception is his *New Republic* study of Faulkner in 1946, twelve
years after their last previous use of his work. His first article for the *Kenyon Review,* "The Present State of Poetry: In
the United States" (1939), explores the two major antiliterary
movements in the contemporary world. Political leftists with
a narrow view of "social significance" have become specialists
in journalism; and many regionalists have risked their integrity
through overreliance on local pieties and peculiarities. Paren-
thetically, Warren adds a caution that seems to describe his
own attitude toward his characters: "This does not imply that
the reader should confront the poem with a virtuous ignorance,
for the reader's appropriate and best innocence, which asks
the poem that it be nothing more than a poem, comes late
rather than early, and it is to be earned." Because the thirties
were reducing literature to letter carrying, young writers were
little interested in older poets other than Eliot, and he was
read only because they mistakenly considered him an apostle
of despair. The leftists themselves unconsciously began, like

Eliot, in neither Marxism nor dialectical materialism but in
"a religious faith based on the brotherhood of man, a myth of
redemption and regeneration." But the decade's vindictive distractions prevented such writers from seeing into themselves.
Poetry had become fragmentary, and bodies of work incon-
siderable, because the "abiding central impulse" behind even
opposite political barricades seemed forgotten or despised as
unserviceable to the cause. The myth required by modernity
exists but is not available simply because men cannot believe
"that poetry is worth writing." The *uses* of poetry, in the sense
of the working world, have exhausted its higher properties and
its authority.

This regard for the autonomy of literature is evident not
only in the contents of the *Southern Review* during the joint
ministry of Brooks and Warren, but also in the rare editorial
that appeared after Pipkin's death in 1941. Howard Mumford
Jones had been trying to rescue literature from the Marxists'
attempt to make it subservient to their ideology. The editors
find him just as guilty of impressing literature into the service
of sentimental Americanism.

When wartime expenses forced the discontinuance of the
Southern Review in the spring of 1942, subscriptions were
transferred to the *Kenyon Review,* and Warren, as advisory
editor, began to publish there a series of articles on contemporary writers. His first study, "Katherine Anne Porter (Irony
with a Center)," pays tribute to a craftsman and old friend
to whom he was later to dedicate his own volume of short stories. What he finds most admirable about Miss Porter's writing
is her ability to present complicated characters in compact
form. For example, Braggioni, the rebel in "Flowering Judas," is revealed to be such a tissue of contradictions that he
comes to symbolize the theme of the story, that ambiguity of
moral reality which "exists in an intricate tissue of paradox."
Similarly, Miranda in "Old Mortality," despairing that she
will ever comprehend fully the involuted legend of her aunt
Amy, presented through the memories of other relatives, decides hopefully but naïvely that at least she will understand
herself. It is implied that Miranda's image, like Amy's, will
be fashioned gradually by the fusion of actual event and the
myth about herself that she and her friends will contrive. Kath-

erine Anne Porter refuses to reduce her people to simple formulas but, knowing the paradoxes constituent of the problem
of self-definition, begins with complicated characters and then
through circumstance and experience, but never in "the poverty of statement, " tests and rallies the thematic line. Warren
has never praised a writer more.

The complexity of literary experience is also the point of
Warren's talk on "Pure and Impure Poetry, " delivered as one
of the Mesures Lectures at Princeton and later, in 1943, published as a major document of the New Criticism. The "pure"
poem is the result of diverse "impure" elements which, however, function to discipline one another in shaping the final
form and in distinguishing it from all that is nonpoetry. Ex-
periencing this otherwise incredible truth in the act of writing,
the poet discovers that he must win his right to convictions by
undergoing resistances, temporary uncertainties, and ironies
comparable to the human process. In turn, the reader must
live through the tensions of the poem. His own experience of
the poem, however, will only approximate the poem's experience of itself, which is the more important.

Yet, in the spring of 1944, providing a means for measuring
the work of Eudora Welty, which escapes the usual inclusion
in genres, Warren asks: "Can we say this . . . of our expectation concerning a piece of literature, new or old: That it should
intensify our awareness of the world (and of ourselves in relation to the world) in terms of an idea, a 'view.'"[2] The fact that
Warren was soon to annotate *The Rime of the Ancient Mariner*
kept him alert to affinities between that work and Miss Welty's,
particularly her tale of Audubon who, in order to know fully
the bird that he loves, feels compelled to kill it for closer examination but consequently can neither know the living bird
nor rejoin human society as he had hoped to, had his knowledge
of bird life brought him popularity.

Nevertheless, despite the attractiveness of her ideas, Warren is not convinced that Eudora Welty has always succeeded
in dramatizing them in such a way that they "intensify our
awareness of the world. " In "The Wide Net" she explores two
important symbols: Man, who has a definition (myth) of himself
but who risks losing it whenever he enters the River, pure and
undefined force. This is her recognition that the dream must

be submitted to the world, "innocence to experience, love to knowledge, knowledge to the fact, individuality to communion."[3] The antipodes rotate on a single axis: "the dream and the world, the idea and nature, innocence and experience, individuality and the anonymous, devouring life flux, meaning and force, love and knowledge." (The dialectic here resembles the course of staggered events in *All the King's Men,* on which Warren had long been working; and the progress through purgatorio developed later in *World Enough and Time* and *Brother to Dragons.)* But this conflict of tensions has not yet become adequately implicit in Miss Welty's work.

In "Melville the Poet" (1946) Warren illustrates the complex of impurities that may constitute a pure poem. Although the academic world had been busy rediscovering everything Melville had ever written, almost no one dared call his poems competent. Warren suggests that what appears to be incompetence may have been deliberate roughening by the author, adding to poetic texture a porous or stuccoed dimension (he himself had used that technique in "The Ballad of Billie Potts"). Melville must have felt the incongruity of easy-mannered verse for the playing against one another of those "fundamental ironical dualities of existence: will against necessity, action against idea, youth against age, the changelessness of man's heart against the concept of moral progress, the bad doer against the good deed, the bad result against the good act, ignorance against fate, etc."[4] Other paraphrases of Melville's philosophy might serve equally as statements of the theme realized in Warren's Pulitzer Prize novel: "Man may wish to act for Truth and Right, but the problem of definitions is a difficult one and solution may be achieved in terms of his own exercise of will and his appetite for action."[5] Cass Mastern himself would have agreed with Melville's estimate that man's deepest composure lies in realizing that each human act participates in all.

Melville's deposed and derelict protagonists, thundering at the gates to have their godlikeness restored, share a family resemblance with Coleridge's mariner, who repeatedly attracted Warren's intellect. Within a few months Warren had published an extended essay, explicating and implicating *The Rime of the Ancient Mariner,* which almost immediately was seen to have been taken as confirmation of the critic's own

theories. Both Warren and Coleridge think of imagination less
as a device for treating illusions than as an active, shaping
function of the mind, source for communion with the truth
through the torsions and equilibrium of form.

A poem will seem to shift in meaning when used to document
alternately the history of language, of literary forms, or of
political ideas, but such perspectives, lying outside the province of literature, badger the poem for private reasons. (When
Warren himself interprets *The Rime of the Ancient Mariner*
as a document conversant with nineteenth-century issues, he
carefully refrains from using this historical fact as any test
of the poem's literary value.) In Coleridge's poem, Warren
suggests as more germane to analysis the allied religious
themes of sacramental vision and the imagination. In this reading the albatross symbolizes the Christian soul, each man's
access to the oversoul. The slaughtering of the bird by the
mariner signifies the attempt of pride to deny the relationship.
The mariner seems to act without motivation, but man by an
act of will is capable of subverting his own faculties of self-
perception; the responsibility therefore still is his. The other
mariners become his accomplices "by making man's conveni-
ence the measure of an act": they think the death of the albatross will make their trip endurable.

The bird, the wind, the moonlight, prompting the mariner's
imagination toward the oneness of the universe, finally force
him to acknowledge his guilt and, repenting, to purge himself
by construing for others what he has undergone. The poet-
mariner, outcast, speaks of his need for communion. Thus
the moral and esthetic concern are aspects of one activity, the
creative faculty, which is spokesman for the whole mind. Imagination as literature is a force binding together perceptions
made available to the reader as world-wide view; it becomes
also symbol for the unity of being.

Some notion of the particular world view that impassions
Warren emerges in the two-part commentary that the *New
Republic* in 1946 carried on Malcolm Cowley's edition of Faulkner. Faulkner's work is interpreted as a legend of the entire
modern Western way of life: its loss of universal sanctions
and the sense of mission. There is in Faulkner no easy re-
course to the past, no complete dependence on precedent, be-

cause the old traditional order was founded on varieties of injustice, slavery among them. Yet its code of obligation did
urge on every man a choice between multiplying the effects
of inherited injustice and honoring each the other's presence,
a chance to define one's self by running the risk of one's humanity. There was a notion of truth in the old order, even if
it was seldom attained.

"Modernism," the decline of man to mechanical process, becomes an age-old problem, product of ambition, which as Warren describes it suggests the dominant motive for many of his
own agonizing characters:

Ambition is the most constant tragic crime, and ambition is the attitude special to an opening society; all villains are rationalists and
appeal to "nature" beyond traditional morality for justification, and
rationalism is, in the sense implied here, the attitude special to the
rise of a secular and scientific order before a new morality can be
formulated. [6]

Faulkner reveals, through the projection of man's image in
nature, that there exists "a contamination implicit in the human
condition—a kind of Original Sin—but it is possible, even in the
contaminating act, the violation, for man to achieve some
measure of redemption, a redemption through love." [7] If man
were more godly, his attitude toward nature would become one
of "pure contemplation, pure participation in its great forms
and appearances"—the attitude of a New Critic, ideally, toward
a poem or novel. But the unloved, unloving "apostles of ab-
stractionism" seldom attain what Faulkner himself calls the
"communal anonymity of brotherhood."

According to Warren, the lifelike quality of Faulkner's characters derives from the fact that, reappearing in several books,
they move gradually toward "a final definition" of themselves,
and they are discoverable fully only in the tissue of their alliances with others, through "polarities, oppositions, paradoxes, inversions of roles." [8] In contrast with the many-leveled
involvement of Faulkner's characters, in 1947 Warren declared
those of Hemingway relatively simple and unvaried, although
the people in the works of both authors seek some sense of human order. Hemingway's earliest protagonists, obsessed with
life's meaninglessness and unable to find ground in their world
for religious faith, acquiesced to the sensation of violence, but

later shaped it heroically to their own terms, through soldierly discipline, athletic form, artistic control. Fidelity to that code is an index to a character's self-realization; usually the individual faces the onslaught alone.

Although the attitudes in which Hemingway would have the reader instructed are dramatic and not abstract, the drama becomes repetitious in Warren's eyes because basic situations and characters are inflexible; the codes, despite their origin in man's universal need for definition, are not profound enough to raise to the order of legend or myth the lives of those who give their allegiance. Hemingway's failure derives from the very restrictions he has so proudly imposed on his imagination.[10]

In Warren's estimation Joseph Conrad is a writer of more consequence because his terms preserve the human predicament in its fullness. Discussing *Nostromo* in 1951, Warren finds typical those characters who try to restore themselves to their own comprehension and to human solidarity. Even the vilest creature has to idealize his existence; although he finally realizes his values are illusions, nevertheless "the illusion is necessary, is infinitely precious, is the mark of his human achievement, and is, in the end, his only truth."[9] He is brought nearly to despair by admission that he cannot remain aloof in his ideal world but must remain committed to action, the destructive element of nature, and must make himself in the image of the dialectical adjustment of morality to action, utopianism to "secular logic," and justice to material interests. (The modulative pattern of self-definition had been used the previous year by Warren in *World Enough and Time.*)

The mediation of two worlds, natural and ideal, is attributed to Robert Frost in a 1954 study of the poet's major themes. Even as Hugh Kenner that year was criticizing *Understanding Poetry* for drawing more examples from Frost than from Shakespeare or Donne, Warren was explaining how the New England poet succeeds in defining "a sort of strategic point for the spirit from which experience of all sorts may be freshly viewed."[10] He is often aware, for instance, that labor brutalizes most when man conceives of reward as something terminating effort, rather than as ongoing fulfillment. Similarly, a kind of emergence through mutual modification is discoverable in Frost's poetry. The contrast between action and contemplation in "Stopping by Woods on a Snowy Evening" does not remain static, in simple debate, but oscillates. There is a sense, over and over in Frost, of the wrong committed by those who sink into natural appetite or into trancelike meditation, into the fact or into the dream exclusively. True art is a magnified dream of the literal world "as it has achieved meaning."

As a New Critic, Robert Penn Warren has long invested greater interest in the approach to literature than in its aftermath. The critic has been assigned, unmistakably, the function not of inventing meager paraphrase to substitute for original work, but of offering those preliminary explanations that will render the original immediately available in all its unique disposition. Esthetic experience is a phenomenon in itself, not to be judged by the efficacy of its re-entrance into the social experience. In reviews and articles, although he did not cease to believe in the importance of society as a shaper of literature, Warren progressively relinquished his sense of the importance of regional reference and of the Agrarian prospect.

Nevertheless, in application the ideal approach, which perhaps ought not to be interested in anything beyond descriptive analysis, was modified by an evaluative "principle of importance." Explication of the works of Katherine Anne Porter accentuates Warren's high estimate of complexity in character and theme to make possible the re-enactment of life's ambiguities; his criticism of *Nostromo* intimates that this complex will assume a dramatic "dialectical configuration"; and his notes on Eudora Welty emphasize the necessity that literature present a world view. But in these authors, as well as in Melville, Coleridge, Faulkner, and others, it is a special, an exceptional world view that has warranted the deepest commitment of his interest: the tortuous self-discovery of an alienated human being, seeking to regain a sense of peace within himself and in the community of men through shared understanding of their failures and hopes. Not all well-carpentered visions have engaged Warren, but only those which describe how human needs exceed human fulfillment and yet, avoiding despair and the reduction of man to naturalistic premises, raise him to that religious dependence which redeems.

Even the New Critics who as Agrarians once were severest judges of the modern scene have not always been immune to

its disease: retreat from responsibility, fear of public commitment. Understandably, they have been wary of having their
fictions compete with the world of empirical verification, where
positivists wait to reduce literary insight to the metaphysical
and therefore imaginary. Consequently, the early New Critics
sometimes pretended that their fictions could not converse
with or complement that other world either. They called each
poem its own best knower and proper evaluator.

Such recognition of literary individuality and the value of
differences does much to keep the singleness of approach in
critical method from becoming formularistic and thus sub-
stantiating Hugh Kenner's charge that *Understanding Poetry*
was constructed to coddle dull teachers and to soothe reluctant
students during the practice of basic reading skills. Nevertheless, when self-realization and inner consistency become the
sole standard for judging a work of art, one surrenders the
right to distinguish the trivial from the consequential, the intransitive from the generative, the existential from the essential, the temporary from the constant, the valid from the inval-
id, the inert from the viable. Whenever judgment is so reduced, an absurd egalitarianism is effected among works in-
comparable because existent on their own terms only. Estab-
lishment of this reduced individuality actually prevents discovery of more profound differences distinguished through assessment by analogy and arrangement by hierarchy.

Warren's own attempt to disengage the social and esthetic
concerns was doomed to failure, given his conviction that in
the soil of society literature is nourished. It was only a matter of time before it would be seen that the cycle of growth
had been only half described. Literature is not a fruit of knowledge which no one dare pick. In that light the articles from
the *American Review* do not quarrel with those later in the
Kenyon Review but prophesy their appearance. The early concept of symbolic regionalism already foreshadows the late
world picture. According to the theory's own warning against
abstraction, the interim distillations of literary theory could
not exist disembodied, and therefore they compelled the choosing from alternative substantial worlds the one on which a man
might risk his literary reputation and more.

Warren has violated the purist code and academic dispassion

of those for whom any poem or novel will serve equally well the clinical demonstration of technique. Perhaps against even his own younger persuasions, he learned to use one talent to test another. The faults of a critical detachment exhibit themselves in his fiction, but so do the virtues of critical scruple, and the working out of verse or book assays the progressively more coherent vision to whose exploration his critical faculties have been dedicated.

Warren's analysis of Conrad is appropriate to himself as well:

The philosophical novelist or poet is one for whom the documentation of the world is constantly striving to rise to the level of generalization about values, for whom the image strives to rise to symbol, for whom images always fall into a dialectical configuration, for whom the imagery of experience, no matter how vividly and strongly experience may enchant, is the urgency to know the meaning of experience. [11]

5

POETRY: THE GOLDEN EYE

After 1922, influenced by John Crowe Ransom, Donald Davidson, and other Fugitives whom he considered more valuable
than any number of Vanderbilt courses, Robert Penn Warren
began to devote more time to versification and less to science
courses. For some years, unfortunately, he was indistinguishable from others suffering the twinges of romantic diction.
In 1923, *Driftwood Flames,* an undergraduate anthology, published his stanzas on "The Golden Hills of Hell" whose line,
"Where lightly rest the purple lilies, " somehow remained memorable for Allen Tate, recalling Vanderbilt days twenty years
later. The summer of that year Warren began to publish, in
nearly every issue of *Fugitive* magazine, what occasionally
could be called rudimentary poetry.

The concentration of these early ventures on dramatic in-
cidents, deputies for massive situations unexpressed, dis-

plays young Warren's fever for history as violence, as in "Crusade":

> We have not forgot the clanking of grey armors
> Along frosty ridges against the moon,
> The agony of gasping endless columns,
> Skulls glaring white on red deserts at noon;
> Nor death in dank marshes by fever,
> Flies on bloated bodies rotting by the way,
> Naked corpses on the sluggish river,
> Sucked from the trampled rushes where they lay. . . .

The way in which the rhetorical pattern of these overwrought iron verses in each case sweeps past the clutch of end rhymes and into the next compounded serial creates the sensation of an anxious leaning forward toward some momentous climax. However, the lines distend themselves with vehemently sensuous but overelaborately itemized detail after detail, arriving finally at some trivial consequence. It is a poetry of effect and melodrama.

During two more years of publication in *Fugitive* the quality of Warren's verse declined. As if trying to stimulate himself with serious subject matter, he wrote often about death and sometimes about drought, but the vocabulary of coiling adders, futile thunders, and gray brain cells remains latent language, petrified imagery smuggled in from the wasteland. Nevertheless he managed to match the least common denominator of a magazine in which Ransom's "Bells for John Whiteside's Daughter" and "Captain Carpenter" and Hart Crane's "Legend" and "Lachrymae Christi" were exceptional entries. It was not until June, 1925, when "To a Face in the Crowd" appeared, that he gave some sign of the writer he was to become. Of all his work in the *Fugitive,* this was the only poem he considered worthy of his first volume (1935) and his *Selected Poems* (1944).

"To a Face in the Crowd" may be read as the culmination of a sequence beginning with a sonnet, "Beyond this bitter shore there is no going," published in April, 1924. The sestet of the earlier poem pictures man trapped on the iron beach between land and sea, in expectation of the "carrion gull." A year later the revised sonnet, having become "Beyond this wrathful shore there is no going, " admonishes each man to pray to "whatever

god he knows." Despite the solemnity of language and the use
of despair and prayer for ballast, neither sonnet seems attached to human occasion, a fault overcome by fuller narrative
treatment in "To a Face in the Crowd."

> Brother, my brother, whither do you pass?
> Unto what hill at dawn, unto what glen,
> Where among the rocks the faint lascivious grass
> Fingers in lust the arrogant bones of man?

Man-poet, the narrator divines that the face, familiar through
dreams, is his ancestral brother's.

> We are the children of an ancient band
> Broken between the mountains and the sea.

The monuments of their fathers silently decree that they de-
scend from the mountains to wrestle with the waters.

> That shore of your decision
> Awaits beyond this street where in the crowd
> Your face is blown, an apparition, past.

Contrasted with the face of this secret sharer, informed by
duty, the contemporary world seems bewildering and imma-
terial. Night and their dark fathers have shared in their proc-
reation; neither can be renounced.

Here for the first time Warren bridles the violence that previously had run untamed. Responsibility for frightful deeds,
not fully foreseen by the mind as it recoils from the encounter
of contemplation, is thrust on man by the precedent of his
forefathers. The fact that others share this burden multiplies
rather than alleviates its consequence. Projected action is
tempered by mature realization of all that must be undergone.
Dramatic tension is enforced by the clenching of grave duty,
deep as guilt, and great reluctance.

"To a Face in the Crowd" was included in the 1928 *Fugitive*
anthology, along with several later poems that had appeared
in other magazines after the *Fugitive* suspended publication.
In "Letter of a Mother," the best of these, the protagonist
wonders if he can disinherit himself, even while he pities the
"mother flesh that cannot summon back/ The tired child."
The choice is between the "illegal prodigality of dream" and
its fragility, both legacies from his mother. If the dream
urges him from her, ultimately the death whose seed she has

also planted in his mortal substance will claim and mother him.
The lines trace the weariness of a mind freighted with this
irony.

The anthology also included two poems in a series called
"Kentucky Mountain Farm, " commemorating the hardness of
hill country life, part of the heritage disavowed by youth. The
landscape itself, in "Rebuke of the Rocks, " instructs the lean
men "That even the little flesh and fevered bone/ May keep the
sweet sterility of stone. " Peace will come to man only after
acceptance of his rank among inorganic matter and a refusal to
reproduce humankind. "At the Hour of the Breaking of the
Rocks, " however, rumors a perennial difference between
rocks and man, who is infused with the restless spirit of the
sea's absolute depths into which the hills themselves will finally
erode. Man's hope now is that this restlessness which resists
brutalization by the elements will devise a prospectus, some
reason for being. In the colloquy of early poems, peace proves
less important than the need for self-exploration.

The Kentucky mountain farm sequence was enlarged in Warren's first volume, *Thirty-six Poems* (1935). "History among
the Rocks" records how sudden death is in a hard land. The
coiled copperhead waits, unsuspected, for the harvests. Just
as enigmatic to modern man are the motives of a past civil
war. With great causes forgotten, man killing and snake killing
seem equally incomprehensible. The natural order of evil is
momentarily interrupted only when Warren remembers, in
"The Cardinal" and "The Jay, " birds caught in the numb pause
between passages of time (prophetic of the characteristic trap
in his novels later).

There is a kind of envy in the description of the hawk in
"Watershed, " high enough in flight to oversee the multiplicity
and divisibility of life. (And there is a kind of yearning, too,
if the bird is taken to be of the same order as those destinate
eagles whose timely appearance Sam Houston repeatedly interpreted as omens. Only in *All the King's Men* is Warren
ready to take his bird imagery cynically, as illusions of flight,
represented by "Jackie Bird" Burden and by diving, swimming
Anne Stanton, who superimposes sky on water.) Below, harried man feels even the granite earth shudder under tides of
the inconstant moon. So, in "The Return, " memory recovers

past joys only as frail dreams, as mutable as one's own image in a loved one's eyes, soon forgotten when the face turns or the eyes close in sleep. (Even youth is a time of innocence raddled with unceremonious initiations. In "The Owl," another portion of the Kentucky mountain farm sequence but one not included in this collection, the sound of a waterfall stops the flow of time for a boy, and "Where time is not is peace." But the abrupt descent of night terrifies him and he flees back into the inexorable menace of the daily world.)

Later, in "The Garden," Warren's protagonist is unable to share either the lover's summer kiss or the debate of jay and cardinal prophesying winter:

> . . . he who sought, not love, but peace
> In such rank plot could take no ease. . . .

In full view of that lost splendor, threatening to become irrecoverable, he can hope only to mortify his desires in prospect that sacramental autumn will "translate/ All things that fed luxurious sense/ From appetite to innocence." His consolation is that peace is incompatible with the demands of identity.

The poise of these poems is that of a man at the instant before wild horses, in ceremony, drag his limbs asunder. It is marvelously managed even in such a complex of associative ordering and dramatic oppositions as "The Return: An Elegy," sequel to "Letter of a Mother," both in structure and in substance. Once more the son catalogues his physical members in the shriveling terms of chemistry and biology, as if such recantation might release him from the self which, because its earlier revolt was a refusal to be·nameless, must return to the home that first lent him family name. The son knows that he will find his mother dying, just as her image has already begun to decay in his mind, associating her with a dead fox lying in the rank gorges. Even as memory bitterly repudiates his dying mother, guilt discomposes him ("the old bitch is dead/ What have I said!"), and he invokes the past, both personal and historical, which once denied deprived him of a precious part. Mother and son both are the dead end of a whole history of that dream pursued by pioneers who first came to "the western slope." Though the houses of these men are in ruins now, and the wet wind snores through the pines, the son cannot forget. He regrets that it is too late to have honored his parents as a boy, "for time uncoils like the cotton-mouth"; and his homing heart offers these waning memories, like a "dark and swollen orchid, " as a final gift of sorrow for his mother. Despite superficial similarities in technique between "The Return: An Elegy" and *The Waste Land,* where Eliot's main line reference is mythical, Warren's is local, his idiom personal, the effect therefore immediate if not permanent. The turbulence of structure, its rapid counterpoint, the compulsive ejaculation of thoughts that betray the son, all communicate the struggle of grief to become pure—a method that was becoming Warren's philosophy. (Experiment with tension through contrast prepared him not only for those metaphysical apparatuses which his next volume constructed, but also for the esthetic theory expressed in "Pure and Impure Poetry, " in 1943, and for the concept of man's winding crawl toward light, the fetal twistings, evident in all his narratives.)

"Letter of a Mother" can be read, in turn, as part two of "Eidolon, " although Warren has never arranged the poems in this order. A narrative sequence is thereby established, tracking a young boy's disaffection with home, his flight, and dismal return. "Eidolon" recounts the unsleeping turmoil of a boy bedded under the rooftree with his "clod-heavy" father and spittle-bearded grandfather, while all night long dogs hunt a stranger in the dark woods. By dawn the white eidolon exorcised has fled, leaving only blood black on may apple. The boy has lost the leaven of his excitement, that apparition which like a courier might have brought a message explaining how the boy can possibly be kin to these relatives, whose gracelessness is like their dogs', "unhouselled angers" unable to perceive a sacred presence. In the dark world of wide-awake dreams, the white eidolon becomes whatever promise the boy can fabricate for himself to clothe the naked future prepared for him by generations past. The intruding dream is driven away. Still in his mind the boy follows it, repelled by his origins.

This cleavage between past and present, home and the wandering son, is prophesied in "History, " plaintively told from

the fathers' point of view. On the verge of a new land that
promised them release from anonymity, they still foresee
how their sons

> . . . shall cultivate
> Peculiar crimes,
> Having not love, nor hate,
> Nor memory.

Their most grievous crime will be unawareness of their own
history, although a few, having beat the brush to rout out
"fanged/ Rough certainty," will stumble on the ancestral jaw-
bone greening in some dim pool, and wonder. For the others
a desert is a wasteland only, not a place of moral preparation
through purgation. Yet, knowing this, the fathers proceed.
"The act/ Alone is pure": in action they find articulation; it is
their flesh if not their meaning; it is the urgency that sustains,
however blindly. When the vision vanishes there is still the
"rugged ritual" that must be served.

The short lines, crabbed by the necessity of end rhyme, gasp
audibly for breath; the words are as wind-scoured and fleshless
as the rhetoric, as if the narrator feels that they are wasted.
Although "History," is more remote than those poems in which
the physical presence of family and unequivocal place stage
the transfixion of man, read in their context it imports un-
common power.

"Letter to a Friend" deplores the wearing effect on interim
man of waiting crouched within inarticulate senses, watching
for the advent of truant peace.

> The caterpillar knows its leaf, the mole
> Its hummock, who has known his heart, or knows
> The trigger of this action, set and sprung?

Though courage is superfluous and hope a burden in a meaningless world, living becomes a habit. Under such circumstances,
to be unfrightened is to deserve greater tribute than triumphal
arches can provide.

These few portions of *Thirty-six Poems* are pediment for a
rubble of epithets and scattered images, only fragmented fore-
shadowings of Warren's major themes.

F. W. Dupee once pointed out that many of Robert Penn Warren's early lines are centered on equivalent images of stone

and bone, "the inorganic that hides out within the organic."
This is particularly true where the early imagery shrinks from
all exertions. If man could rid himself of flesh he would no
longer be compelled to submit to knowledge and its attendant
duties. He could wink at night dreams filled with "unaimed
faceless appetite" and at memory, the endless query, "is their
wrong/ Our wrong?" so like the epigraph from Housman in
Band of Angels. Man's uncertainty finds emblem in repeated
coilings: the Orphic maze of recollection, the unsuspected copperhead, time itself in process. Stunted lines and hard-edged
words are an attempt to reassert minimal confidence. Throughout, the hawk hangs aloft, symbol for an enviable insight, taking the light even as darkness settles on earth ("To a Friend
Parting"; "Watershed"). The poet tries to sharpen his inspec-
tion to such a minute point that it cannot be violated by change,
as in that snapshot of the beloved, "So Frost Astounds":

> You were maintained in the green translucence that resides
> all afternoon under the maple trees.

But, as "The Garden" warns, such mesmerism presages not
love but peace.

At the same time man resists this shrinking of self to stone.
He scratches himself again and again with violence to be certain
that he bleeds. He resents forgetfulness and ignorance as if
these rob him of life. He will not let assassins remain "nameless and/ With faces·turned" lest he himself be one. He can
claim a self only if he acknowledges the possibility of guilt,
which presupposes choice. The vocabulary everywhere pro-
claims the long and ever present history of evil, but there is
always the suspicion that by renouncing this history one also
relinquishes the possibility of good.

Stone is peace, but peace unearned is not the same as innocence. It is capitulation to the inorganic. Man, to be man,
must take his chances in the world, come uncloistered in Conradian commitment to action, seek to rediscover virtue. In
"Man Coming of Age, " having watched death settle throughout
the night "in the room of no-love" to which he has returned,
man wanders the hills and woods, trying to retrieve the self
he once was, when love perhaps *was* conceivable and more
crucial than peace, which after all is only absence.

Resistances yoked together within the language ("Truth, not truth, " "ambidextrous regret, " "arrogant chastity of our desire, " "the grape unripening, ripes") and within characterizations (in "The Return: An Elegy" the son is uncertain which is more substantial, the hatred he has for his mother or his sorrow at her death) describe human exigencies. Such polarities, characteristic of this interim struggle, rehearse the later "logic of experience." In *Proud Flesh* (1939), the verse drama that first played out the grievous errors of the extremely deceived man of action and the man of ideals, the conflict of opposites became visible as well as verbal in the antagonists. (Only in the novel and later dramatic versions did middleman Jack Burden step out of the shadows.)

After the sudden growth in poetic control exhibited in *Proud Flesh*, discomposure in *Eleven Poems on the Same Theme* (1942) is clearly subject matter and no longer the discomfortable method of a poet in search of his subject. Single-minded and hard-muscled, all of the poems except "Question and Answer, " which is written in the cropped style of "History" *(Thirty-six Poems),* conform to tight traditional patterns of precision. There are no experiments with turbulence, as in "The Return: An Elegy" or "Letter from a Coward to a Hero." Nevertheless, the sequence composed at the same time as *At Heaven's Gate,* which is also contrapuntal, has the range of a prolonged fugue, each part an exploration of that original sin which every man commits. (This is the "contamination" which Warren in 1946 analyzed in Faulkner's works and to which in his study of the Ancient Mariner he counterproposed "communion" as the means of man's redemption.) By 1942, Warren had become fully aware of what his subject matter was, and was to be.

"Monologue at Midnight" tells of "joy and innocence, " now past, among the pines. Only the companions' shadows, like inescapable guilt, have endured through day and moonlit night in every season. "Or was it guilt?" Nor is their own identity certain now: "are we Time who flees so fast, / Or stone who stand, and thus endure?" In "Bearded Oaks" probing questions are suspended while the lovers lie submerged in diminishing marine light beneath the trees, symbolic of the urge to be unborn, unbothered, unnamed.

> All our debate is voiceless here,
> All our rage, the rage of stone;
> If hope is hopeless, then fearless fear,
> And history is thus undone.

It is a world of negative curvature, slowly receding before the positive arrival of night. The air makes "nameless motions" at this hour when the pain of knowledge must be parried. In the present stillness they practice the peace of eternity. Such a mood, however, is never more than momentary in Warren. The landscape of "Picnic Remembered" remains the same: purity and innocence are associated with a marine amber light that buoys the protagonists' relaxed bodies, so still and seemingly preserved that they can "mock time's marvelling after-spies." But on this occasion darkness is both climax and threatened conclusion. Their desperate calm is token of death, not innocence preserved. Hearts turn to "hollow stones." Or is it possible that they are already dead and their "dearest souls" somewhere re-enact the pleasure of the picnic remembered?

> Or is the soul a hawk that, fled
> On glimmering wings past vision's path,
> Reflects the last gleam to us here
> Though sun is sunk and darkness near
> —Uncharted truth's high heliograph?

The hawk, symbol of hopefulness, is as usual enigmatic. Although it can be seen, what it sees cannot. The poem does not assert; it questions.

The illusion of buoyant relief now broken by the descent of moral darkness, the next five poems perform another dramatic cluster, with Anyman in an attempt to name his terror aimlessly pursuing the spoor of his own experience. He envies the mad killer of "Crime" his incapacity to recall the act committed. Both have wanted happiness, "peace in God's eye"; but whatever the mad killer buries is buried, "nor is ever known/ To go on any vacations with him, lend him money, break bread." Anyman's crime, however, awakens seasonally. The very letter that he ignores just as he ignores its sender "names over your name"; despising its grief, he multiplies his own. The resurrected toad's "bright jewel" now is associated with "the precious protuberance" on the forehead of his grandfather, whom he has tried vainly to forget. His first

homesickness, recognition of his sin of betrayal by desertion,
is over, but the wrong itself will not let him rest. "Oh, nothing is lost, ever lost!" As if to cleanse himself of his past
self, he rarely leaves forwarding addresses, and he hears
with pleasure of the death of an old acquaintance, but memory
patiently, sadly, lingers "like a mother who rises at night to
seek a childhood picture."

In "End of Season" Anyman seeks to wash away "the accus-
tomed nightmare"; but St. John the Baptist is a stranger to
the contemporary scene, and no country health resort—beach,
spiaggia, playa, plage, spa—can serve as surrogate. Nor has
any language been invented to replace words of salvation. The
only alternative is to avoid all occasions for communication by
choosing solitude and the submarine world, "the glaucous glimmer where no voice can visit." But he knows that his mail will
ferret him out, summon him back to a world without communion. Only the global eye of hope, unwinking, is unseasonal and
steady: Anyman prepares for confession.

"Revelation," a flashback, recapitulates mankind's happy
fall:

> Because he had spoken harshly to his mother,
> The day became astonishingly bright,
> The enormity of distance crept to him like a dog now,
> And earth's own luminescence seemed to repel the night.

So the peaceful "submarine glimmer" of childhood innocence
is shattered, and the natural order ravished as when Sulla
smote his mother Rome. But "in separateness only does love
learn definition" (nearly the words of the Scholarly Attorney,
explaining creation to Burden). This the boy has learned: that
"love's grace" is redemptive. However, the next poem, "Pursuit," actually precedes "End of Season" in progress of meaning, so that the labyrinth turns inward again and has no exit.
Although the protagonist is a sick man in a sick world, he col-
lects no portion of profit from this knowledge. The corner
hunchback barely tolerates his interest. In the outer room of
the clinic the others' eyes, withdrawn or bold, isolate him
further. The doctor, unaware of that love which "is a groping
Godward, though blind," merely prescribes a change of scene,
a trip to Florida where Ponce de Leon sought extenuation of

flesh alone. In the sunny port of no importance Anyman suffers the same old circumstance of loneliness.

Surrounded by others equally catatonic, man shrinks to his irreducible self, represented by the bare-bone structure of "Question and Answer." His counsel to himself, "let the heart be stone," is a request for neither death nor despair but for endurance, strength to recall how Moses brought forth the grace of water from rock. But, if the heart is too impatient to be stone, let it be a bow from which the lover-arrow may "fly/ At God's black, orbed, target eye." Let man assume those postures of prayer to whose efficacy tradition gives testimony. See if word of love does not beget a lover.

While "Question and Answer" discovers its final, graphic image only after tortuous exploration, "Love's Parable" is from the start an explanation of metaphysical passion, making experience and idea, flesh and ghost, matrix to one another. Once its lovers were like aliens, sharing hopes though not language. Exchanging loyalties, they practiced being center of each other's orbit, until this daily miracle grew so commonplace that they abused it. Only at its loss did they realize how precious their possession was. In "our garden state," joy prospered at the expense of innocence, until the "inward sore/ Of self" had already cankered to the bone, and love turned to hate. Now, by habit unable to separate, they merely infect one another, wondering whether they brought ruin into the world or the world ruined them, and begging restoration: "for there are testaments/ That men, by prayer, have mastered grace."

The proximity of this poem to those in which religious vocabulary is decisive cannot be accidental. The sense of a first sin, rejection of complete unison, which corrupts some antique garden substantiates Howard Nemerov's reading that the lovers here are man and God:

Grace may at any time be given, but cannot be sustained without awareness. The paradox is, that this awareness must be (in the experience of the two lovers) gained at the expense of grace: the shock of disillusion and the knowledge of self, of separate being, combine to make the initiates despise the paradise they have already lost. Mere knowledge of cause and effect (scientia) will but aggravate the disaster. Hope resides in resignation, wisdom, prayer. Yet the experience of

the fall is necessary, in a way, for without awareness grace cannot
be sustained. . . .[1]

The motif of the "fortunate fall," mankind's consolation, expressed in "Revelation, " is echoed here.

Eleven Poems on the Same Theme ends by robbing man, in
"Terror, " of two alternative consolations: war and scientism
(symbolized by the reverence of Alexis Carrel for his test-tube
heart), both incapable of explaining man because incapable of
an "adequate definition of terror." American volunteers kill
now on this side, in Spain, now on that, in Finland, moved by
the same "passionate emptiness and tidal/ Lust." They are
considerably less human than Macbeth, who at least could be
conscience-stricken.

In a rare self-explanation, Warren later wrote:

. . . the business about the chicken heart seemed to summarize a
view current in our time—that science (as popularly conceived) will
solve the problem of evil by reducing it merely to a matter of "adjustment" in the physical, social, economic, and political spheres.
That same day I recalled a remark made in some book by John Strachey that after science had brought "adjustment" to society it would
then solve the problem of evil by bringing man a mortal immortality,
by abolishing disease and death. It struck me as somewhat strange
that Strachey should equate physical death and evil on a point-to-point
basis, and should thereby imply that good and physical survival are
identical.[2]

Nazism and fascism glorify, paradoxically, these contradictory
elements: violence and death, and "salvation through . . . the
'rational' state." Both elements are evasions of "that proper
sense of the human lot, the sense of limitation. I should call
that sense, when it is applied inclusively, the religious sense—
though I don't insist on this."[3]

The central method of *Thirty-six Poems* is to project man's
part in the world's evil through images of rotting vegetation,
animal life in ambush, and the skeletal measurement of man.
In the most successful poems these become correlatives for
man's relationship with man, usually the son's division from
his parents. Only in "The Garden" and "Eidolon" is it intimated
that the wrongheadedness of life might require more than sociological investigation.

In *Eleven Poems on the Same Theme,* however, the presentation of evil is subtilized, with the weight of meaning moving out of single epithets into the full cadence and controlled stanza. Vestiges remain of the "carnivorous orchid" and "arsenical meadows" and of bone and stone; but the poetry relies on them less and less. Instead there is a constant illumination of sense objects by great volumes of light. Sometimes darkness succeeds the light, but only at a crawl. Sometimes it persists, as ominous presence, even in the all-day sun or submarine glitter of the beach; but that is part of the maturing vision. Although occasionally man recognizes the symbols of his fortune, they only aggravate his misery, because *he* is the darkness and cannot know which way to walk. In broad daylight the mystery appalls, its awesomeness deriving not from a catalogue of venoms but from unrelenting guilt, the unnamed shadow invisible in overlapping light. The meditative quality of this inquiring verse is saved from immobility by metaphysical conjugation, the erecting of a hierarchy of states to be symbolized.

The tragic sense is heightened, presumably, whenever evil in human nature is described in terms larger than the anthropological. Nevertheless, although the meaning of Warren's poetry at its fullest is not available without some understanding of the religious language used, the poems themselves insist no more than he on being interpreted solely on their merits as predetermined doctrine. When such terminology is employed, often it occurs short of the poem's climax, so that it functions chiefly as a suggested explanation of the painful division being described. The emphasis remains on the constancy of the problem itself, experience of its universality, the need to acknowledge it. The very inviolateness of the ingrained doctrine, its timeless composure, makes it serve as alternative and dramatic countermovement to those actions which survive essentially "unaimed" and nameless. Like the more obvious structures of the poetry, it restrains the remainder of violence and exacts the hazardous balance of tensions joined.

So scrupulous and single-minded is the presentation of *Eleven Poems on the Same Theme* that its successor, *Selected Poems: 1923-1943*, seems hastily arranged. The major principle of division is simply between "early" (roughly, to 1934) and "late" poems. The former group conforms to the order established in

Thirty-six Poems, itself nearly haphazard. The "late" poems, when organized at all, are stationed according to likeness in external structure. No longer are the poems intended to be read in succession. Even the old disposition of *Eleven Poems on the Same Theme* has been dismembered. The new disharmony indicates an attempt to prop weak poem against strong. If this is true, it is self-criticism, but no solution, since strength is sapped rather than shared.

The volume is also harmed by three new but far from satisfactory poems. "Variation: Ode to Fear," slack-shaped, grotesque in its humor, performs the disservice of reducing its real subject, evil, "with me *in utero"* and ever since, to the company of common ailments.

> When the dentist adjusts his drill
> And leers at the molar he's going to fill,
> Murmuring softly as a mother,
> "Just hold tight, it'll soon be over,"
> *Timor mortis conturbat me.*

Stoicism invoked to withstand such trifles (a parody of William Carlos Williams' "The Use of Force"?) dwindles to a minor order. (By contrast, "It came from your mother's womb," the poem Slim Sarrett writes in *At Heaven's Gate,* alone in his hotel room after the accidental murder of Sue Murdock, has the impaling impact of "Crime.")

Sections of "Mexico Is a Foreign Country: Five Studies in Naturalism" reflect the same hobbled sensibility. In Part I the displaced tourist, "robed in the pure/ Idea," typically retreating West, tries to flee his own violent wrathful act (unidentified and, perhaps as with Oedipus, as yet anticipated only). But he is prevented from the peace of purchased innocence by the equivocation of Mexican landscape: butterflies that circle the "precious flower" of his head also flutter over some "death-gaudy" dog; and the pink cloth tenderly covering a dead child's face in Jalisco has the practical purpose of warding off troublesome flies. Part II parodies this search for detachment with the sleepy announcement that "here even the bladder achieves Nirvana, / And so I sit and think, 'mañana.'" Part III, stiffening its back in a show of dignity, contrasts the newcomer with the old native who (like the hunchback in "Pursuit") has no needs, asks for nothing. Nor has the Mexican

anything to offer the newcomer, so different have been their
histories. The insecurity of the displaced stranger finds its
symbol in "the crow-bait mount, the fly-bit man" that plunge
across the cobbles toward no known address. "'Viene galopando
. . . el mundo,'" observes the native. Things are in the saddle.

Part IV describes the day-long drill of soldiers, "gallant
little formulae":

> The little drum goes rum-tum-tum,
> The little hearts go rat-tat-tat,
> And I am I, and they are they,
> And *this* is *this*, and *that* is *that*. . . .

Their endeavor to seem invincible deputies of despotism is
belittled by "The buzzard, absolute/ In the sun's great gold
eye. . . ." Like that of the daylong onlooker, their life is an
absurdity: the regimented and the disengaged. Unfortunately
the poem, by mimicking its subject too closely, becomes equally absurd.

However, when this slenderness in attitude reappears in Part
V, it no longer can be justified as fashionable satire. The
theme demands a stalwart idiom. Man and mango fruit are
brothers in their guilt, their human-vegetable part in a world
corrupt and ripe for decay. Their dilemma is that they must
purge their nature *through* their nature. Each is conscience
to the other: "the mango is a great gold eye, / Like God's";
man is an *"agent provocateur."* But what they are being punished for is ultimately God's own "monstrous, primal guilt"
as creator. If they could once forgive God, they might be "blest
in that blasphemy of love we cannot now repeat." They might
be capable of communion on the day that division ends, creature against creature, and creature against God. Knowing
shame but not its final cause, man acknowledges God only as
scapegoat (as Hamish Bond in *Band of Angels* was later to
blame the world for its wickedness, until he realized that talk
of human helplessness is self-pity or, worse, that it deprives
a man of any self to pity). If evil is universal and everlasting,
its cause must be divine. Yet such denunciations do little to
ease the misery of existence. Man cannot help feeling that if
he could forgive he might be forgiven.

In three sections of "Mexico Is a Foreign Country" the ideas are not witnessed by supporting structure, a failure due to the author's refusal to accept the seriousness of his own satire on the inadequacy of naturalism as a philosophy. The execution of contrast necessary to establish controlling tension is not sufficient. Terms that should be opposites gravitate instead toward the weaker. Consequently, Warren's point of view and not the naturalist's is put at a disadvantage.

The longest and apparently the latest poem among the selections, "The Ballad of Billie Potts," is a fugal arrangement of narrative and commentary. The ballad itself concerns an old folk tale from western Kentucky. Billie's father is an innkeeper who ambushes, kills, and robs men traveling westward alone. When Billie himself tries to help one day, he fails and is forced to become a renegade. Years later, after he returns, bearded and rich, his parents unwittingly slay him for gain. After they learn that the body might be their son's, they dig it up fearfully and find that it bears his birthmark. The narrative line is deliberately roughened to such an extent that its chop-rhythms sometimes seem more manneristic than candid, more "primitivized" than casual. Nevertheless, the intensity of characterization and the convincing quality of clannish affection assumed throughout rescue the narrative from its tendency toward poetical horseplay. Part of that impulse, of course, is appropriate. The tale is so ancient that its pathos is intentionally threadbare; it is a "fiction"; the characters are "grotesque"; it is only a joke that happened to somebody else long ago. The function of the commentary is therefore to make truth out of fiction and extend the skin of guilt to cover man.

The commentary begins with the "galloping world": a stranger driving past uncoiling sloughs, contemporary man on the move to nowhere, incapable of understanding the pioneer push westward by men whose shadows were their law.

> The answer is in the back of the book but
>   the page is gone.
> And grandma told you to tell the truth but
>   she is dead.

Their quest was endless—to their children, pointless; history stands still: "And the testicles of the fathers hang down like old lace."

The American dream was to leave behind "the old shell of self" by entering the "land of the innocent bough . . ./ Think of your face green in the sub-marine light of the leaf. " Yet, whatever the new name, whatever the change in face, "the name and the face are you, " as the reflection "of your deep identity" in any stream will confess. "Under the image on the water, the water coils and continues": there is no sanctuary.

The American dream was to be able to begin over every day, to absolve oneself from old duties:

> For Time is motion
> For Time is innocence
> For Time is West.

But daily changes sliver man. Constant altering of profession converts the mind into compartments, neurotic cells. Finally realizing that his substance has been wasted, he returns home to his source for replenishment. Now, in the dark pool of memory, that former self is hardly visible. The very belief that childhood innocence is possible even for children is a sin of pride that must be expiated. The prodigal grows "weary of innocence and the husks of Time. "

The eternal instinct to return unites all life in a design far grander than man's dreams. "In the great unsolsticed coil" of sea, the eel performs the ritual of migration:

> The salmon heaves at the fall, and wanderer, you
> Heave at the great fall of Time. . . .

As birth was the beginning of death, so death may be rebirth. The need of man for God is matched by God's need for man. Though the Father may turn out to be an "old man/ Who is evil and ignorant and old, " still he must be honored from the knees as progenitor, fountain of the family of man, as man's birthmark testifies. That identifying human flaw is his luck, his proof that he was made in an image stern and ruthless, nevertheless divine.

The apparent blasphemy of "The Ballad of Billie Potts" relates to the "blasphemy of love" mentioned in "The Mango on the Mango Tree, " according to which it would be sacrilegious for man to admit the existence of God, only to love him as an equal. His attitude, as the ballad's commentary advocates, should be that of a dutiful son to his father, to the tempestuous and undisputed Old Testament God. Trust in transcendent design, in the rightness of whatever divinity has done, brings man to a greater innocence—freedom from pride, the silencing of doubts—than he has ever hoped for. Even if the "old man" is read not as the ultimate Creator but as his deputy, Adam, homage is an act of total heritage, humiliation preceding regeneration.

In "Ransom" *(Thirty-six Poems),* Warren wrote, "Our courage needs, perhaps, new definition, " the courage to explore the possibilities of love in tragic surroundings, a kind of stoicism. In "Terror" *(Eleven Poems on the Same Theme),* he wrote about men "born to no adequate definition of terror, " men incapable of confessing the reality of evil in themselves, yet (like Jerry Beaumont—John Brown) ready to assume the role of avenging angels. Courage and terror mirror each other. Now a third term for the equation is offered in "The Ballad of Billie Potts": "our innocence needs, perhaps, new definition." What man lacks is not innocence by flight or denial or presumption of righteousness, but that paradoxical innocence which comes with the acceptance of guilt, of sin, permanent to human nature. It is right that man pay violently for his violence.

The failure of both the backwoods father and the traveling stranger to recognize their own exemplifies the inarticulateness of modern society, the breakdown of a common language which Warren's poems have noted elsewhere and which sometimes vexes him, as author, as well as any man. Compelled, the poet speaks; but even in the act, he retracts himself from full expression, realizing that he will not be understood completely.

Because the theme of this long poem is paradoxical and grim, the strategy of its early parts provides questionable preparation for the conclusion. Although its boisterousness has already been explained and in part accepted, its excesses detach it from its commentary. The method is that of yoking rather than of weaving. If the ballad and the sections in free verse had been made reciprocal commentaries, reflecting each other's truth in the manner of particulars and their generalization, indivisibility might have been achieved. In effect, after the vain attempt of the ballad to carry Warren's burden, another poem had to be written and spliced into the first.

John Crowe Ransom once remarked that the parenthetical structural parts constitute "a gloss far more implausible than that which Coleridge wrote upon his margin. "[4] By not trying to compress a whole complex of meaning into the folklore of the ballad, Warren has avoided the dangers of allegory, but the way in which the present ambiguous alliance allows false interpretations is a danger equally grievous and not always circumvented. Nevertheless, "The Ballad of Billie Potts" remains one of Warren's most important and interesting works.

The narrative immediacy of "The Ballad of Billie Potts" shows the influence of Warren as novelist. In *Night Rider* and *At Heaven's Gate* he had already experimented with the use of a commentary, the story within a story. For nearly ten years Warren devoted himself to fiction before returning in 1953 to narrative poetry with the book-length *Brother to Dragons*.

At the time of the appearance of his *Selected Poems,* he had considered writing a novel about the brutal ax-slaying of a slave by the nephews of Thomas Jefferson, prophet of human perfectibility. But he decided that thinness of circumstance and the refusal of crucial historical parallels (Meriwether Lewis's suicide, and the shocking murder) to annex each other would fail the natural demand of a novel for heavy-grained texture and final resolution. [5] The material was too muffled to speak for itself without an interpreter, and already Warren was attempting to avoid commentaries, cripplers of fiction. In the summer of 1950, Warren blocked out action for the stage. [6] Jefferson was to serve as chorus, brooding over the event in much the same manner as the choral devices in *Proud Flesh,* his 1939 play which after many seasons of change became *All the King's Men.* Again, however, thinness in plot was only too evident, and, for a play, the role of Jefferson was disproportionately large. The collaboration could not survive premature handling of materials still not assimilated.

Finally, Warren saw the possibility of constructing a dramatic dialogue in place of a play, "to get out of the box of mere chronology, and of incidental circumstantiality. " In this way he could keep alive both the "old horror" and the role of Jefferson as a timeless spectator; and he could add the poet, "R. P. W. , " as a kind of "interlocutor, " providing the wider perspective of modern man, who also has to "face this ter-

rible thing in his own blood." Poetry allowed a reduction of
circumstance to the minimum required for conviction. Nevertheless, he faced the new problem of keeping his episodes
sharp in both their immediate and symbolic senses, and therefore of finding a double-leveled language for his characters
and of redeeming action by debate, just as he has always urged
the mutual absorption of will and idea.

Brother to Dragons assembles real and fictitious persons
to discuss and dramatize "human constants": the place of evil
and, notwithstanding, of aspiration in human careers. The
central incident narrated is the ax-slaying of a slave by two
Kentucky brothers, Lilburn and Isham Lewis, nephews of
Thomas Jefferson, during that exceptional time of floods,
earthquakes, and pestilence, December, 1811. However, natural violence is presented as a sibling to the human violence
in which Jefferson is said to share. Nature's derangement,
as in the poem "Revelation," plays no favorites. The brutality
itself is undercut by being recalled rather than re-enacted, so
that the action's symbolic value can emerge.

At first Jefferson appears merely embittered by the fact
that his own relatives should have stripped him of the idealized
picture of human beings he memorialized in the Declaration of
Independence, and of the West he promoted through the Louisiana Purchase. He had never been wholly naïve, of course; the
gargoyles of Gothic France represented for him a human actuality. Yet the mathematical precision of the Roman archi-
tecture at Nîmes (as inviolable as the orderly drill of anonymous Mexican troops) had led Jefferson to believe in a natural
human innocence that could be liberated. Since that day, however, having been introduced to the minotaur in man, he regards all love as a disguise to the "immitigable ferocity of
self." He wishes that he personally had brained his nephew
Lilburn, to prevent these most precious ideals from being
robbed of possibility.

Gradually, however, it becomes plain that such bitter renunciation is no different from Lilburn's own condemnation of
his father, perversion of his wife's offered love, and rejection
of his former wet nurse. Lilburn has loved only his mother
and in her name kills the slave who deliberately steals her
Virginia heirlooms. His mother has already died, stricken

by the enormity of his cruelty to others. Nevertheless, her ghostly flesh returns, accepting the price of her having loved him, and tries to obtain him justice in the poem's debate. The deed is separate from the doer in her condemnation.

The significance of the debate enlarges with the appearance of Meriwether Lewis, come to accuse Jefferson of being the cause of his suicide. Having been convinced by the Founding Father of man's nobility and of pristine innocence in the West, he had explored Indian lands, only to discover sickness and savagery. The greatest disillusion, however, came later, when as territorial governor in St. Louis he was falsely accused of embezzlement and was driven to self-destruction. He accuses Jefferson of having disseminated the concept of nobility merely to magnify his own image. Jefferson's vanity has already been proved by his repudiation of Lilburn Lewis.

Gradually Jefferson is convinced, after Lilburn's mother Lucy charges that such repudiation makes her brother an accomplice in his nephew's crime. The exquisite pain of wisdom makes him say:

> Now I should hope to find courage to say
> That the dream of the future is not
> Better than the fact of the past, no matter
> how terrible.
> For without the fact of the past we cannot
> dream the future.
> . . . .
> It would be terrible to think that truth is lost.
> It would be worse to think that anguish is
> lost, ever.

Again, he says:

> . . . if there is to be reason, we must
> Create the possibility
> Of reason, and we can create it only
> From the circumstances of our most evil despair.
> We must strike the steel of wrath on the stone
> of guilt,
> And hope to provoke, thus, in the midst of our
> coiling darkness
> The incandescence of the heart's great flare.

Robert Penn Warren, as character in his own lines, has challenged the unqualified nature of Jeffersonian idealism and would substitute a faith which by being informed makes per-

missible hope in redemption, that glory which he calls repeatedly "the only/ Thing in life." Despair is not the proper
exit from human vanity, nor is interchangeability with nature,
although man must in fact live in the world. Instead, through
comprehension of his own aged father's tested attitude toward
life, by accepting the necessity of ultimate imperfection and
failure, Warren purifies vanity without extinguishing it completely. For without the dream, that myth of self which answers the cry for identity, man could not act. Both the agony
of will and the anguish of option are prerequisites of achievement:

> . . . if responsibility is not
> The thing given but the thing to be achieved,
> There is still no way out of the responsibility
> Of trying to achieve responsibility.

But action unsustained by faith is unprofitable, and only if we
are

> . . . aware of the incorrigible and blessed need
> To give even evil the justification of good,
> And thus affirm the good, do we have the possible
>   courage
> To confront the necessity of virtue.

Only through recognition of each man's complicity in all human
history, of those portions in his nature that are forever fixed,
of the required direction toward fulfillment, can he ever begin
to earn the new innocence and freedom, the unselfish selfhood.
Salvation lies in the service of this paradox.

Although, to prevent *Brother to Dragons* from becoming mere
repudiation by Jefferson of his old dream, Warren broadened
the roles of Lucy and Meriwether, Jefferson remains in the
author's words "the real protagonist, the person who had to
come to terms with something." The poem might easily have
been converted into an ode praising the Jeffersonian ideals that
underlie so much of Southern tradition: self-reliant agrarianism or the optimistic view of human nature that argues for
such a program. Instead, these ideals are measured against
the acts of man, historic facts that must have shaken Jefferson
himself, and their modern counterparts. The book is an attempt to discover "an adequate definition" for "the glory of
the human effort": a hypothesis, based on the characters' joint

experience, which can account for the coexistence of good and
evil, thereby both justifying and directing the survival of man.

In the foreword to *Brother to Dragons* Warren explains his
use of the chronicled fact complemented by imaginary re-cre-
ation by arguing that "historical sense and poetic sense should
not, in the end, be contradictory, for if poetry is the little
myth we make, history is the big myth we live, and in our living, constantly remake." We aspire to the incarnation of ideals. Since man's access to knowledge is drastically circumscribed by his senses and sensibility, poetry properly employed becomes as legitimate a method for illuminating experience as history: "poetry is more than fantasy and is committed to the obligation of trying to say something about the
human condition." In a world where comprehension is by that
very condition necessarily incomplete, action is impossible
without myth.

In *Brother to Dragons* conclusions evolve naturally from a
debate in which intense physical action and vigorous intellec-
tualization alternate, just as the characters themselves, dis-
putants from several temporal realms, converse without in-
terference from deep and permanent antagonisms. The *per-
sonae* are present not as enactments of unique individual attitudes but as part of that fluent exchange of passions and ideas
among men which makes credible the recognition of their mutual moral involvement. The problem for the author is to make
each separate characterization valid while rendering all of the
characters ultimately inseparable. It is solved without the
promotion of any single person as spokesman or seer; Robert
Penn Warren himself, as both author and character, becomes
one among many provoked by a common and obligatory interest
to listen and to speak.

The structure of *Brother to Dragons*, therefore, is that of a
symposium, the natural rising and falling inflection of any
man's life, Warren's, for example. Or, to use a metaphor developed later in his Columbia University address, its movement is that of "continual and intimate interpenetration, an
inevitable osmosis of being." The importance of *Brother to
Dragons* in Warren's canon lies in the clarity of its comment
on those terms of the human paradox which need redefining—
complicity and innocence, necessity and freedom. Their grad-

ual apprehension in Warren's earlier novels reaches a climax
in this long poem. In each book revelation comes too late.
Perse Munn and Jerry Beaumont are slain at the moment of
partial understanding; Jack Burden and Jerry Calhoun resolve
to learn from their errors but need a breathing space before
the long beginning over. In *Brother to Dragons* "R. P. W." carries the vision forward; and, although the poem ends again with
that vision as threshold only to "the world of action and lia-
bility" rather than with its being tested in that world, its am-
plitude exceeds what the novels provided. The poem's further-
ance of the inner eye's horizon makes understandable, perhaps even better than Warren's recent personal history (after
the moral shock of his first wife's mental illness, his re-
marriage in 1952 and the birth of two children), the final sense
of deliverance in *Band of Angels,* as well as the tender lyric
quality of many of the poems in *Promises: Poems 1954-1956.*

Writing of the possible articulation of Conrad's physical agonies with his central intuition of man's perilous ropewalk above
an abyss, Robert Penn Warren once cautioned that "an act of
creation is not simply a projection of temperament but a criticism and purging of temperament." What risk Warren chances
in his Pulitzer prize volume, *Promises* (1957), originates not
in his attempt to mitigate that Conradian vision through the
"astonishing statement of sun" and apocalyptic moon, but in
his abandonment of anonymity, his provision of public ballast
for affections personal and private.

The poems speak, and are themselves part, of a legacy divided, as the dedications specify, between Warren's daughter
Rosanna and son Gabriel. He has now given them not only life
but knowledge of that indebtedness which goes with the expense
of memory and the course of blood: kinship. They are instructed in the lives of others who died that they might have
their chance: Warren's parents, Ruth Penn and Robert senior,
seen side by side through the luminous transparency of ground;
his maternal grandfather, Gabriel Telemachus Penn, retired
cavalry captain, C.S.A., stern hangman of bushwhackers; and
his other grandfather, whom he never saw, volunteer private
in the Tennessee and Mississippi campaigns; those epic heroes,
Houston and Bowie; and the faceless ones who "wrestled the
angel, and took a fall by the corncrib." Warren's achievement

is that these poems become more than a gathering of clans. By extrapolation they represent whole histories of the human project.

Those lines tendered to Rosanna are deluged with sunlight, those to Gabriel with the moon. There are lyrics and lullabies; more happiness than the poet has ever before conceded; hope. Counterforces in the dialectic upheaval have become counterparts. The day of creation is shared by, rather than divided between, the newest generation, girl:sun and boy:moon whose prophetic radiance replaces those torrents of blinding guilt that drench the conscience in *Eleven Poems on the Same Theme*. Yet the only illusions granted are those necessary ones which keep man moving. "Grace undreamed is grace forgone, " the poet counsels. The little girl in the ruined fortress has much to redeem with her laughter. All around the sea-salt crops off the late season flowers. From next door comes the crooked wave of a defective child, the "triptych beauty" of whose sister Warren resents because it expects to bless away effortlessly the "filth of fate." Only the laughing girl's youth can protect her momentarily from the responsibilities of time and the history of the human condition. Only the tall light of dying summer allows temporary reprieve.

The burden of remembrances placed on the boy is greater, since his will be the line of declared descent. For him the father commemorates particularly nights of the past which, transfigured, were moving relentlessly forward, committed by unspoken promises, to enact *this* present out of all other possibilities. How many times, like an Adam but without instructions, did he himself stand before the tree! How many snakes were crushed in the grain field and forest; how many dragons from hell escaped! Human inheritance, as Conrad knew and Warren affirms, has its unholy origins against which moonlight knowledge and the "sunlit chance" are asked to persevere.

Between these polarities of hope and knowledge, brightness and dark, promise and actuality, the poems lie, conforming to patterned lines of force. In only one previous collection, *Eleven Poems on the Same Theme*, has Warren ever approximated the thematic indivisibility of his latest volume, despite the fact that the varieties of poetic experience have now become more

numerous. Many of the figures contribute a secondary reso-
nance to deceptively simple poems because of their earlier appearance in the Warren canon. It was Warren's father, drows-
ing in the wayside car, reconciled to his own failure and therefore immune, whose place in *Brother to Dragons* measured
Warren's sleepless chase toward the boundaries of innocence.
The Gillum family's mass murder by their berserk father has
its counterpart in the crime of a minor character, in *Night
Rider;* "Summer Storm (circa 1916) and God's Grace" acts as
corollary to the short story "When the Light Gets Green." Its
aftermath, flood's destruction, was described in "Blackberry
Winter." Here were also first portrayed Grandfather Penn
of "Court Martial" in all his vigorous dignity, astride his har-
rowed country world, and the tramp in "Dark Night of," whose
very otherness, a conjuring of the boy's own alienation, lured
him from thoughts of home to seek himself. Finally, "The
Dark Woods" sequence re-enacts the "unappeasable riot" in
"Eidolon" of the boy who hears the nighttime visitation of a
stranger and becomes restless. Even the sea gulls of Italy and
Warren's "hawk-hung" solitude among the crags with his wife
are reminiscent of frequent hawk images, horizon-eyed but
silent, in the earliest of his poems.

Through the dimensioning in depth that such repetitions construct, these figures are seen deployed in the continuous act
of defining themselves and the themes they represent. "The
world is real. It is there," young Warren is convinced as the
avenging cavalry ride out of the sun into his boyhood eye. The
poet has demonstrated that what is genuinely universal, neither
statistical truth nor the abstractions of history, exists even in
the particulars of one's own flesh.

The colloquial quality, the casualness of several poems can
be explained in part by their reliance on family images. However, the wryness of the most seemingly off-hand lines suggests a deliberate roughening, for the same reason that Warren once said Melville roughened his verse: because truth is
not easily trapped; it assumes contradictory shapes even while
being handled; it exudes a slippery substance called ambiguity.
And evil wears the disguise of familiar things. The sequence
"Ballad of a Sweet Dream of Peace," for example, which begins like a conversation over the peculiar antics of a Southern

granny, quickly develops into scenes of bestiality from some inferno. Incongruity becomes a mode of vision, with idiom rubbing other elements into a shape of meaning.

In "The Reading of Modern Poetry" (1937), Warren wrote that all poetry is dramatic at root, even when it is not narrative. In the sum structure of this book, the drama is managed by putting opposites in each other's coil and letting them be mutually absorbed. All of the poems to Rosanna have Italy as their locale; most of those to Gabriel, Kentucky. Nevertheless, two poems in the latter section specify the Italian scene. Are these displaced poems? They make no mention of the boy, yet they belong with the poems assigned him because in common they treat initiation into horror and "fish-flash" perceptions of how it must be assuaged. No situation is foreign to this uniform experience. Moreover, Gabriel's section discloses the only condition under which Rosanna's joy can be restored, through acknowledgment of the dark filth of blood, in full-grown comprehension.

In an age of broken promises and lost honor, "When posing for pictures, arms linked, the same smile in their eyes, / Good and Evil, to iron out all differences, stage their meeting at summit, " it is easy to be sinister or a cynic. Only a man who has followed himself and others closely is mature enough for faith. Warren, who has debunked the rash presumption of human perfection by Jefferson and the immigrant's dream of rebirth in the West, has yet to make the mistake of arguing that constant failure proves the futility of effort. Rather, he has criticized American culture for its worship of success. Some things are worth the failure, and this is the only promise that a foundering father can honestly make: that there is good reason to have faith in hope despite man's record of evil. These new poems are not naïve but make a refrain of multiple motive: the joy of the horror at a bullbat's death, or the tramp's "awfulness of joy" in pure despair. Yet it is precisely this sense of complicity, this sharing of human weaknesses, which, like the compassion expressed for all those cruel and unloved in "Mad Young Aristocrat on Beach, " cleanses man and prepares the possibility of that fullest image of kinship, sacramental reunion. This has long been Warren's version of the "fortunate fall. "

The growing child will separate from the parent because
such is the meaning of birth, and that pain, therefore, is good.
Only in the risk of separateness can the progenitor's love be
proved and fulfilled. It takes courage to mean:

> You will live your own life, and contrive
> The language of your own heart, but let that conversation
> In the last analysis, be always of whatever truth you would live.

(Perhaps as critic he has learned that one can conduct a reader
only so far.) As reward one has only the conviction that he has
given life, not withheld it. Children then become their own
promises, standing as straight as two statements, which *could*
be named Rosanna and Gabriel:

> The sun is red, and the sky does not scream.
> . . . .
> The moon is in the sky, and there is no weeping.

But every leavetaking brings the wayfarer, through the cir-
cuitous coil of endangers, closer to home. Robert Penn Warren's development as a poet is a journey from the physical
realm to the metaphysical. Pure violence was his first subject matter, as if it held some promise for a special sense of
reality. But its density was a matter of decor only, a species
of abstraction belying the appearance of sensuousness. By con-
centrating too narrowly on the vocabulary of invented outrage,
he achieved only an effect of forced immediacy. Gradually,
however, the act of particularization found usable correlatives
in Warren's own experience: the Kentucky hills and their inhabitants, the severing of traditional ties as the wanderer
leaves home and discovers unfamiliar landscapes.

John Crowe Ransom (who otherwise abhors the "biographical heresy") has attributed Warren's choice of theme to the
real loss the man felt after being separated from southern Kentucky. It is true that "To a Face in the Crowd," the first disclosure of bitter division repented between sons and fathers,
was written at Vanderbilt just after Warren had moved (about
fifty miles) from Kentucky to Tennessee; and that the address
acknowledged on occasion in the *Fugitive* is still Guthrie, Kentucky, not Clarksville, Tennessee, It is equally true that War-

ren developed his "Kentucky Mountain Farm" sequence and the whole series of "prodigal son" poems while he was in California, Connecticut, England, and Italy. However, the poems themselves (and the prose) must be final judge whether or not these few facts from the author's life are sufficient and necessary cause for the lines he wrote. The poems make clear that what Warren saw and felt in innumerable leavetakings and wayfarings parallels convictions reached on more subtle occasions. As a result his poetry becomes more than personal, more than a diary document. It is available to the recognition of each reader. As Warren explained in "Original Sin: A Short Story," man outlives ordinary homesickness. The other kind, the apprehension of his nature's moral peripheries that he recalls from his undeniable private past but that awaits him too in future ambush, can never be cured.

Perhaps it is modesty on Ransom's part not to recognize in Robert Penn Warren's thought analogues of his own work, especially *God without Thunder,* in which Christ himself is represented as a sort of prodigal son. Man, argues Ransom, will rediscover a proper religious sense only when God the Son (symbol of sacrificial brotherhood) returns to God the Father (the demanding patriarch, lawmaker beyond appeal); when man will submit again to the stern Godhead of the Old Testament, whose mysterious ways might well seem, to the blindered temporal eye, "evil and ignorant and old." Yet because this Godhead is first, final, and sustaining cause it must be acknowledged. The introduction to *I'll Take My Stand* (for which Ransom was largely responsible) also indicts each man as Cain and designates each day Ash Wednesday.

From the main line of Warren's thought, expressed in poetry, emerges a system of similar themes, performing as metaphor to one another. Following the dream of a strange and more exciting self, the son leaves home, shortly to discover that, although he has dressed himself in a new personality, the claim of his past self can never be denied. Psychologically, man's night and day worlds mirror each other; many of Warren's poems observe this interchange. There is no exit from the image of fact multiplied. Man must accept as a continuum all the distributed selves he has ever been—an onerous decision, requiring acknowledgment of his first deliberate wrong, desertion of the family mores. This is the individual's story.

It is recapitulated in terms of mankind and the mass (rather than the personal) unconscious in poems such as "History," which asserts the presence of the past, the obligation modern man has to the aspirations of all previous civilizations. Sociologically, the formulation is still valid. The movement from "Eidolon" to "Original Sin: A Short Story" traces the abandonment of the agrarian community with subsequent migration to the city. The flight is never successful because urban life is too impersonal, too disoriented, to act as proxy for the past self's continuing demand for recognition. In "The Ballad of Billie Potts" the city supplies symbols of fragmentation. The American dream of new lands and new natures, which as an index of man's deeper needs at least had an authentic motive for existing, has ended in the unreality of metropolitan civilization. It is the natural creature—bee, goose, salmon—whose instinct beholds great designs in the universe. Such imagery invokes religious correspondences. Search for innocence in the West and the intuitive migration to spawning grounds are projections of an innermost human impulse. Neither baptism nor anonymity can remove man's primal guilt. Innocence can come only after forgiveness, and forgiveness only after full understanding and humble contrition; it cannot be demanded but only hoped for. Excessive human self-reliance threatens to deprive God and is a form of denial. Evil is the symptom of man's ultimate dependence; grace, his capacity to welcome that subordinate role. Stoicism can be sublimated, even man's suffering being offered as express sacrifice.

These are the levels of meaning that confirm one another in Robert Penn Warren. They are the "fictions" that support each other's truth. Although Warren himself may not insist on his poetry's religious significance, the poems themselves implicitly do. The religious vocabulary of the earliest work (such as the "unhouselled angers" of dogs in "Eidolon") may owe more to manner than to intention—the early *Fugitive* poems of Tate also impress such terminology into their service. However, the appearance of such language in Warren's later poems, which are controlled and conscious, can hardly be explained as accident. Repeated concentration of hieratic imagery in advance of the poetic climax is a sign not of indifference but of a decision to avoid direct didacticism. Warren's first concern always is with presenting a drama of the spirit, rather than with propagating any pre-experienced or specific sectarian doctrine.

While certain of the earliest poems wonder admiringly at human capacity for suffering, others composed in the same period already cry out for justification of pain. Warren's growing technical craftsmanship has been invoked by the ultimate demand that causes beneath phenomena shall be unmasked. Correspondingly, the center of gravity has shifted from separate epithet to more substantial expression and the invention of forms. At the same time expanding subject matter has explored the diversified soils of human behavior, intending not so much to relieve suffering as to understand it. In the process of identifying this problem, Warren suggests that suffering can be made meaningful only by recovery of the sense of sin and by man's acceptance of the necessity of evil. Such is the nature of his inherited defect that man inevitably causes suffering. Its presence makes his existence possible. Evil conspires to define man: the fiction of Robert Penn Warren makes this conclusion unavoidable.

6

FICTION AND BIOGRAPHY:

THE ORNATE WEB

John Brown: The Making of a Martyr (1929)

In the aftermath of World War I, the Southern states, already profoundly knowledgeable in the course of postwar "reconstructions," set their literate citizenry the task of recalling chronicles of their past as an example in conduct, proper and improper, for the whole nation. One result of this new self-awareness—new to the extent that it was not defensive but at times so scrupulously critical in its findings that it earned the resentment of more sentimental Southerners—was that several of the Vanderbilt group were assigned the reassessment of regional character in terms of its past stalwarts and scalawags. Histories once written exclusively by Northerners now had to compete with Southern versions made available in several biographies: *Stonewall Jackson: The Good Soldier* (1928), *Jefferson Davis: His Rise and Fall* (1929), and *Robert E. Lee* (1932), all commemorated but not quite celebrated by Allen Tate; Andrew Nelson Lytle's *Bedford Forrest and His Critter Company* (1931); and Robert Penn Warren's *John Brown: The Making of a Martyr* (1929).

Although these authors were not historians by profession but, at the time, only apprentice poets and makers of fiction, they did represent a philosophy, later expressed in *I'll Take My Stand,* which could admit Southern faults, appraised as abandonment of the most distinguished principles of the region and participation in the corruption of local integrity by the national will. Warren was particularly qualified by his wide reading in American history since childhood, an interest that he maintained while doing graduate study in literature at Berkeley and Oxford. His conception of history as "the big myth we live" is already evident in this early biography of a man whom history had made, according to Warren, a mock Messiah. (This attitude would later find official disclosure in the foreword of *Brother to Dragons* and be confirmed through peripheral narration by historians in *World Enough and Time* and "Circus in the Attic, " as well as through the choice of Burden, student of history, as central intelligence in *All the King's Men.)*

The figure of John Brown, in Warren's interpretation, becomes so complicated that he seems not only self-contradictory but even unmanageable. In an attempt to distinguish fact from legend, Warren consulted a number of biographies, memoirs, and general studies, and, although he concedes the conflicting nature of a few crucial sources, through a multitude of comment he tries to reassure the reader that the consensus being presented bears no stigma of doubt. Such intrusions, however, have a reverse effect. They indicate that the editor must intervene because the facts, though culled with caution, will not speak for themselves. In addition to this private selectivity, Warren has jeopardized the reader's earnest judgment by the use of fictional devices such as reporting the most intimate thoughts and emotions of John Brown without reference to their presumed origin in his letters or journals. The few footnotes that accompany the text are a printing error, explained away with an apology. However, even when John Brown and his children are cited, their words cannot be the final arbiter of their own truthfulness because of conflicts in their statements.

Instead of recording this circumstance objectively, Warren
has taken such contradiction as license for whatever interpretation he chooses to make. To the author's misfortune, the
very evidence that the breadth of his study admits questions
the identity thrust on his subject.

John Brown's father is pictured as an Ohio frontiersman
living on the patronage of New England factory owners who
opposed slavery in the South because it threatened their monopoly of wealth, made possible by high protective tarrifs. John
was a land speculator until an expected canal failed to be constructed on his property; then he became a cattle drover and
unprincipled (as well as unsuccessful) wool merchant, recoup-
ing some of his losses by teaching emancipated Negroes on
the New York estate of Gerrit Smith. Although he himself had
once paid fines rather than drill as a civil guardsman, in pam-
phlets and speeches he began inciting armed resistance to the
Fugitive Slave Law.

After five of his sons squatted on free Kansas Territory,
John Brown joined them, ostensibly to prevent incursions of
proslavery men from Missouri (he now carried a gun) but perhaps more realistically to see if "something would not turn up
to his advantage," as a daughter put it later. Finally his armed
gang of "Liberty Guards" made their murderous sweep through
Pottawatomie Creek. Although he later denied it, Brown himself shot the first of the slain. His son and namesake, who had
not joined the raid, was driven slowly insane by the burden of
his father's guilt. Nevertheless, the old man prospered, at-
tracting a press agent and sufficient outlaw forces to intimidate
the government marshal.

Returning from the field after further raids, unappreciated
by a people already at peace, Brown used donations given for
defensive purposes to train a dozen men in his grand scheme:
conquest of the South with slaves as his soldiers, Yankee dis-
unionists his benefactors. The point of attack was Harpers
Ferry; he did not realize that there were few Negroes in the
area. Like most abolitionists he "thought of slavery in terms
of abstract morality, and never in the more human terms of
its practical workings." However, even if there had been Negroes in the area of the arsenal, Warren maintains that they
would have had no cause to revolt.

The first man killed by Brown's "liberators," ironically, was a free Negro. Townsmen cut off the attackers from escape until Colonel Robert E. Lee of the United States Cavalry arrived, and J. E. B. Stuart personally captured the traitors. At his trial Brown could not plead insanity without discountenancing his lifelong passion for recognition. Others, however, made the plea for him, citing nine cases on his mother's side and six among his first cousins. Gerrit Smith himself went to an asylum in 1859. Nevertheless, John Brown, seizing his chance for martyrdom, went quietly to the gallows that same year.

Throughout the biography, depending on the moment's need, Warren chose to treat Brown now as a resourceful mercenary (horse thief and business speculator), now as a completely irrational madman. Repeated reference is made to the mental sickness of Brown's first wife, of John Brown, Jr., of Gerrit Smith, and of Realf (an early raider who was raising money in England at the time of the assault on Harpers Ferry). The attempt to discredit John Brown is undisguised. What is not attempted is a sober effort to determine the exact condition of person and action, summarily labeled insane and half-insane. In his final analysis Warren perversely has refused to relieve Brown of any guilt by declaring him a paranoiac. As a criminal he deserved execution.

Even in this judgment, however, Warren is partial. Although he acknowledges that both John Brown and his sons repeatedly denied that the father personally slew Boyle, the Pottawatomie settler, rather than admit doubt Warren arbitrarily accepts the accusation of Townsley, another of the raiders. His method is narrative, unobstructed by the hesitations expected of a historian. His main intention seems to be to burn John Brown in effigy. A young writer's recklessness is revealed in the reliance on Negro stereotypes, the offhand manner of presenting views on slavery, and his haste to exonerate as "executions" the mutilations performed by the Virginia mob on several raiders.

The partisanship of the narrative dismisses prematurely persons of some importance. The moral intent of the traitors is negated only through association with Brown, a man of clouded mind. But why dispose so quickly of Dangerfield Newby, free

Negro, who died at Harpers Ferry to rescue his wife and children from slavery? Or of Watson Brown who, having written
his wife concerning a slave near their Virginia hideout who had
hanged himself because his wife had been sold into the Deep
South, added that he himself could never come home while such
human cruelty lasted? He, too, died at Harpers Ferry and deserves a place in the moral reckoning.

Aside from such partiality, *John Brown* rehearses certain
formulations later characteristic of Warren's fiction: the man
who, like Perse Munn, seeks to define himself through violence; the man who tries for a time (as Jack Burden did) to
justify villainy by social determinism, while the author himself insists that any causes external to man lie only in God's
inscrutable will: man's role is conferred, not assumed. Furthermore, there are suggestive resemblances between the description of John Brown's first raids and those narrated in
Night Rider. The death of Boyle in the biography is not unlike
the killing of Bunk in the novel. Although the two books were
published ten years apart, when *John Brown* appeared Warren
was already at work on "Prime Leaf, " the novelette that foreshadows *Night Rider*. Brown became progenitor of all later
irrational agonists, the ambivalents, torn nerve from flesh
in ceremony by their own divergent passions. Willie Stark is
a more scrubbed and sanded version; but among the overlapping
plans of Warren has been the possible reappearance of this
archvictor-victim, John Brown, in play form.[1]

Meanwhile, as preparation for the writing of historical fiction, *John Brown* was influential in the Warren canon, though
its native value as either history or fiction must remain in
doubt. Until his two-part narration of the Mexican War, in
1958, Warren refrained from attempting any official chronicles of action. The interim taught him, with every short story
and novel, to observe, to respect, to document, to verify intuition by fact and fact by intuition, to inform vision through
revelation.

The Circus in the Attic and Other Stories (1948)

During his undergraduate days at Vanderbilt, Robert Penn
Warren had written several short stories that he disliked so
thoroughly that he decided to abandon fiction permanently. But

the friendship that developed with Katherine Anne Porter during the late 1920's, while Warren was at Yale, helped to change his mind. At the same time he had been impressed by the fact that Caroline Gordon was publishing stories about his own region. While he was away at Oxford his thoughts of home grew more lustrous, so that when the editors of *The American Caravan,* which had already printed his poetry, requested fiction, he remembered the tobacco country of his childhood, the turbulence of its economic wars that sundered son and parent, and wrote "Prime Leaf."[2]

The Circus in the Attic and Other Stories, collected in 1948, corroborates that early turning homeward. Most of Warren's short fiction is an ingathering of Southern rural life. His best stories have been adult reminiscences of durable childhood events, combined retrospection and introspection, the older scrupulous mind infecting with its guilt the reopened flesh of the past that has never quite been lost, or wholly lived in.

Of this group, "Blackberry Winter," held in such esteem by its author that it was published as a book in 1946, justifiably has already entered the histories of its genre. The story is narrated by a man in his early forties, recalling how his immaculate boyhood mind, at nine, had watched only with curiosity the city-clothed stranger who, snapping the silence of green twilight suspended under forest trees, approached his father's farm. While the man earned his feed by burying chicks and poults drowned in the latest storm, the boy watched with neighboring farmers their possessions stream irrecoverably, in a swollen current, past the fields of flooded tobacco plants. Still, his father sat straight in his saddle.

Yet the world had changed. The boy found a yardful of trash washed out from under the cabin of his father's "prideful" help, and old Jebb predicted that the cold snap in June would go on. The Lord had tired of sinful folks and was blessing the earth with earned rest. Later when his father, explaining that he was unable to hire anyone now, still offered a dollar, the stranger cursed the farm and left, dogged by the curious boy whom he also cursed. "That was what he said, for me not to follow him. But I did follow him, all the years." The boy has been initiated into irrevocable manhood in a world of time.

"Blackberry Winter" makes no attempt to romanticize rural

hardships. Its concern is with intuition more than with senti-
ment. Flood, the drowned poults, the dead cow, the ruined
tobacco crop—these are expected. They are countered with
calmness, by women replanting flowers in their wake and by
men who stoically compare their calamities with those of General Forrest's cavalry. But just as the displaced stranger fails
to comprehend such composure, so does the boy consider it
too commonplace to notice. The flood, the hillmen's hunger,
the "woman mizry," all are no more than personal inconveni-
ences, preventing his going barefoot. Only the mean, defeated
stranger can engage his curiosity about the meaning of a man.
Leaving, not literally but imaginatively, he moves into time,
the unforeseen world of change, beyond the charmed circle
of childhood's "submarine" forests. His action is the natural
motion of birth, of parturition. Yet, remembering it, he feels
a sadness beyond nostalgia: guilt at having come so late to an
appreciation of his family and its undramatic daily weather-
ing. While reaching out to make the strange familiar, he has
let the customary become mysterious. The farm is quickly
lost, his parents die, his playmate is imprisoned. Now any act
of attention or of contrition seems ineffectual. Even old Jebb
who endures like Tiresias or ancestral memories is immor-
tally aware of mortal suffering and human loss, the expense
of knowledge.

To this same moral landscape belongs Grandfather Barden
of "When the Light Gets Green," whose portrait, taken alone,
would seem cropped. Nothing remains of his ex-cavalryman's
physique except a thin posture of dignity and a sure hand on
the horse. During a heavy hail in the summer of 1914, threatening his son-in-law's tobacco, he collapses, and later waits
to die upstairs, unloved. His grandson lies, pretending to love
him; although Barden dies not then but four years later, the
boy feels ashamed of his inability to love and his rejection of
the old man who had no son of his own. The now adult narrator is puzzled by his own sadness and shame. Everything remembered about the old man is pleasant, except for what the
boy feels about his grandfather's shrunkenness. Is this pity,
or involuntary self-pity, the twist in the loins at the realization of imminent disability? (It is an ominous green that shines
before the calamity of storms; after his lie, the boy cannot

P. 93-94

face himself in the dresser mirror, which is "green and wavy like water. ") Is it an incapacity to associate himself with age and change, the required disaster that makes him reject the old man? In both this story and "Blackberry Winter" there is a curious nostalgia for a past, painful because its obligations are beyond comprehension. The sense of kinship works in se-cret.

In "Christmas Gift" one of Milt Alley's sons is shown the same respect given the father, "white trash" hillsman, in "Blackberry Winter. " The boy is shy and burdened. En route to deliver his sister of an illegitimate child, a doctor lets the boy roll a cigarette and in return receives a stick of candy—mutual tokens for those who survive adversity.

Measured by the authentic simplicity of such stories, "Good-wood Comes Back" and "The Patented Gate and the Mean Ham-burger" seem contrived. Goodwood, after drinking his way out of professional baseball, finally marries a girl who has what he really wanted all the time, half interest in some out-country land. One day her brother kills him because "bad blood" had developed between them. The cause of violence is never explained except for the hint that Goodwood loved solitude too much. He should have farmed his land instead of spending his time off in the woods shooting or fishing. But the narrator seems unsure of the significance of his story. The characters of "The Patented Gate and the Mean Hamburger" are again hard-living would-be yeoman farmers. After thirty years of labor Jeff York finally owns a small farm with a gate that can be opened without getting down from a buggy. But, because his wife's one pleasure is hamburgers, he sells his farm, buys her a stand, and hangs himself on his patented gate. She happily learns in time to fling "a mean hamburger. " The con-clusion, by paring down her character to grotesque dwarfdom, destroys the credibility that the story maintains as long as Jeff is its center. For sacrificing so much for such a woman, he himself is whittled down until his suicide becomes more bewildering than pathetic.

The same indeterminate interest unsettles "The Confession of Brother Grimes" and "A Christian Education. " In the first of these stories Warren's cosmic web philosophy appears to be parodied. When preacher Grimes's relatives suffer sometimes without apparent cause, he admits that God is punishing him, through them, for dyeing his hair black over twenty years. More provocative but equally elusive is the confession of the narrator in "A Christian Education." Silas Nabb, raised to ignore all provocation, nevertheless one day on a picnic cruise attacks a boy who has harassed him with dirty jokes and in the commotion falls overboard. The boy-narrator makes no attempt to save Silas until forced to do so. Swimming down, he wants to lie in that remote silence, looking up, "trying to see where the light made the water green." But the drowned body's touch forces him up to the surface, shrunken with guilt. The fact that much later Nabb's brother, not brought up a Christian, is imprisoned for shooting a man forestalls any attempt to interpret the story as a text on child education. As a result the Nabbs seem nearly superfluous in this story whose one convincing scene is that in which the narrator acknowledges the enormity of his crime. Yet his own attitude toward the story he tells is ambivalent. In the death and rescue scenes his manner is candid; reporting on the Nabbs he is distant, sarcastic. His own confession comes accidentally, the reader's attention having been directed meanwhile toward people whom the narrator neither knows nor cares to know. As a result the characters are made to appear eccentric, although it is the narrative line itself that is off center.

What happens when the "central register" of a story is only a semiconscious character is clear in the contrast between "The Love of Elsie Barton: A Chronicle" and its sequel. Elsie is a woman of mystery even to herself. Her life seems bent on fulfilling some ineluctable pattern to which she must patiently acquiesce. When she is violated by Ben Beaumont (who understands neither himself nor his interest in her), she refuses to struggle. Their subsequent marriage makes her feel even more "trapped in that alien body." Ben's passion is as much an involuntary reflex as is his wife's passivity. Confronted by the unrelieved incomprehension of these characters, the reader has to invent his own cause for pity. "Testament of Flood," however, gains by being told through the mixed feelings of a young boy who loves and hates Elsie's daughter. Filled with a sense of his own ugliness, yet wanting this beautiful girl who dates older men, he is suddenly saturated with gossip about her and realizes that already she is dead and tragically inaccessible, and he in his knowledge and impotence older than anyone alive.

An equal irony certifies the characterizations in "Her Own People." Fired for her temper, Viola, a Negro cook, lies in her rented bed waiting to die unwanted. She has no other home but death. Her employers are angry with her because she has made them examine themselves and their own niggardly relationship with life. The home for which *they* are sick is the one they were never married enough to build.

The two stories about academic life included in this volume develop the theme of the rejected past introduced in other stories. "The Life and Work of Professor Roy Millen" studies a man whose childhood has been difficult, his young manhood painful. When a student maneuvers him into saying that he once visited Paris, he becomes so enraged with his own lie, the denial of his early life, that he repudiates the student rather than recommend him for the requested Paris scholarship. In "The Unvexed Isles" a professor's temptation to reject the truth of his origin is complicated by the discovery that his wife finds attractive the sophistication of one of his students. To keep his wife, the professor is at first prompted to behave with equal sophistication. Instead he reminds them all of the modest midwestern farm that was his home, and his wife is trapped by his honesty. For a moment after the student has left in dismay, the professor, fearing the silence that frosts the interval between his wife and himself, feels profoundly homesick for the first time. But he senses, too, that the home to which one returns is never the home he left. Home is a spirit that each two people must construct on some past image. Whatever his wife is, insufficient or merely tired, he is also. Yet even these resources for building a life together are better than pretenses. Such a conclusion is more compelling than that of its companion story largely because the introductory action, by refusing to stay withheld in one man's mind, allows what it symbolizes to affect and alter the contents of the three minds involved.

Short fiction has never satisfied Warren's love of and respect for circumstantial detail and development. His best short stories have been incomplete; divided halves in search of each

other. Both early and late, he has trained for his longer works
with novelettes: 1931, "Prime Leaf"; 1947, "The Circus in
the Attic." In the later, sprawling story, having successively
isolated himself from his heroic ancestry (he is the only sur-
vivor of Bardsville's first settler) and his possessive mother,
Bolton confines himself to the secret carving of a soft-pine
circus. It has become his personal monument to honor what
he most desires: something undemanding, to which he can belong (as the town has its own monument to glorify itself in two
Civil War "heroes," one actually too drunk to run from the
Yankees, the other a temporary turncoat). He has always been
afraid to explore the motives for his own "civil wars," knowing that under the rational answers will be "the blank-faced
need swaying in the dark, coiled like the spring of his being."
He contents himself with his circus and with keeping an inadequate history of the county (he has never known even his pioneer ancestor's name). Then for a while he identifies himself
with his stepson when the boy is drafted. But after the boy's
death, as victory in war approaches, fewer people listen to
Bolton's enthusiasms, and, when his wife and a certain captain
are killed in a highway accident together, he retires to carve
another circus in his lonely attic. His daughter-in-law, re-
marrying, discovers guiltily that she loves her new husband
even more than she did the old, but her joy is too real to be
denied. Nor does it matter. In some future all those who lived
will be equally blessed by the blurring of memory.

Perhaps the novelette is intended to mean that history is a
circus, an entertainment, a projection of each man's mind
carved to suit its own half-seen needs. History deserves to
be satirized when it pretends to be exact and omniscient, instead of admitting to the erection of self-satisfying monuments. No man knows with complete intimacy and accuracy
his own motives. No man can enter and survey the mind of
another. Consequently history is elaborate myth or the feeble
interpretation of external action only.[3]

Such a reading of "The Circus in the Attic" could find parallels in the attitude of the historian-narrator in *World Enough
and Time,* or the philosophy of history in the foreword of *Brother to Dragons.*[4] Nevertheless, even if these resemblances establish the intention of "Circus in the Attic," the novelette is

still hobbled by having to adopt the method that it satirizes. The characterizations are so disproportionate in interest assigned them that Bolton survives as the central figure only by force of accident. The storytelling method is so hopelessly remote from extraordinary human insight that it seems to assent to, rather than censure, the notion that all men are equally unimportant—that each simply has his own source of intoxication, his own dark compulsion and destiny, his own mystification.

Warren's earliest novelette is equally extravagant. Its whole first section of dialogue is ballast better overboard. Once under way, "Prime Leaf" is essentially a straightforward tale of action about a family's near division during the tobacco wars. Old Man Hardin steps out of the farmers' association rather than use force against objectors to price fixing. However, his son, whom he had originally convinced to join the association, refuses to quit immediately. Their reconciliation occurs when young Hardin kills a man raiding the Hardins' property. The old man rides with him part way to town, honorably bringing him to justice and bringing justice to him, but on the way the father is ambushed and killed. After its awkward beginning, "Prime Leaf" explores with powerful intimacy the divisions and alliances of its inhabitants.

What makes "Prime Leaf" an exceptional story in the Warren canon is that none of its characters wonders who he is or what the nature is of man, God, or society. Although most of the short stories have the same locale as the novelettes—Kentucky and Tennessee—the impression repeatedly given is that of an alien world. The narrator, after having rejected this background early in life, discovers now, as he tries to recall it, that in turn it has rejected him. Although he left in order to "define" himself, he feels that his present life is either false or inconsequential. He suffers genuine nostalgia in recalling his youth, though its circumstances were hard or even perilous. He remembers the dignity won by the poorest of hillsmen. His motives for rejecting home now seem obscured. Yet he blames only himself, believing that there can be no identity for him without obligations. In order to prove that he has an existence at least partially independent of ancestral forces fused in him, he necessarily must couple a sense of guilt with his sense of loss. The presence of evil in his life is dim but undeniable, and he is one of its sources.

Even where motivation is darkest, it is this concept of the individual struggling to emerge from determining forces and yet somehow merely multiplying their efficiency which provides a near-tragic tone to the more successful stories of Robert Penn Warren. The others fail when the characters are so unaware of their own situation that no feeling in them, or consequently for them, can result. It is not unnatural for a writer to try to express the irrational acts of subterranean man, for who needs a spokesman more than the mute? Yet Warren has seldom found short fiction adequate to the aura of associations that subsumed incitements require. Perhaps also, in some part, he claims for the author areas of the unverifiable, those psychic portions unexplained by science and often never dreamed of by Freud. In this area myth, however finite, is privileged to move, but often no myth is forthcoming. Such stories become mere chronicles, parodies of Warren's concepts. There is puzzlement without sadness, an alien world with no competing vision, dark compulsion without resistance. As a result such stories seem bad copies of Sherwood Anderson's "grotesques," which Warren once criticized for presenting motivation in terms of oversimplified but still unexplained impulses.

Night Rider (1939)

Night Rider was the first of Robert Penn Warren's novels to be published although he had previously written two others, both close to his own youth: one concerned with Kentucky farm-family life before World War I, the other with a small-town school.[5] Like "Prime Leaf," which had appeared ten years earlier, *Night Rider* makes effective use of Warren's birthplace as its scene, a Kentucky county that participated in the tobacco wars of 1905-8.[6] Two characters, Mr. Christian and Captain Todd, bear the names of counties involved, and, despite the fact that Warren was born in the first year of the civil conflict, he has retained remarkable memories of a state guard encampment at his home-town railroad station.[7] Nevertheless, as the author's own introductory note warns, the novel is not meant to be read as an allegory in Southern economic history, nor, despite its opportune publication, is it limited to interpretation as an indictment of proto-fascist terrorism. Perse Munn is the spectral man of the twentieth century, and the local social turmoil is employed to reveal and reflect divisions within the characters themselves. This ingathering of forces is responsible for the qualitative difference between the novel and the novelette that preceded it.

Mr. Munn (as he is usually called, except by his wife—a sign of Southern gentility and a symbol of his remoteness from reality) apparently galloped through uncharmed adolescence in pursuit of adulthood, so little of the past or of kinship clings to him. He recalls only childhood hunts and an ageless widowed mother, competent farmer and taciturn companion except for rare lunges after her son's withheld love. She died, for him, long before her death. Life begins only after his return to Bardsville from law school in Philadelphia. Covetous of the power that mob oratory gives such men as Senator Tolliver, a father figure in his ambitious mind, and attracted by organizer Bill Christian's excitement, which his daughter Lucille warns is more important to him than his talk of individual rights, Munn lets himself be hired by the newly formed price-fighting Association of Growers of Dark Fired Tobacco.

Munn's initial disgust with the conscriptive brunt of crowds on the Bardsville train fades as he realizes how easily mobs are led by those they think their servants. Yet he cannot help wondering if they recognize him only because he has borrowed their identity. Is it not *their* sureness with which he has identified himself and which he has merely presented back to them through his words? He moves among them like a drunken somnambulist.

Characteristically unsure of himself afterward, Munn is disappointed that his wife is pleased with his choice. They seem to stain each other with their strangeness: often he watches her in her secret sleep, or hurries home in the hope of surprising her before she becomes what she is in his presence. Growth of the organization comforts his doubts only briefly: "At what moment could a man trust his feelings, his convictions? At what point define the true and unmoved center of his being, the focus of his obligations? He could not say. And who could say?" He envies Captain Todd, former Confederate cavalryman and now association member, who "could be confident

because he had no confidence in things and events, " these being
blind. Munn himself, meaningless alone, submits to the movements of his world. In his lovemaking he practices cruelties
on his wife in order to feel the assurance of power that absent
love is unable to give.

Yet, despite his personal bewilderment, Munn is intuitively
assured of the innocence of dirt farmer Bunk Trevelyan, accused of murder, and an illegal night search in fact discovers
the murder weapon in the shack of a Negro. Trust in his judgment falters, however, when Senator Tolliver defects from
the group. Feeling betrayed in the act of worship, Munn pre-
fers to believe that the Senator sold out from fear of bankruptcy
and not in protest against imprudence or in prophecy of violence.

Some "darkly coiling depth within himself" continues to tor-
ture his wife, making her world as unstable as his. And within
a few months there is more illegal night riding, this time by
the Free Farmers' Brotherhood of Protection and Control, an
inner circle mustered around Dr. MacDonald and his father-
in-law, Professor Ball, quoter of agrarian classics but seeker
after peace with a sword. (Ball, like John Brown outrider for
a meatax-wielding God, keeps his own hands disguised under
antiseptic bandages.) Men like Trevelyan replace Tolliver.

Although Munn has submitted to violence in the hope of self-
realization, his night self remains distinct from its daytime
counterpart. After a dark night of destruction, Munn can hardly
believe that the report in the morning paper concerns the same
event. He begins to wish for "that little world where everything was motionless but seemed about to move, " a world that,
as a boy, he had discovered in a stereopticon. Captain Todd,
whose firm bearing Munn has long envied, quits the secret
association when he no longer knows who his own people are.
Munn, feeling that betrayal is complete after Bunk Trevelyan's
attempts to blackmail another rider disprove all previous assumptions of his innocence, helps to murder his former client.

In the fall, enviously watching the serene migration of grackles, he recalls his homesick student days in Philadelphia where
his only relative was Ianthe Sprague, now almost as anonymous as their obscure common ancestor. She liked to have irrelevant and unconsecutive passages from the newspaper read

to her. Like some species of marine life lodged among random currents, she had withdrawn from events; but the grackles could live among events, still defined and undisturbed. Munn, deserted now by his victim-wife, turns in desperate longing to a secret life with Lucille Christian who, ironically, has been attracted to him because she thinks he is self-sufficient, while she, like Ianthe Sprague, refuses to contemplate time and change.

Troops are stationed in town after MacDonald leads a mass burning of tobacco warehouses, during which young Benton Todd needlessly dies because of a tactical error by Munn and has to be brought, a corpse, to his stricken father. Munn's blind impulse to injure is mocked by imitation: farmers with private motives borrow the night-rider tactics, razing Munn's own house when he declines to fire Negro tenants. That same night he loses Lucille, after her father has collapsed from the shock of discovering her (screaming, "I don't belong to you! Or to anybody!") in Munn's deserted bedroom. Thoroughly shaken, Munn makes no effort to rescue MacDonald when the latter is cornered by deputies, and refuses to risk damage to the case by acting as defense counsel. Munn's own truth, the actual moment of the warehouse explosions, becomes confused by the contest of conflicting testimony, all purporting to be equally true. The final turn of the screw comes when he is falsely accused of murdering the principal prosecution witness.

Escaping to the back-country home of Willie Proudfit, hard-working godly man who welcomes him, Munn tries to let thought strain into his rinsed mind only "like light into a submarine depth." He has already forgiven Professor Ball, who had let Munn appear to be the murderer, for the sake of his daughter's husband. He can see the old man, somnambulant, putting aside the murder weapon and staring at his white-bandaged fingers, unbelieving. But understanding of another's guilt feelings does not purge Munn's own. He has a recurring dream in which his wife presents him with a fetus whose features are Bunk Trevelyan's, and the actual birth of their child is a strange, indifferent incident in his utter isolation.

Proudfit tells Munn of his earlier life, his dream of the West, his wayfaring, and the slaughtering of buffalo in Oklahoma wallows and in Kansas. Finally aware that his body had become a machine part of his gun, he returned to the green land and pool and waiting girl that had appeared to him once in a delirium—the Kentucky from which his family had been wandering for years. The prodigal was home, his soul grown back to his skin. The moral of his *exemplum*, however, makes no impression on Munn.

When her father dies, Lucille returns to Munn for warmth, but they discover (together for the first time by daylight) that they have nothing to offer each other but the promise of death. To justify all his previous acts, Munn plans one final violence: to hunt down and kill Senator Tolliver, whom he blames for his original involvement but whom he pretends to stalk for insulting Lucille with his attentions. He hardly recognizes the unafraid old man whom he apprehends in a burned-out, ruined house. They confront one another like Lord Jim and Brown at the conclusion of Conrad's novel. Although Munn is convinced that he must kill, through the outrageousness of execution to know the reality of himself, the futility of killing Tolliver is clear. Each has sucked his strength from the crowd and still is empty. To fulfill the death wish that, in the name of justice, has been secretly his ambition all along, he returns to the dark outdoors and fires, in order to draw a murderous answering volley from the soldiers who have tracked him down.

The setting of *Night Rider* is the dark of mortal understanding. Proudfit's story-within-a-story provides the *exemplum* of a forgotten ethical imperative: to desist from ruthless exploitation of human and other resources and rededicate oneself to the painstaking, personal labor of one's fathers. The world of the novel is alien and unreal to its principal inhabitants, each of whom has diverged from this grand design. As an out-of-state student, Munn feels derelict; later he fails to know even his own wife with any intimacy. He tries to devise by an act of will a more than intermittent self, first through mass action, then through violence (elements glorified by Fascism, as Warren had observed in Mussolini's parading black shirts and later described in "Terror").

Because the chosen ways are self-defeating, however natural the need, Munn becomes less and less the self he wants to be. As his sensitivity toward individuals is forfeited to the surge of crowds, so his willingness for responsibility is overshadowed by his zeal for power which progressively encroaches on his control over his inner self. He kills Bunk Trevelyan; violates his wife; betrays Christian; and nearly assaults with blind brutality his wife's aunt, a bystander during the town raid, and a Negro hosteler. Those whom he has envied most for their self-assurance suddenly undergo a startling change. When Tolliver and the former Civil War officer Todd reject the secret organization's betrayal of first principles, Munn, once their admirer, blames Tolliver for his own dilemma and is responsible for the death of Todd's son. He seeks support from MacDonald and Ball, only to find that the former intends to flee to the West and the latter is trying to implicate him in murder. Nor can he appropriate Lucille's strength, since she has been relying on his. Even Proudfit, who has purified himself by excess, cannot communicate his righteousness. Munn seeks to restore his cause by one last violent deed, to glorify his death.

Senator Tolliver's weaknesses are Munn's own. Both need, rather than actually lead, the masses. Both put price (money or power) above principle. Both consequently are drained of personal affection. Munn cannot regenerate himself through the death of a man who is his alter ego. He cannot persist in his pose as minister of justice without punishing himself. His permissive suicide is the culmination of his gradual annihilation as a person.

The principal device employed by Warren to dramatize this night of the soul is the placement of the majority of the action in literal darkness. Munn observes his wife while she sleeps; he betrays Christian with his daughter in the night. Bunk is slain in the dark; the riders destroy the crops of farmers who reject their proposals at night; Munn himself dies in darkness. Even midday brightness gravitates toward the symbolic values established by night. Time and again Munn is made aware of the vast emptiness of the daylight sky, the hollowness of his life at any hour. He sees that night thoughts reflect the day in the same way that dreams read back significance into his waking moments. The novel is valid as a document of both private and social psychology, but it justifies itself as more than case history by its resolute system of representations.

Munn's attempt through will and party politics to escape the
obligation of making his life meaningful in motion is symbolized
by static submarine imagery as well as by short flights backward to childhood fantasy, detached from the fullness of any
past: the stereopticon's frozen innocence, remembered wood-
land serenity on childhood hunts, and at the moment of death
the blood-drowsy distortion of soldiers' voices into "the voices
of boys at a game in the dark." Such images are epitomized
by Ianthe Sprague, whose obsession with fragmentary news is a
deliberate attempt to conduct her life so that order—and therefore change or disorder, equivalents to her—will not intrude.
Hers is a living death, as Munn's also becomes: he is known
usually as Mr. Munn, a function or formal annex, not a man.
Eventually, however, he cannot escape the consequences of
the fact that man does exist in time, where things develop or
decay; the image most conversant with man's condition is not
the motionless pool, after all, but the web, as he had once
sensed in the coalescence of individual wills through the Association of Growers of Dark Fired Tobacco.

Despite this extensive use of imagery to dramatize, full
force, the corrupting influence of power on man's all too willing "dark fired" mind, *Night Rider* can tell only half its story
from the point of view Warren has chosen. Because Mr. Munn
can know so little of himself and his world, an *exemplum* of
the alternative way has been inserted near the end, in a fashion
so contrived that it seems an admission by the author that
his major characters cannot convey that theme alone. Furthermore, because Mr. Munn's sensibility is obscured, he can
give the reader only an experience of evil; he cannot direct
one's insight into its innermost causes. Although the symbols
employed have a natural consanguinity and are not multiplied
to the point of appalling density, their range is too small to
reproduce that *history* of resonances which a longer narrative
might have provided. Structure has been sacrificed, unneces-
sarily, to texture. There is a lively tension created between
the cinematic clarity of "action" scenes—invocations of the
mob, outlaw raiders, holocausts—and the dimness of self-
examination. Unfortunately the effect is largely to invite too
much attention to naturalistic appearances, by such emphasis

lending violence a superreality—the very illusion the novel had
hoped to dispel.

At Heaven's Gate (1943)

Eleven Poems on the Same Theme, which described the
crimes of "unnatural man" against his own and the world's
reason for existence, was followed within a year by the publication of Warren's second novel, *At Heaven's Gate,* whose
characters are also violators of the natural order, as if they
would unfix that very humanity which the implications of history have so painstakingly assigned. After the materials had
begun to gather, their thematic shape was suggested by the
seventh circle of Dante's Inferno, scene of the punishment of
those doing violence to nature's intentions: usurers (Bogan
Murdock), homosexuals (Slim Sarrett), and, with liberal variation, all the others trapped among deep, concentric, descend-
ing rings. [8] Many of the ideas and most of the imagery of infection had already been tested in *Proud Flesh* (1939), Warren's
first play, in which Willie Talos (predecessor to Willie Stark,
fallen monarch of *All the King's Men)* is a counterpart to Murdock. Each in his own way has the "faculty of fulfilling vicariously the secret need of others, and in the process . . . discovers his own emptiness, " as Warren later expressed their
relationship. [9] In all of these works each person pursues his
separate sin of incompleteness and incomprehension. [10]

To complicate *At Heaven's Gate,* through contrast, in alternate chapters there is the slow revelation of Ashby Wyndham's progress as a pilgrim. He, too, has been selfish, having
sinned against an actual brother. But, though his search for
redemption has all the signs of failure that any human effort
at perfect atonement might exhibit, even in his trials he finds
a peace beyond the other's understanding. He has experienced
the possibility of honesty; the rest, declaring the necessity
for self-knowledge, take temporary sanctuary in a life of lies.

Sue Murdock, a Tennessee financier's daughter whose stifled
cry, "Oh, what am I?" (anticipating Amantha Starr's livelong brooding in *Band of Angels)* finally finds public utterance,
has been a persistent admirer of student-poet-boxer Slim Sarrett's self-possession. Although she does not yet belong to

herself, she rejects the thought of being the property of her
father or of his employee Jerry Calhoun, whom (in a formula
of betrayal to be repeated in "Circus in the Attic" and *World
Enough and Time*) she once coldly forced to violate her in the
room beneath her father's. She had first been drawn to Jerry, a
young geologist in her father's oil-search office, by the certainty of his smile, but her interest plunges him back into inherited clumsiness. In spite of his own successful years in
college football, he is reminded constantly of his father's mus-
cle-bound floundering and his Uncle Lew's clubfoot. If he had
known his ancestors better, those latecomers who found the
best lands already taken, he would have resented them, too.
Once as a boy, to acknowledge his debt to great-aunt Ursula,
who had raised him, he had bought her a shawl and wept openly
in her presence. But secretly later (like the narrator in "When
the Light Gets Green") on the stable lot he poured out all the
vile words he knew, in repudiation of his aunt. Having rejected
his family in this way, he cannot consider wholly undeserved
the "something like homesickness" he felt during the lonely
years of college football, even after rich alumni offered to pay
his way into fraternities.

Among the employees at Murdock's bank, bond, and insur-
ance business, only Duckfoot Blake appears to have any human
sympathies. However, his family alienate Jerry because he
envies their childplay and banter and perhaps because they
are too like his own long-suffering family whom he has already
decided to surpass. Although Jerry's Uncle Lew reminds him
that old Angus Murdock became rich through land speculation
and that later his son Lemuel shot a man for political cause,
Jerry is pleased with his membership in Murdock's gun club,
an index of his rise.

(Simultaneously a spiritual, rather than social, progress
is being chronicled by a wayfaring backwoodsman, now prisoner
both of his conscience and of the law. Statement of Ashby Wyndham, Sheriff's Office: only extreme faith can feel God's love
behind man's vain reachings, the taking off of one sin and putting on of another. Ashby is the poor descendant of godly folks,
Porsums on his mother's side, left with a brother and a farm.
When Marie, an orphaned transient, neglects him he whips

her mule to death and then has to hire out to the Massey Mountain sawmill to repay her.)

Concupiscence, Jerry discovers, is no corridor to deepest
familiarities. He and Sue, frantic lovers, are always uneasy,
alert to interruptions, the very disquietude and threat of change
which have driven their spirits to their bodies for comfort.
Moreover, with Sue unaccountable acts of cruelty alternate
with sudden passions, "like the minute was all there was, like
there wasn't any yesterday and there wasn't any tomorrow."
She is capable of making her grandfather weep by demanding
bluntly why he shot his old political rival. Still, when Jerry
feels obliged at last to introduce her to his family, she sur-
prises him by ignoring drops of coffee dried on cups, shakes
his father's greasy hand, and, despite gobbets of food or spittle
on the old face of his aunt, kisses her. These people are the
source of strength which she mistook in him, and she announces
their intended marriage.

(After Marie becomes heavy with child, Ashby decides to
sell his half of the farm and go away with her. When his brother
Jacob objects to the loss of their homestead, Ashby hits him.
Jacob refuses his share of the price that Massey Mountain
Company offers and leaves estranged. When Marie nearly dies
in childbirth, Ashby, feeling punished for unworthiness, is
tempted to desert her, worried that his human love has not
been confirmed by God love.)

Displeased when Jerry defends her grandfather's worthiness
to have a mountain park named after him, Sue in desperation
appeals to Slim Sarrett, but he can tell her only the natural
history of his own loneliness. (Jerry, he assures her, is only
a fantasy invoked by her special needs.) After the death of his
barge-captain father, he had joined a street gang, expecting
fulfillment in the rage of crimes. From his mother, dispos-
sessed of any sense of past or future, Slim had learned the
falseness of nostalgia and of hope for immortality. A "multiplicity of fathers"—his legacy from her prostitution—and the
detachment of a poet's life console him. His apartment is the
scene of nearly uninterrupted diversions (Sue snuggles among
his coterie's envied "unchangingness" like a child in deep hi-
bernation, under a comforter, rejecting morning). Neverthe-

less, his interest as host is as clinical as his college work. Apparently unconscious of its applications to himself, he has isolated Shakespeare's major dramatic theme, the hero's defective self-knowledge, and has asserted (much as Warren himself did that same year) that poetry is the secretion of impurities in the self's attempt to become pure.

Sue's mother secretly envies her decision to leave home. Unable to think of her husband's youthful body as more than carrion, now unloved though once "vessel of a great tradition" (her ancestors, too honest to make money off land grants and Continental paper, have left her unprepared to be a financier's wife), she looks for solace in drink, pretending to be submerged in deep, relinquished waters, the backwash of time.

(When Massey Mountain Company announces a pay cut, a union man named Sweetwater calls a strike. Private Porsum, backwoodsman and former war hero, now company president, makes a personal plea to the strikers and is called a hireling by Sweetwater, whom Ashby therefore angrily strikes, provoking a riot. Ironically, Ashby is one of the men subsequently fired. He and his wife make public confession of his wickedness, as in the company of other outcasts they search the countryside for his fugitive brother.)

Briefly, Sue leaves her own "dim, subaqueous world" outside of time after Slim defends her from her father by accusing him of "the special disease of our time, the abstract passion for power, a vanity springing from an awareness of the emptiness and unreality of the self which can only attempt to become real and human by the oppression of people who manage to retain some shreds of reality and humanity." Impressed by his strength, Sue becomes Slim's mistress. He has never made love to her before, although he has studied her closely in her sleep. Later she discovers his homosexuality, and still later his lie: his father, a wash-machine salesman in Florida, is still alive.

Despite a fleeting reconciliation, she has finally renounced Jerry as a mere proxy for her father. (The Calhoun and other homesteads in Happy Valley are being foreclosed by Murdock enterprises, but only Duckfoot is incensed enough to resign.) Consequently, after Slim, Sue can turn only to Sweetwater for sheltering strength. His commitment to a cause, to an active life, makes possible a resolute callousness toward a relic past in which he felt he had no part and the desertion of his first wife. A professional rebel, he refuses to marry Sue although he causes her pregnancy and, picturing their unborn child enwombed in its ancestry which it will some day have to rescue from absurdity, tries to balk Sue's alcoholism. She is only reminded of her father's tyranny and, surfeited with rejection, has an abortion performed.

(Despite Ashby's interposition, a policeman is shot trying to imprison the evangelists. Taken to prison, Ashby makes his written statement, wondering at the will of God without questioning it.)

When a reporter confronts Porsum with a true and sworn copy of Ashby's words, he feels compelled to explain why the man was fired by Massey Mountain Company. Struck by Ashby's humility, Porsum remembers how, in Germany, prayer more than a sharpshooter's eye had made him a hero. He attempts to have his innocence restored by admitting publicly the corruption of Murdock's enterprises. A second chance for heroism presents itself to Porsum when he tries to prevent the lynching of a Negro falsely accused of Sue's murder (panicked by her delirious talk, Slim has suffocated her and then fled to New York to write dispassionately a poem about the everpresence of evil in man); but a brick strikes Porsum, toppling him, dead, to the ground.

Jerry, sickened by Murdock's use of his daughter's death to distract public attention from his finances, tries to find his way home. At night he is aware of the "coiling immeasurable depth of darkness outside" into which he had once fled, and on his old mattress he sinks back into the shape of his former self. "Something in the old self which had lain there had driven him out, but if you are going to come back, why do you leave?" He has no answer; but he realizes that, even while he was trying to make of Bogan Murdock a substitute father, his own inadequate and uncertain father, whose death he had willed, had understood and forgiven.

Meanwhile, to regain his stockholders' confidence, Bogan Murdock poses with the remains of his family, invoking the memory of men like Andrew Jackson, Southern ancestors whose reckless courage the modern financier has inherited.

While his daughter has led from one mirage to another a
cavalcade of characters variously requiring self-definition,
Murdock remains steadfast and impregnable in his self-deception. To the end he stands aloof, apparently unmoved by the
travail and miscarriages of others. Explaining why Murdock
will never be brought to justice, Duckfoot describes him as a
"great big wonderful dream. And you can't put a dream in jail,
son." While ambition leads harassed Perse Munn to self-destruction, Murdock's survival is suggested as a professional
achievement. He is the finance capitalist *par excellence*, incapable of qualms, epitome of a culture. In a novel whose re-
volving sections represent persons worrying each other to
death, there is no stream caught from his consciousness. He
has achieved immobility. That is the receipt for his wealth:
a subtle, prolonged form of suicide.

Murdock's attempted association with the heritage of Andrew
Jackson therefore officiates as travesty. Although the finance
capitalist, too, is responsible for men's deaths (through provocation of violent strikes, depressions), unlike the fighting general he assassinates by proxy. Having tooled his emotions to
a point beyond friction he can never be loved as Jackson was
loved, although he is hated as Jackson was hated. The flag
of tradition that Bogan Murdock waves is a manufactured one.
Only he can deny the terrible truth that his grandfather grew
rich through land speculation and that his father killed a man.
To justify himself he will memorialize them. This is the fig-
urehead which, having courted Jerry's loyalties away from his
own clumsily honest family, suddenly threatens to deprive
Jerry of his very homestead and birthright.

However, even as Jerry gravitates toward Bogan, Sue repudiates her father for his weakness and for her own. A great
share of the novel regards her search—through Slim, through
Jerry, through Sweetwater, her thoroughfares—for immutable
strength and integrity. Each fails her. Slim, the poet-boxer,
seems at first the ideal union of thought and action, but sport
to him is *evasive* action; his New Critical interpretation of
Shakespearean tragedy only nags his own spiritual deficiencies.
Slim's sexual ambivalence is symptomatic of deeper contortions; his invented personal history is attempted wish-fulfillment. He is an exhibitionist. At the same time, the particulars

of that history supply sufficient justification for his isolating himself from both his true and his imaginary family. Sometimes close to intimate self-recognition, Slim's knowledge merely multiplies his agonies. Sweetwater, in turn, is too strenuously opposed to all conventions, even those constitutive of the orthodox family structure and homely lineage that Sue requires, to be valuable to his mistress.

Malcolm Cowley once characterized Sue as the typical lost girl of the 1920's who, having rejected her father at the whim of Freud, must also discard her lovers as they threaten to become surrogate-fathers in their relationship with her. What such an interpretation, with its emphasis on submerged sexualism, overlooks is that not only Sue but all of her lovers have rejected their parents. They cannot replace what she has lost with what they no longer have. Jerry and Sweetwater have slammed their memories shut on their earlier lives. Slim (like Murdock) has gone further, falsifying his past to suit his present needs. All the characters are fugitives from a human condition which they cannot escape and which they are not strong enough to live with either. Not acquiescence but reduction by assimilation is the only means to immunity. Sue's conscription of Jerry to assist in her violation in the room beneath her father's is no simple Freudian maneuver. It is outrage answering outrage, the present reproaching the past, and nearly recreating it in the act. Like Lucille Christian in *Night Rider,* she fumbles for warmth in others, extinguishing its occasion.

The only person whose strength Sue appraises correctly is Mr. Calhoun. However, comfort from him cannot come except through Jerry; and by the time that Jerry is prepared to accept his own family as she already has, to shake his father's greasy hand and kiss the gob off Aunt Ursula's face, Sue has been murdered. Outside heaven's gate, the assessment of man is shaped according to his treatment of others. Whoever knows himself can prophesy the final judgment.

The major characters of *At Heaven's Gate* are versions of the same corroding incompleteness. Slim warns Sue that Jerry is largely a fantasy created by her need. But it is equally true that Murdock is "something you and I thought up one night." Product of the popular imagination, he cannot be destroyed without mass consent to a share in his guilt. Murdock's whole financial empire, in fact, is a mirage sustained by the will of society. Not only is Slim himself an invention of his own need, but his analysis of visitors to his apartment follows patterns of wish-fulfillment. Even Sweetwater, supposed antiromantic, cannot believe in himself without believing in a cause which will allow him to forget his sins against humanity. To all those who literally or figuratively watch over each other's sleep, hoping to enter the dream of another, there is no one to say, like Cass Mastern in *All the King's Men:* "It is human defect—to try to know oneself by the self of another. One can only know oneself in God and in His great eye."

As compensation for their incompleteness, the spiritually disabled resort to oppression or to displays of physical prowess. Jerry, the football player; Sue, the horsewoman; Sweetwater, the union roustabout; Slim, the boxer; Bogan, the middle-aged man with a youthful body: only the soul will not respond to their calisthenics; its hygiene is beyond the order of their knowledge. By contrast, as Sue herself occasionally realizes, those in the novel who are physically crippled are humbled but by compensation are rewarded with the faculty of honest self-appraisal and clarity of public vision. Clubfooted Uncle Lew, paralytic Aunt Ursula, mangled Rosemary, the almost pathologically awkward Mr. Calhoun, Duckfoot Blake—these are the purgatorial invalids, the victims who cannot retaliate. But in their combined worth and long-suffering lies the human answer to the predicament of the others. To their number must be added Private Porsum and Ashby Wyndham, backwoods kinsmen. Ashby never succeeds in recovering his brother Jacob so that they can be reconciled; yet in the web of things his confession-prayer does restore Porsum to the virtuous ways of their common ancestors and threatens to level the imperial walls of Murdock.[11] In these fault-ridden and common folk, gauche amid the ambidextrous city life of the Murdocks, lies whatever hope there is in the novel.

Unlike *Night Rider, At Heaven's Gate* is narrated by a rotating multiplicity of observers, most of them the spiritually crippled. Each is individualized and has his own resource of speech. Although in one sense they speak as a single person in a tumultuous outcry of unsatisfied need, nevertheless theirs is a babel of voices. They are nearly as remote from each other as the uncommunicating characters in Virginia Woolf's *The Waves*. Their cry, dislocated and ignorant in its protest, alternates throughout much of the book with the solitary voice of Ashby, sustained by his recognition of duty and his troubled attempts to work the cryptic word of God. In *Night Rider* the counterpart to Ashby's chronicle is intrusive and contrived, an aside to the reader. In *At Heaven's Gate*, however, the presence of Ashby's story is not only plausibly arranged but does, in fact, serve to reanimate Porsum's sense of moral obligation and therefore to quicken Murdock's financial disintegration, though not the collapse of the cultural mode it represents. By dispersing Ashby's testimony throughout the narrative, Warren has prevented it from blocking the progress of the novel. At the same time he has managed by contrasting language and motives to mold the story of city-aggravated anguish into dramatic shapes. It is the antithesis by means of which the dialectic must progress. Nevertheless, by strategic placement Warren prevents the ideas of the backwoods chronicle, although attractive because of their language, from separating radically from the others and thus becoming the message. The climax to Ashby Wyndham's portion occurs before, rather than after, a whole series of influential scenes: Mrs. Murdock's frantic accusation of Porsum in an attempt to earn a lover's reputation, however illicit or untrue; Porsum's ironic death; Sue's abortion and strangulation; Jerry's return to his former self. Ashby's story is no more a detached commentary on the life of Bogan Murdock than is any other in the multitude assembled.

A greater clarity also proceeds from the lessening of the "coiling darkness" imagery in *At Heaven's Gate,* The characters are more fully drawn and motivated than those in *Night Rider*. Although Jerry, for example, is never sure of his original reason for rejecting home, mistaken vanity is the suggested and sufficient cause. Only by accepting what he had been could he ever be anybody.

In search of familiar figures from local history to add density (as Dante had done before him) to the composite inhabitants of his own Inferno, Warren borrowed from the actual careers of such men as Luke Lea of Tennessee, onetime United

States Senator and convicted bank manipulator, imprisoned
for the multimillion-dollar failure of the Asheville Central
Bank and Trust Company. Like *All the King's Men*, however,
At Heaven's Gate suffers none of the official restrictions proper
to biography or history, but only those which an author's personal view of human nature imposes. The great difference between Bogan Murdock and Willie Stark lies not so much in their
differing degrees of ambition as in Warren's growing comprehension of how a populace makes its appalling masters
possible.

All the King's Men (1946)

Within a year after the assassination of Louisiana's home-
spun caesar Huey P. Long in 1936, while Warren was still
an instructor at Louisiana State University, he felt impelled
to write a play about a man corrupted by the very power he has
invoked against corruption. Long himself, whom Warren knew
as a political phenomenon rather than as a personal acquaintance, was never more than one installment in the character
of Willie Stark as he emerged. In Mussolini, who paraded his
legionnaires on Roman streets in the hope of battle and plunder,
Warren found a variant of the man "whose power was based on
the fact that somehow he could vicariously fulfill certain secret needs of people about him." He was already thinking the
thoughts that, in "Terror," would become wonderment and
outrage at the fascist habit of equating glorified violence with
success, death with practical adjustment. Alexis Carrel's experiments with immortal chicken hearts were the *donnée* for
what Warren later described as "the theme of the relation of
science (or rather, pseudo-science) and political power, the
theme of the relation of the science society and the power-
state, the problem of naturalistic determinism and responsibility, etc."[12] Pragmatist William James was another of "the
figures that stood in the shadows of imagination behind Willie
Stark."

By the end of 1939 Warren had completed his mixed verse-
prose play, *Proud Flesh*, first produced seven years later,
on the suggestion of Eric Bentley, at the University of Minnesota during Warren's term there. By then the material, re-
worked, had already been published as the Pulitzer Prize nov-

el, *All the King's Men*. A year later Warren's adaptation of
the novel was staged off-Broadway; he had approved, with qual-
ifications, the motion picture script, directed by Robert Rossen, which became a 1949 Academy Award winner; and a "final"
version, tentatively called *Willie Stark: His Rise and Fall*,
having been premiered in Dallas late in 1958, was produced
off-Broadway as *All the King's Men* during the autumn of 1959.
If Jack Burden is a contemporary Ancient Mariner compelled
to speak to compensate for the last-minute inarticulateness of
Willie Stark, Warren is an even stranger Ancient Mariner
whose tale to the wedding guest is each time varied. The playwright's explanation is consistent with his long stand: "in trying
to dramatize the novel I found myself, by the logic of the contrast between dramatic form and fictional form, re-interpret-
ing, re-thinking, shifting emphases. . . . If you begin to alter,
however casually, a form . . . you are bound in the end to
alter meaning."[13] So possessed has Warren become by the figure of his most successful nominee for tragic stature—the
American demagogue, mirror of mobs, through whom each
man creates his own doom—that he has portrayed him in every
medium he has ever practiced: poem, drama, novel. Yet of all
these versions only the novel can surpass the imaginative language of *Proud Flesh* as a means of characterization and in-
direct narration.

Proud Flesh employs a chorus of surgeons, onstage throughout the play, not to mediate between it and the audience, but
to quarantine the play's meaning, to sterilize communication
of anything personal, sentimental, or metaphysical which might
infect that anesthetic state which the chorus terms the general
happiness. Only Dr. Adam Stanton is not complacent by profession. Shocked by the cancerous spread of corruption under
Governor Stark's monocratic rule, he confesses, "We are the
dark/ He is in the dark." However, his blunt accusation that
Stark's proposed eight-million-dollar hospital for the poor is
intended only as an occasion for publicity and graft is answered
by the governor's offer to make him director of the hospital,
to insure that it remain undefiled. Although the chorus is satisfied (an early version read: "Do you ask if a liar compounded
the previous medicament, an adulterer whetted the scalpel?"),
Stanton, who has seen "sun glint the rotten water under the

tangle, " is too much aware of the nameless evil within Stark which "uncoils slime into stone. " The surgeons argue that Stanton must not pass judgment since "you are not other than he. "

In the midst of this indecision, Jack Burden, an old newspaper friend of Stanton, announces that the doctor's sister Anne has come to plead the case of an orphan group. Adam is angered by their advice that he accept Stark's offer. Together they recall old times on the beach, when "the fish hawk rose, he rose into light, " and they themselves "swam in light like the swell, " until that world's truth seemed everlasting. Anne insists that what they planned then, to help mankind, is all that can outlive childish dreams, but is sufficient: "If it's good, it's good, good in itself. . . ." When she accuses *him* of vanity, for rejecting Willie, Adam is shaken: "There's a tooth that gnaws, and gnaws our definitions. " Finally he tells the governor's secretary, Sadie Burke, that he will accept the directorship.

After flexing his muscles in public before the hospital is constructed ("Blood on the moon! . . . Your need is my law . . ."), Stark refuses to contaminate the building contract with henchman Tiny Duffy's graft and then defends Anne's good name by throwing a glass of whisky into Tiny's leering face. The governor has been so successfully dishonest that he can afford honor now. Yet he warns Anne when she is in his arms that "to make bricks, somebody's got to get down and paddle in the mud. " Anne trusts that he is strong enough to accept responsibility; she is reassured, too, that he is capable of affection by the look on Willie's face when word comes that his son Tom, having broken football training, has been picked up safe in a nightspot. The chorus of cynics, however, knows that love is a physical function only, costumed by the lover's theatrics.

At the football stadium while Stark is busy buying Fourth Congressional District votes for a "little sweetening" from the hospital contract, Tom Stark is carried off the field badly injured. The chorus diagnoses the cause as carelessness: "Like father, like son—that's a good definition of fate. " Just as Willie has ignored the infection of his polictial organism by hirelings, the boy has neglected to stay fit through exercise. Willie's divorced wife Lucy comes to plead that he release Tom from his personal ambitions, but, recalling the nameless compulsion that blew through his childhood, Willie cannot allow his son to be commonplace. In ruthlessness, Lucy sadly declares, those who "have no inward answer" find their last delusion. But she cannot escape her love, even when it is not returned. Like Eve, she has earned the "purgatorial knowledge" that devotion lives "not in surrender but labor."

Shocked at Stark's subsequent marriage proposal to her, Anne rejects him. She has needed his needlessness, the warmth of his momentary blaze "in the affirmative instant, out of time." Now she begins to suspect the emptiness within him, which he himself will acknowledge only at the death of Tom. Confessing his doubts to Lucy ("I've heard in my mind/ Blunt horrors lurch and grind, like streetcars . . ."), he falls and is comforted by her. Immediately he tries to reinstate the life he had before Sadie and Anne, before the days of "sweetening." But the "coiling atoms" of his passage have already crystallized, and it is with a degree of satisfaction that he accepts the end which has been fashioned.

Through Tiny, Sadie betrays Anne's scandalous affair to Stanton who, disillusioned, despairing, and even convinced that somehow he has mothered this disaster, confronts Willie in the capitol corridors, shoots him down, and lets himself be shot to death. The chorus grandly withholds judgment of Willie because it believes that "anything which tends to promote the health and happiness of society, by any means, even by means which *seem* to be immoral, will in the end be conducive to morality, and can in the long view be called moral."

Stanton does not kill Willie from outrage at the governor's civil policies. Nor are Willie's power politics treated by the play as more than a dramatic symptom of an amoral science-society. Appropriately, the man of science slays the politician he has produced, occasioning his own destruction and thereby fulfilling the death wish inherent in such a society. The survival of the chorus, its very invulnerability to the play's processes, make it the ultimate adversary, the object most criticized. The playwright's problem was to counterbalance the massiveness and homogeneity of the chorus by individualizing the portraits of Adam and Willie, and thus to avoid writing a Punch and Judy, Pilate and Judas morality play. Although Stark was originally named Talos, Warren later explained in his "Note" on the novel, after the "brutal, blank-eyed 'iron groom' of Spenser's *Faerie Queene*, the pitiless servant of the Knight of Justice, " it is on its personal rather than personified and abstract level that dramatic engagement is achieved, through the blind contest of Willie's selves for supremacy. His character is therefore required to be as complicated as the restrictions of poetic drama and Warren's sensibility in 1939 allowed. He is knowable only through the actions of the play rather than in simple predictability before the curtain rises. In Anne Stanton's renunciation scene the crowning irony is disclosed: Willie has been assigned the satisfaction of needs which he himself in his emptiness shares. He can be the crowd's epitome but not its savior.

The same motif—cold flesh imploring warmth from the equally cold—was being developed, simultaneously, in *Night Rider*, where the same failure of selfishness to substitute for love obtains. But the death wish of Perse Munn, aspiring man of action, is transferred in *Proud Flesh* to Stanton, the disillusioned idealist. Willie exceeds his counterpart Perse not only in demagoguery but later in self-awareness, and is struck down in the midst of trial regeneration. His conscience, resurgent, has left him defenseless in a roving world of his own making. The real weakness of the play is that it does not recreate the past in which that conscience once stood erect and was audible. The possibility that Willie had been a reformer was yet to be invented by Warren. The Willie of *Proud Flesh* is not the richly enigmatic and divided man of the novel in progress, but a figure of lesser dimension, harried by ambition to the boundaries of irresponsibility and rescued only by the shock of seeing his future die in the death of his son. His ex-wife's sufferance and sacrificial love are offered him for imitation, but contrition cannot restore original innocence; without being surprised by the fact, he dies for his crimes.

Stanton's character is in many ways more fractured. Although a doctor, he is alienated from the pragmatics of the chorus because of his idealism. His sense of the incongruity of the present world contrasted with what he holds possible fills his mind with images of rot and stench and pus. He bitterly realizes that the political corruption surrounding him is mere

symbol for every man's corrupt spirit, but he will not suc-
cumb. He will not surrender to the scientist's confusion of
morality with expediency. Only his sister's defection defeats
him, forcing him to admit the admixture of good and evil not
only in the world as a whole but in each person and particle
of that world. There is no absolute purity, no "good-in-itself"
(nor moment-in-itself) such as Anne tries to recover from
their childhood. For Adam there is no saving degree of difference between his own imperfection, once acknowledged, and
the "essential deformity" which is Willie's. He feels compelled
to remove them both.

Stanton therefore dies without achieving the equivalent of
Willie's revelation, recognition of the value of restraint. In
considering him strong enough to accept responsibility, Anne
has misjudged the governor. Until his last moments he is *too*
strong to accept responsibility. Nevertheless, before his death
he has begun to earn his right to live. Stanton, on the other
hand, having encountered at first hand the adulterated com-
position of human life, destroys himself for being human. The
play's dark lines are properly his. The world's stench fills
him until he is inseparable from it; he cannot endure suffering.
Nor has he any resource of consolation such as that which Willie and Lucy, reconciled, begin to discover in compassionate
understanding. The poetic transformation of Stanton's torment
compensates for the play's infirmities: the disproportionate
role and exaggerated self-satire of the chorus; the inadequate
characterizations of Sadie Burke, Jack Burden, and Tom Stark;
the occasional self-parody, by excess, of the poetry in the
mouths and minds of characters such as the highway patrol-
man, who are incapable of its splendor.

By 1943, having already depicted "the desiccating abstraction
of power" in the person of Bogan Murdock, Warren began to
consider Willie Stark's story in terms of a novel. During the
same long months thereafter, he was doing research for his
textual analysis of Coleridge's *Rime of the Ancient Mariner*.
Its theme, the sacramental vision, became accessory to his
own developing "life web" philosophy of human interactions.
Gradually, therefore, interest shifted from the solitary father-
image to those whose need participated in its erection. Huey
Long, he was to write later, "did not spring full-blown and

ravening on a sweet and virtuous society. "[14] The people of
Louisiana made him possible. For that matter, it is likely
that many who rejoiced in his assassination secretly hoped
to expiate their own sense of guilt (for not defeating him at
the polls, for not even wanting to) by transferring all responsibility to their elected scapegoat. Because Warren did not, could
not, know "what Long was like, and what were the secret forces
that drove him along his violent path to meet the bullet in the
Capitol, "[15] he wrote instead of Willie Stark, whose successful
ruthlessness and charming ambivalence "give a holiday to a
part of our nature—give it a canter and then rub it down and
put it back in the barn. "[16]

But in *All the King's Men* the gradual shift is evident from
the king to his man: Jack Burden, insignificant bystander in
Proud Flesh, comes to realize that the story of multiple events
that he has been narrating is his own. His wisecracking manner
makes him seem detached. As a student of history, a reporter,
and a political researcher he tries to perfect neutrality. Yet in
each capacity he becomes more and more deeply, personally
involved. Just as the portrait of Willie goes beyond that of
Murdock, because of the governor's attempted regeneration
and the whole complex of invented circumstances that make
this attempt credible, so the characterization of Jack is superior to that of Sue, who is satisfied with renunciation of her
father. Jack's task is more difficult than mere rejection: to
understand Willie, and himself in Willie, and both in the world,
largely against his will. Jack's identification with Willie is
never complete, not primarily because he is outraged at Willie's measures but because, throughout, he resists accepting
Willie's reminder that "man is conceived in sin and born in
corruption and he passeth from the stink of the didie to the
stench of the shroud." Adam dies, Jack is born, when the fact
that man is not immaculate finally is impressed on them by
Anne and by Judge Irwin. The prenatal imagery of the novel
is finally revoked with the birth of Jack into "the awful responsibility of Time." Strangely enough, that beginning marks
the cessation of motion for him.

From Willie Stark's car, driven at high speed by his body-
guard, Sugar Boy, Burden describes the Mason City countryside, ravished by industries. But he makes no association be-

tween them and his boss, culture images of a reckless exploitation. His humor is that of a spectator, the innocent bystander. Listening to Willie, once simple county treasurer and now governor, work over a small-town crowd, Burden feels some inner fetus of himself, blind and warm, rejecting birth, regretting that "the end of man is to know." At Willie's old farmhouse (left unpainted for effect but with a commode constructed indoors) the governor's wife Lucy shares Burden's wonder at where the essential Willie has been lost. What remains of the Lincolnish boy who tried to study while the wind off the Great Plains set something coiled inside him to growing? Jack can understand how a man might be repelled by his parents' possessiveness. But why does the same force that sunders us, reunite? Calling himself an idealist ("What you don't know don't hurt you, for it ain't real"), Jack allows himself no more than curiosity.

Jack's own home at Burden's Landing is as wrenched and partitioned as Willie's. The athletic young executive who is his mother's current husband can win no affection from him (like Slim Sarrett, Jack suffers from a multiplicity of fathers), and the days of his love for Anne Stanton, a neighbor, are over. Now she is merely the sister of his friend Adam. Only Judge Irwin, always a fatherly figure to Jack, can attract him. But the occasion of this visit is the judge's support of the opposition ticket because Willie's rule is corrupt. Unable to shake Irwin's convictions, Jack is ordered by the governor to unearth the unholy truth that must lie somewhere in the judge's past. Neither suspects that the web he shakes will trap him.

First, however, Jack rehearses the Boss's own past: his defeat at the local polls in 1922; the justification of his demand for reform when a schoolhouse fire escape collapsed during drill; his subsequent invitation by Tiny Duffy to run on a straw man ticket for governor. His long-winded speeches on facts and taxes at every whistlestop won no votes, but Sadie Burke, assigned to be his adviser, doublecrossed Duffy and told Willie he had been betrayed. Full of liquor and livid anger, Willie warned the crowds that they were dupes like himself. By 1930, with Sadie's help, he was governor and Tiny Duffy was his salaried whipping boy and other self, reminder of the rites of expediency.

Jack, who covered the early Stark story as a reporter, returned afterward to the Great Sleep, that sublime unconscious-
ness which he had summoned also just before his doctorate in
history was to be finished and, again, just before walking out
on his wife, Lois. It is a precious heritage from his mother
who constantly tries to make "a little island right in the middle
of Time, " for example, when Jack wants to ask about his father, the Scholarly Attorney, who hands out leaflets in an evan-
gelical mission. Jack used to tell his father that, since Life
is Motion Toward Knowledge and God is Fullness of Being,
God is Complete Knowledge and therefore Complete Non-Motion
and Non-Life: to worship God the Father is to worship Death.
(But while Jack, safeguarded by such sophistry, brooded on
History from somewhere out of time, Willie whipped the crowds
into usable frenzies or corrupted minor officials, even though
in doing so he alienated both his wife Lucy and his honest attorney general, Hugh Miller.)

In retreat from the present excess of parents and division
of loyalties, Jack devoted his college years to the history of
his Civil War ancestor, Cass Mastern, who with a Mrs. Trice
betrayed the hospitality of her husband and thus became accessory to his suicide. A female slave, because she discovered
their secret, was sold downstream by Mrs. Trice; Cass, guilt-
stricken and wearing his profane wedding ring around his neck
like an albatross, searched for her. Unable to dam the flood
of circumstance he had loosed, Cass set his Mississippi slaves
free, in spite of the warnings of his more practical brother,
Gilbert. Then, realizing he had sent them to greater misery
in the North, he volunteered as a private in the struggle over
secession, wishing on himself every humility and taking no
lives. Dying at last in the battle of Atlanta, Cass wrote: "I
do not question the justice of God, that others have suffered
for my sin, for it may be that only by the suffering of the innocent does God affirm that men are brothers, and brothers
in His Holy Name. " He had touched the gossamer threads of
life's web, in whose center glitters God's eye. But Jack, careless of vibrations, laid aside the journal, he recalls now with
curiosity, and, "like a driver groping downward into dark water, " entered on the Great Sleep. (His denial of the past is so
nearly complete that he is embarrassed by ex-soldier Judge

Irwin's hobby of building ancient catapults and ballistas, which once fascinated him. Like Slim Sarrett in *At Heaven's Gate* he wants to be able to say: nostalgia is a crime against life as a dynamic art.)

Jack's second attempt at historical research is more successful, although no one will help implicate Judge Irwin. (The Scholarly Attorney is too busy ministering to a former circus hanging man who has never recovered psychologically from his partner's fatal fall; and Anne's "deep inner certitude of self," Jack feels, prevents her from being surprised into answers.) Recalling a time when Judge Irwin was insolvent, Jack discovers that his revered friend's fortune derived from stocks of a utilities company shortly after, as state's attorney, he had dismissed a case against the company. Irwin had been rewarded further by being made company vice president, replacing the attorney for the utilities, who, convinced of his uselessness, finally killed himself. Slowly Jack is forced to believe, as Cass Mastern did, that nothing is accidental: "I eat a persimmon and the teeth of a tinker in Tibet are put on edge. . . . We have to accept it because so often our teeth are on edge from persimmons we didn't eat."

When Adam Stanton (a romantic who dismisses the world whenever it fails to conform to his mind's tidy picture of it) is undecided about accepting the directorship of Stark's hospital, Jack tries to reassure him that, like a love sonnet dedicated to a married woman, some things are good in themselves. When this fails, he shows Adam and Anne photostats linking Judge Irwin and their own father, the former governor who had refused to act on his knowledge. Anne asks only that the evidence be withheld from Willie until the judge can explain.

Willie defends his methods before Adam by professing that good has to be made out of bad because in life there are no other raw materials. His concept of good Willie makes up as he goes along. (Yet he fights to keep the hospital undefiled as if he were honoring the fiction of his own fundamental innocence.) Adam capitulates, though unconvinced by Willie; and Anne, remembering her father's complicity, becomes the governor's mistress.

Shocked that he has handed Anne over to Willie through some "obscure and necessary logic," Jack drives furiously West, as if to undo fact by flight. He has finally lost "that image of the little girl on the waters of the bay, all innocence and truthfulness," which had first awakened love and veneration in him. Actually, he had lost Anne when that same image of virginity had made him hesitate to violate her, naked in the undisturbed quiet of his mother's house. She had rejected him not for his nobility but, sensing his fear of the future, for his irresolution. All that summer of their youth he had been drifting with events, never expecting that their climax would require decision. In full flight that time, he had hastened into a substitute marriage with Lois, who required little that animal nature could not satisfy but who, consequently, meant no more in the end than any well-adjusted sex machine. Now the impulse to withdraw into mechanism tempts Jack to unlearn this wisdom. He returns from the coast having convinced himself that life is only "the dark heave of the blood and the twitch of the nerve." Yet he is skeptical when Adam tries to prove that cauterizing a patient's twitch by prefrontal lobectomy can change the man's personality. The sense of having sinned against Anne is too strong. A man must act, and then not blame those acts on body functions or on fate. Having looked at himself, for the first time Jack can see the potential of evil in Willie's powerful face, spread on every billboard.

The web trembles: Willie demands the photostats in order to use Judge Irwin's influence to quiet a potential scandal involving Tom Stark's illegitimate child. The judge admits his guilt when confronted by Jack. Later, at home, Jack's mother wakens him with a scream: the judge has shot himself. Jack has killed his own father! For the first time he realizes that his mother is capable of vigorous and genuine love. She has never been able to care for anyone except Irwin, but he could not desert his sick wife while she lived. Although "truth always kills the father"—the revered ikon, the patently divine—with the respect that understanding brings, *two* fathers are restored to him: Irwin, and the Scholarly Attorney who had known, and privately grieved. Ironically, Jack has also become sole heir to the estate created through the judge's dishonesty.

With Judge Irwin gone, Willie can protect his son from scandalous exposure only by compromising the hospital contract to silence the blackmail of political grafters. But when he tries to "fix" the football coach too, forcing him to use Tom although the boy has broken training rules, Tom's spinal cord is crushed. Reduced to helpless infancy, he is doomed to an early death. Conscience-stricken, Willie is attempting frantically to reverse the course of his life—to curb corruption and to return to his wife—when Adam Stanton, responding to a call about his sister, shoots down Willie in public and is himself killed by Sugar Boy. (It is vanity, vain idealism, in Adam as in the Jefferson of *Brother to Dragons,* which convinces them that removal, by violence if necessary, of those who challenge their ideals is an act of justice.) Willie dies believing that things might have been different, might have come undone.

Later Jack discovers that Sadie, angered by Willie's renunciation, told Tiny Duffy how to betray him. Although Jack, believing in Willie's lost greatness, is tempted to send Sugar Boy out for revenge, he decides at last that he would only be making Tiny his whipping boy as Willie had done. Moreover (in another duplication of the Lord Jim-Brown recognition scene), Jack realizes that he is far from being an avenging hero; that he and Tiny are "twins bound together more intimately and disastrously than the poor freaks of the midway." When he lies to Mrs. Burden, reassuring her that Judge Irwin was never dishonest, Jack understands better the dilemma of the "true lie," the terror of having to improvise values, after the fashion of Adam, man of idea, and Willie, man of fact, each destroyed ironically by the answer in the other, because of "the terrible division of their age." History may be morally neutral, but man is not. There is no escape from choice or the conditions of action.

Since Anne is also now prepared to live with her past, they are married. The Scholarly Attorney tells them:

Separateness is identity and the only way for God to create, truly create, man was to make him separate from God Himself, and to be separate from God is to be sinful. The creation of evil is therefore the index of God's glory and His power. That had to be so that the creation of good might be the index of man's glory and power. But by God's help. By His help and in His wisdom.

Thus he confirms the judgment of Cass Mastern: "It is human defect—to try to know oneself by the self of another. One can only know oneself in God and in His great eye." After Jack finishes his book on Cass Mastern, he and Anne expect to re-enter "the awful responsibility of Time."

The epigraph to *All the King's Men,* from Dante, is synoptic of Warren's theme: "By curse of theirs man is not so lost that eternal love may not return, *so long as hope retaineth aught of green.* " The curse of man is his identity, which is his sep-arateness and therefore his incompleteness. Man's duty is to rededicate himself to God in whom completeness lies. Because any future is the outcome of its past, man is necessarily more aware of the probability of imperfection than of the possibility of perfection. That humbling state of being warned is required, but so is the will to hope and work for salvation, whatever the agony. Only in that way can Humpty Dumpty (or the fallen aeri-alist whom the Scholarly Attorney attends) be put together again.

This is disclosed to Burden while he is assembling other people's lives. If human nature exists, whatever one discovers about any man becomes valuable as self-discovery. The posi-tion of Burden as narrator resisting the significance of events produces a special kind of suspense. As a professional re-searcher (historian-reporter) he is forced to accumulate in-formation, but he affects callousness in registering these facts for the files of the political machine. Earlier he could resort to the Great Sleep or to a belief in the Great Twitch, behavior-ism. But this mask wrinkles with the features of truth, be-traying Jack's real sense of loss in having been deprived of parents and of Anne.

Particularly is he unable to deny his share in Anne's de-spoiling. His confidence that he could keep her innocent for-ever was as much a delusion as the Great Sleep or flight to the West: both have to accept time, change, and the necessity of choice. It is Willie's resoluteness that attracts both Anne and Jack. But they discover that a man armed with a meatax and ruled by expediency may develop an irresponsibility of his own. Jack finds in himself a further resemblance to the Boss: occupational corrosion of their previous humaneness. The Great Sleep is an attempt to avoid human involvement; Jack's detective talents become so automatic that they can be employed even against old friends; and he admits having contributed to Lois' conversion into a sex mechanism (". . . I forgive you for everything I did to you"). For his part, Willie openly makes objects to be manipulated out of Tiny Duffy, hireling Byron B. White, Sadie Burke, his own family, and the whole body politic. Such clinical diminution of human values, like the neurosurgeon's insensible detachment from the personality whose alteration is at his skill's command, is the real evil in which Willie participates.

Stanton's decision to assassinate Willie, whom he knows only as an abstraction, characterizes the objective scientist in him. To Stanton, Willie is a cancer, not a human being. The doctor's temporary substitution of "pure force" for "pure idea, " therefore, is no reversal since both positions are remote from the human median. What Adam's action does allow, however, is the double irony of a man's being killed by his favorite weapon at the very moment he has decided to lay it aside—a dramatic assertion of the penalties attendant on evil self-willed. Although Willie dies ignorant of Adam's motives and perhaps of his own, yet when he insists on his deathbed that life could have been different he is accepting the notion that his will has always been to some degree free and that he can be blamed or credited to that extent for actions now formally his. In this manner he attempts to rescue identity, to prevent himself from being reduced to mere function in a mechanical universe. (The respect that Burden, as well as Warren, pays this gesture is made unmistakable when Willie's dying words are contrasted with the closing dialogue in *The Sun Also Rises*—Jake's cynical answer to Brett's sorrowful-passionate plaint that things might have been different.)

Jack, similarly restored to personal responsibility, ceases to act as pure response. When his research ends in the death of his own father, his pretense at neutrality stops. Fortunately he is left alive to benefit from his knowledge, to recover *his* past in his parents and *the* past in his comprehension of the web of kinship, to orient his values by the hard Christianity offered by Cass Mastern and the Scholarly Attorney.

As narrator of events both physical and metaphysical, Jack Burden is necessarily presented as a complicated figure, capable of thought and speech on two levels, the tough-realistic

and the poetic, reminiscent of the dual style of *Proud Flesh*.
The rhetoric of the Cass Mastern interlude represents the
longest stretch of objective narration. Although told by Burden, the voice is that of the anonymous historian in *World
Enough and Time*. The presence of Cass Mastern's story is
properly prepared for and, despite its length, does not delay
the "local action" of the novel any more than does the extended
story of Judge Irwin's bribery. Yet its withholding of emotional commitment makes it seem at first only a commentary
on the novel. Nevertheless, the distance is deliberate, functioning to signify Jack's ambivalence. The very effort required
of him to speak with unnatural objectivity of Cass Mastern is
secret acknowledgment of the significance of the *exemplum*. It
is an index of his resistance, part of the novel's characteristic
subtlety.

As in *Proud Flesh*, the novel's preponderance of images of
filth and infection, drawn from a world of hospitals and government corruption, mirrors elements natural to the human
condition. Submarine images, the Great Sleep, the western
flight, mark vain attempts to escape that condition. Its acceptance and affirmation of a morality beyond pragmatism,
the theme of regeneration, is conveyed by symbolic action:
Cass Mastern's pursuit of purgation; the care the Scholarly
Attorney gives to the childlike former hanging man. While the
other images are static and repetitive, those of rebirth have
direction and climax. Willie's ruthlessness occasions the death
of his son and himself, but the alternative to unrestrained will
is not suspension of action (ventured by Jack, Anne, Mrs.
Trice, Mrs. Burden) or retreat to pure idea. It is will—choice—
modified by natural necessity and controlled by moral vision.
Assurance of identity, the ambition of so many characters, is
elusive because it is not unchanging as they think. It is a name
for direction, an appreciation of origin and destination. The
vector of regeneration in this novel diagrams the movement
toward identity.

However, although a moral imperative is expressed by the
structure of symbols, the good that is to be willed and done is
never explicitly defined. After the deaths of Judge Irwin, Willie
Stark, and Adam Stanton, the narrator reviews his relationship
with each of these as well as with the living, as if separating

out all his lifelong contradictions for the final years ahead. He seems determined to live the good life in spite of evil circumstance. Unfortunately, when last seen, Jack is still a man of thought, with action only anticipated. How will his changed world picture change the world? What is the aftermath of knowledge? Evil is a condition of good, he knows. But once, in Jack's presence, Adam asks Willie: What is good? Later, Jack himself nearly asks Adam: Where do values come from? In the novel itself only negative definitions of good are demonstrated: one should not treat men as less than human; one should expect to pay for his share of life. Knowledge becomes nearly unknowable in a world where even identity depends on some assumed continuum among apparently discrete and conflicting selves ("direction is all") and where "meaning is never in the event but in the motion through event." Human behavior, traced by such shifting coordinates, is necessarily ambiguous. Jack soon discovers that "a man's virtue may be but the defect of his desire, as his crime may be but a function of his virtue." Certainly he finds less to admire in a weak saint, the Scholarly Attorney, than in a strong sinner, Judge Irwin. (Consequently, he compares the judge not with Cass but with Gilbert Mastern, slaveholder, colonel of rebel cavalry, Reconstruction railroad builder: self-made entrepreneur "always at home in any world.") There is the old implication here that man must take the full risk of his humanity. The fallen can rise to blessedness, but the untempted, meditating on immaculate plateaus, give off little light. Nevertheless, at the end of the novel the earlier questions remain, and the keenness of the questioning spirit seems to have faded with Jack's skepticism. Has he experienced at last the "holy emptiness and blessed fatigue of a saint after the dark night of the soul," as he once sarcastically described the Great Sleep?

One may suppose that Jack's willful faith and the agony of time will derive the answers as circumstance matures. Will such answers be minute revelations, reflections of some absolute and fixed nature when seen in composite? Or will they be truths for the moment, another way of saying with Willie: We make up what good is as we go along? Or perhaps Jack's is an evasion, not just a postponement. His poise before the plunge is indistinguishable from sheer fatigue or the weakness of still insufficient resolution. According to his convictions, his hope should be greener than ever, but despite his convictions he has never seemed less vigorous, less prepared for birth than at the end of the novel. Instead of passing into the "awful responsibility of Time," Jack Burden speaks with the calm of one ready to lie down now with Anne and share with her the long, long sleep. It requires a faith equal to Jack's in Willie to believe that this is only the last effect of the purge that must precede the great appetite.

Warren has often speculated whether or not the author ever succeeds in writing exactly the work that he intended. Still, *All the King's Men* and *Proud Flesh* remain Warren's most significant efforts in wrestling with the problem of civil corruption of the soul. They are superior not only to the "Kingfish syndrome" as previously described in Sinclair Lewis' *It Can't Happen Here,* Dos Passos' *Number One,* Hamilton Basso's *A Sun in Capricorn,* and Adria Locke Langley's *A Lion Is in the Streets,* but also to subsequent dramatic versions. The off-Broadway staging of Warren's novel in 1947 suffered from multiplicity, cluttering the theater with so many scenes from the book that motivation became summarized and unconvincing. In this version, even the achievement of continuous movement through blacking out all stage areas but the one briefly committed to each of twenty-four scenes only compounds the sense of spliced action, dizzying and incoherent without the novel as referent. The chorus of surgeons in *Proud Flesh* has been reduced to a single Professor of Science who occasionally comments on the progress of events or debates with Jack Burden on the forestage, but his presence creates as many dramatic problems as it solves problems of narration. Overabundance of episodes becomes a substitute for characterization, the demagoguery of Willie Stark is allowed to dominate *All the King's Men,* and nothing can quite put the play back together again. The play tries too hard to imitate the novel, and in process it loses any resemblance.

The film version of *All the King's Men,* which Warren had neither written nor advised, was nevertheless advertised with his signed recommendation: "In this picture, I think, there is intensity without tricks and pretensions, and always a sense of truth: such a thing as this could happen in a world like this."

Several critics chose to interpret "a world like this" to mean Hollywood—not just the modifications required when a story is translated from one mode of expression to another, but the necessary compromise enforced by an industrialized art customarily spastic in its sensibility. The blame for each change was laid on Warren, despite the fact that Robert Rossen had sole responsibility for writing the screen play. Presumably the Robert Meltzer Award was presented to the novelist by the Screen Writers' Guild because the scenario borrowed heavily from the book for its dialogue. Rossen and Warren were often together during the retakes and editing of the movie, but at no time was Warren's opinion requested or desired. Nevertheless, he felt at the time that the movie, though its conception differed from his, was effective on its own terms until the concluding scenes, and it was this opinion that he had wanted his comment to convey. [17]

Important portions of the context of plausibility established during the development of the story from *Proud Flesh* to the novel were lost again in the movie, notably the individualized characterization of Stark himself. The motion picture governor has nearly reverted to type. Too often he acts the fascist bully wrapped in a little Southern hokum, divested of Jacobean metaphysics and stripped of soliloquies on those unseen rakes that scrape the muck of mind. The figure of Stark is larger than a bootleg ganglord's, but far inferior to Ahab's.

Perhaps the critical confusion that followed, then, was not unnatural among those who knew what the screenplay sacrificed but knew nothing of its authorship. Parker Tyler, however, who was acquainted with the facts about Rossen, preferred to explain the atrophy of Stark as Warren's self-incriminating way of washing his hands of a dictator, his own father-surrogate, who in the novel had become his lyric hero: supposedly, Huey P. Long. Tyler's failure to distinguish between Long and Stark can be attributed in part to the fact that both the film and the general public blurred the two figures until they merged into a single archtype. However, the critic with equal justice might have offered Stark's untidiness in the novel, his conflicting natures, as an index of the author's swerving attitude. Lost in the business of identifying real with fictitious personages, Tyler overlooked the function of ambivalence in Stark's characterization, rather than in the author. Stark is a man of mixed and warring qualities, and his appeal is to the duality of the audience itself, its yearning for the meatax (whether as victor or victim), despite the final show of moral abhorrence and rejection of the once heroic wielder. In the novel Burden enacts this role of the participant-spectator in order to involve the reader's own sense of guilt and understanding in the tragic horrors. But the cosmic web as confirmed by secret paternity collapses, in the motion picture, through substitution of Judge Stanton for the now-absent Judge Irwin, and the Cass Mastern story is omitted altogether. Consequently, the audience never has to undeceive itself; it can assassinate Willie Stark without seeing its face suddenly on his effigy; it is never purged of its own ambivalence. This is the flaw of the movie which permitted critics to attribute their own confusion to Warren.

His "final" treatment of the story, *Willie Stark: His Rise and Fall,*[18] in many ways returns to the scenic simplicity of *Proud Flesh* although it lacks the poetry of the earlier play and of course retains the dominant roles that Burden and Irwin have evolved from version to version. (In *Proud Flesh* Judge Irwin's part did not exist; his creation is foreshadowed only in Willie's reference to a corrupt Senator Crosby who has been driven to suicide by notoriety.) By eliminating the choric comments and by limiting the action to twelve scenes, Warren avoids the cumbersome form that made his staged novel, *All the King's Men,* impracticable. Earlier experiments with flexibility have been continued and improved. Subordination of props and sets provides the mobility necessary to shifts in scene without lags in action. Audience involvement is managed by having actors both narrate and play their roles.[19] Massive suggestiveness is made possible with relative economy.

However, simplicity has once again cost the father-son relationship of Jack and Irwin and the reconstructed past of Willie, without which the final will toward reform seems like a plot contrivance. Willie's brusque intrusion at the moment of Judge Irwin's confession to Jack is particularly destructive to his potential appeal for forbearance. In fact, foreshortening robs most of the characters of those humane preliminary moments that evoke sympathy. Sadie's hatred of Anne overshadows her own suffering; Judge Irwin's suicide, in the absence of precedent facts of his past, appears to be only a less subtle version of Adam's: neither can live without self-deception. But the most serious change is in the characterization of Willie himself.

Yet this change is at least conceptually valid. In both plays, *All the King's Men* and *Willie Stark*, the Boss is permitted to add in the epilogue: "Being a man, I did not know what I was, nor what might be the fullness of man. But being a man I yearned toward that definition, even in the dark night of my ignorance." What prevents this from being the mere rhetoric of apology, from man defeated? Jack's faith in Willie, without which he could not bear to watch the living and the dying, could not bear to be a man, might be only another in a history of delusion. In the play, Jack is not the same explorer of souls as the narrator of the novel. He has even dared to accuse Stark of using the hospital to simulate piety, just as he has always used his patronage of Tiny. There is little beyond his need to justify Jack's faith and therefore little reason to ask the spectator to respect that faith. Is it Willie's startling self-denial before his final public gathering that enjoins our belief ("What man knows the truth of his heart? But I shall look in my heart, and I hope to find some love for you")? His self-incrimination in the hope of finding enough innocence to be able to look them in the eye? Sugar Boy's refrain is a warning: "The B-B-B-Big B-B-B-Boss—he k-k-kin talk so good!" Is it, however, perhaps a promise, too?

In his public confession, in his dying assurance that "everything might have been—different," in his epilogue summation, the words of Willie can at last be trusted *because he does not trust himself*. At the precise moment of clarification and expected regeneration, he finds himself doomed by habit: ". . . you start, and then you find it is just the same. . . . You find you're just heaving yourself around like you did. You find yourself saying the same things." He has killed a part of the essential Willie before Adam ever draws the assassin's pistol, and paradoxically it is Willie's self-understanding that rescues him from condemnation.

And it is this which warrants respectful regard for his last invocation, though it is not a harangue in the thumping tradition: "But being man I yearned toward that definition, even

in the dark of my ignorance. I say this not for extenuation or
for forgiveness, for I have no need now for those things. All
I need now is truth." Despite the limitations of *Willie Stark:
His Rise and Fall* as independent drama (only the decline is
shown), this single insight into man is earned and possessed,
inaccessible to loss. In it lies the heart of the truth, beyond
moralization or expectation, toward which Warren long has
been working: the wonder of man, his own executioner.

World Enough and Time (1950)

In 1944, while Robert Penn Warren was consultant in poetry
at the Library of Congress, Katherine Anne Porter brought
him a pamphlet dated 1826 and entitled *The Confession of Jereboam O. Beauchamp.*[20] Warren spent five minutes reading the
record and six years fashioning the novel. Aside from the biography of John Brown, he had not ventured beyond the contemporary scene. But his imagination, which had several times
already grasped the image of a whole continent and culture in
Kentucky, now telescoped past and present in a myth of man's
constancy more subtle than the mere contrast of times in *The
Ballad of Billie Potts*, just completed. With a poet's craft of
compression, as he explained in 1950, "I began to think of the
political struggle of the time as a kind of mirror I could hold
up to the personal story." By satirizing present errors under
their past guises, he took his stand against tradition as blind
worship of the backward glance.

In Willie Talos (Stark), central figure of *Proud Flesh*, he
had earlier described the groom of justice, self-appointed redeemer through reforms, crucifying in the name of high conviction. The epigraph for *World Enough and Time*, drawing
on the same cantos from Spenser's *Faerie Queene* in which
Talos appears, indicts romantic Jerry Beaumont, night-riding
champion of wronged womanhood, through implied identification
of his role with that of Talos' master, the righteous knight of
justice, Artegall himself. Unlike Stark and Murdock, Beaumont is not cast as one whose passion is to become a public
monument. His tormented role is so private and subtilized
that the reader risks embracing the young man as a martyr
even after Jerry has learned he is the victim of himself. Jerry's youth and naïveté make his crimes seem the awkward

mistakes of innocence. He is so well deceived by his own motives (in contrast with the seasoned evil wisdom of Willie Stark)
that he may be forgiven too soon, without understanding, by
someone made numb to irony by the mode of narration. There
are two narrators: an anonymous and neutral historian tabu-
lates the facts in an objective discourse; Jeremiah discloses
his own story in frantic subjectivity. Beaumont is Adam Stanton
if Adam had survived to be brought to trial for murderously
defending the image of immaculateness in a woman's honor.

Studying Jeremiah Beaumont's confession, the historian-
narrator is disconcerted by the difficulties of reconstructing
the whole truth. Jerry seems to have invented an elaborate
melodrama so that its excitement and design might affirm his
hopes of emerging from the "ruck of the world." The grandiose
manners he affected as trappings sometimes reveal less his
actual form than his desperate simulation. The very existence
of his confession indicates how strong his pride was at the
height of delusion, since he offered himself, no other, as author of his ruin. (Similarly, John Brown preferred death to a
mitigating plea of insanity; and Warren, discussing Conrad in
his Columbia address, recalls how the other Brown, in *Lord
Jim*, elevated massacre to the status of retribution to rescue
the image of himself as man, subject incorrigibly to dreams
of vindication.)

Jerry was born in Kentucky, in the first year of the 1800's,
an unformed time during which Bible and dirk, pistols and Plato
still competed, perfect symbols for his own confusions. One
of his own earliest memories was a picture of the burning of
a woman martyr, whom he could never decide whether he
wanted to help kill or rescue. Unhappy with his father, an un-
fulfilled and driving man, Jerry used to wish he could hide in
the great green wooded silence, unattached to time or generation. Or, while visiting his maternal grandfather's tumble-down
mansion, he would hear bugle notes from passing riverboats
and feel some dark compulsion to leave home and follow. Now,
with the loss of the Beaumont farm after his father's death,
Jerry is named his grandfather's heir provided that he will
change his name, thus avenging the old man against the out-
lander who had stolen his daughter. But Jerry, choosing to be
a renegade like his mother, insists on his name and a rebel's

birthright. He will not borrow any man's identity, so thoroughly
does he enjoy even the tribulations involved in searching for
his own.

For a moment, exalted by the evangelistic exertions of Co-
rinthian McClardy, a "devil-breaker" who represents God as
a bear grappling for the throat of the soul, Jerry can touch an
icicle on a tree and feel the communion of all created things.
But, warned by a more doctrinaire brother that God's kingdom is not of the senses, he loses the joy of faith until Mc-
Clardy returns. Then, quickened by the passionate sting of
the preacher's words, he joins in the frantic orgies of the
crowd, sprawling in the thickets with "another creature, " a
hag, he later discovers. Convinced that neither earthly estate
nor heavenly mansion awaits him now, he tries to come to
terms with the more accessible world. He thinks he is now
an initiate, a practical, rational man.

Thus at seventeen Jerry is introduced to Colonel Cassius
Fort, a tried Jeffersonian and, though lowly born, a congress-
man, beneath whose austere manners is the melancholy face
of a man secluded with his secret self. It is to this man that
Jerry apprentices himself as a lawyer after his mother's death.
Because Fort treats him as a son and because Jerry has only
the name and the pride of his original father, the young man
agrees with Fort to accept the replevin act, which grants hard-
pressed farmers a year's stay of sale for debt.

Through Fort, Jerry meets young Rachel Jordan, whose
family home would have been lost except for Fort's help. Feeling cheated because her mother's memories of childhood splendor impoverished the feeling between her parents, Rachel
tries to run away from home but has no place to go. She tries
instead to find some way to punish her mother by outrage (the
spiteful vengeance, later, of a Hamish Bond). She writes in
her diary, "I think she is afraid of me. And she does well to
be afraid. I am afraid of myself." She has accepted the inti-
macies of Fort in the hope of escaping through love to some
world secure against sudden change and deprivation.

Wilkie Barron, a young man of calculated naïveté, reveals
these facts to his roommate, Jerry, in the manner of one whose
courting love has been betrayed. Shamed by his foster father's
unworthy act, Jerry wins the company of Rachel by subterfuge,

as if in hope of restoring the priceless image of her virtue and of standing with her against the world, their enemy. He cannot accept her refusal of marriage, though he knows the impediment: a stillborn child whose father is Fort.

Meanwhile, Wilkie musters Jerry into the proreplevin ranks under Skrogg, an early rebel against parental tyranny and now a fearless editor whose dueling pistol settles whatever the word cannot. (He appears almost unworldly in his idealism. Only later is it revealed that he was part of the world after all: on his dead body a chain-mail vest is found.) At the county election polls, Jerry fights to save Skrogg's skin in a mêlée and is shocked as much by his own show of violence as by Wilkie's brutality. But later, in the room where Fort must have possessed Rachel, he is eager to kill his fatherly rival. An opportunity comes when he has made Rachel tell "of her own will" the story of her child and has made her agree to marriage if he kills Colonel Fort. Not the child's birth but its death has saddened her. Still she requests what is expected of her.

Jerry is sure that the gratuitous act of risking his life for the sake of justice will define and justify the "midnight pulse" that compels him. (The historian-narrator accepts this motive: "Explanations can only explain explanations, and the self is gratuitous in the end.") But Fort, though slapped publicly, refuses to duel and leaves Frankfort by stealth rather than be horsewhipped by his "son."

Jerry can also be kind. When Rachel's mother complains of being unloved, Jerry, though nauseated, manages to kiss her brow, despite the fact that for weeks her watchful eyes have accused the joy of the lovers from the shadows. When Rachel herself complains that no one ever loved anyone in that home, Jerry secretly possesses her while the old woman dies alone upstairs. After the funeral they are married and enjoy simple pleasures on their plantation. But the memory that Fort still lives harasses Jerry—and rumors that he himself has married Rachel for property. Where is his truth now? Only by washing in the blood of Fort can Jerry prove his nobility. His decision is confirmed when Fort announces that he will uphold the Kentucky constitution against the replevin group; Jerry has been its unsuccessful candidate. He is prepared to invent the necessity for revenge in spite of occasional scrupulous questioning of his own motives: "Did he want power clothed in duty and justice, or justice and duty clothed in power?"

For her part, Rachel is so content with her new pregnancy that she reproaches Jerry for having forced her to require Fort's death. Then two broadsides reach Jerry: one publicizing Rachel's seduction by Fort, the other apparently from Fort himself, claiming the father of her firstborn to be a mulatto slave. Jerry is too late to prevent Rachel's seeing the second handbill. She suffers a miscarriage and, confusing Jerry with Fort, rails without discrimination against their lovelessness, the fact that both men have filled her womb with death. The imputations of the wife he needed as fellow victim stirs Jerry's self-pity. At last he finds his duty clear. The pure idea of his mission, which he has allowed to protect him from the world, must become fact, justice in the flesh. For Rachel's protection (though there is no love between them as he leaves on his mission), he decides to kill Fort by stealth.

In Frankfort he identifies himself before murdering Fort in the dark doorway of his house. Then at inns on the road home, deliberately confusing his listeners as if he has the facts secondhand, he convinces himself of his innocence. Like a knight, waving the blood-red pennant of his wife's sash, he spurs his horse into their yard. That night he dreams of the West, where once he had almost taken new lands, and where silent trees "let only a green light down like light under water when you dive deep and where everything is still." His innocence thus ratified, he surrenders himself as a witness next morning. En route to Frankfort, through his own overconfidence, evidence in Jerry's favor is deliberately lost by his escort. He himself steals and destroys other contradictory evidence.

At Frankfort the replevin party offers an attorney, Mr. Madison, and so does the opposition, afraid of being accused of making political gain from the charges. Their help is offset by Sugg Lancaster, a complete stranger who offers himself as state witness, a kind of Rosencrantz come to convey the captive Hamlet.

Fort, it is revealed, was killed on the eve of announcing that a compromise can be effected between the Old Court ("the law will counsel man") and the New ("man must keep changing laws until justice gives him satisfaction"). The confusing political overtones of the murder and Mrs. Fort's refusal to identify Jerry's voice (to escape becoming the unloved wife in a romantic revenge trial) strengthen his feeling of guiltlessness.

When Madison treats him like a son, Jerry allows Rachel to travel with the counselor to talk with possible witnesses, but later he thinks jealously of Madison as another Fort. Jerry is consoled by the resemblance between his dark inward dungeon cell and the childhood womblike cave where he had often withdrawn, absorbed into the secret, private truth of the prenatal like a body that sinks forever into uninhabited, amniotic seas.

When he discovers that Sugg Lancaster has tried unsuccessfully to bribe Jerry's servant to testify falsely, Jerry also pays him to perjure. But the servant refuses to be bought by either, and the court is informed of the bribery. After a multitude of lies, a truth is told. Wilkie betrays Jerry by suggesting revenge for Rachel's seduction as a motive. Within ninety minutes Jerry is declared guilty. He admits the act but not the guilt.

Although legal proceedings against Rachel are quashed, she lives with Jerry in jail. Jerry's only hope for justification lies in discovering the handbill written by Fort, which provoked the assault. Lawyer Hawgood wants it, too, as proof of truth, a higher end than innocence.

Two passions now occupy Jerry, as the time of execution approaches: an indefatigable assertive lust for Rachel (for life, like a hanged man's last demonstrative ejaculation!) and a compulsion to write down his story, to uncover what must have been inevitable because it happened. Although he decides that Wilkie's love for Rachel was the first cause of all his calamities, Rachel denies knowledge of such a love.

Munn Short, their keeper, tries to comfort them with the reminder that the death of the body may occasion the rebirth of the soul. Once long ago he had lain with the wife of another Kentucky backwoodsman. Caught in the fields by the Indians, she was killed and he knifed. Her husband later found Short alone, nursed him back to health, and bided his vengeance. But, after Short told him where his wife's body could be found, he was satisfied. Short decided that only by putting the mark of Jesus on his brow could he take off the mark of Cain.

Jerry's days, however, are so distorted by the coming of death that he denies life meaning. Just before the execution Dr. Burnham, his childhood tutor and Fort's friend, arrives to read his face, to see the truth. Reproaching the old man for ever teaching him Rome's code of honor, Jerry begs for poison as compensation now. Burnham brings laudanum, but it only acts as an emetic.

When hope is gone Wilkie helps them break from prison and sends them into the canebrakes. Movement on the water, into the deep western swamps, is mere removal to a new uterine remoteness. Jerry dreams again of absorption by a current without destination. No longer trying to analyze Wilkie's motives, he sinks into the timeless forest world.

The wretched settlement of Gran Boz, old hunchback pirate, and her great unsatisfied desire for love and a child gradually drive Rachel from her reason. Again and again she steals another woman's infant, which she cannot even suckle. Jerry is content to sleep with the mother, finding union with the rest of mankind in his sin and its venereal symptoms. His debauch so completely occupies him that, when a Frankfort cutthroat comes to sell him the handbill he sought, he wonders if truth is more desirable than peace. It is his pride that finally goads him. He becomes so outraged at the disclosure that not Fort but Skrogg and Wilkie had fabricated the handbill—and therefore his gallant revenge is negated—that he accuses Rachel of taking part in this inglorious treachery. Her defense is counteraccusation and suicide. Dying and no longer distraught, she forgives him.

Jerry sees the pointlessness of accusing Wilkie, who, fruit of some dark eternal evil or mask of the world itself, his antagonist, must not be made an excuse. Jerry has his own crime to acknowledge. He rides on alone, with the "kind of knowledge which is identity." It is not a legal pardon that he seeks. His crime, the crime of self and of existence, is unpardonable. Arrogantly he had tried to purify that self by withdrawing from the active world to the realm of ideas. Then the abstract end was made to justify violent means: world redeemed idea when he killed Colonel Fort. Finally in the canebrake he had embraced the world, regardless of ideals, satisfied with the guiltlessness of animals and thus with being less than man. This is his history of errors. Welcoming his soul's punishment, he still has faith that there must be some way by which word and flesh, loneliness and communion, can be reconciled without contamination.

Before he can reach Frankfort Jerry is overtaken by the cutthroat sent by Wilkie and is decapitated. Wilkie buries the husband's head in Rachel's grave and then, enigmatic to the end, after a successful career shoots himself "tidily through the heart, without a single spatter of blood on the floor." Yet he does not destroy Jerry's manuscripts even though he knows that their truth, however romanticized and even confused, must circumvent his own.

Today injustice still propagates itself in Kentucky as elsewhere, but like Jerry some men keep faith in the worth of suffering, at least to the extent of wondering—was all for naught?

World Enough and Time illustrates a distinction, made early in *An Approach to Literature,* between facts from a coroner's report and the truth of fiction. In the nineteenth century several American authors found the actual events related in *The Confession of Jereboam O. Beauchamp* an attractive source for their own adaptations. Charles Fenno Hoffman's novel *Greyslaer* made a Revolutionary romance of the action; Edgar Allan Poe used the public whipping and the plan for westward flight in an unfinished Elizabethan verse play, *Politian;* W. Gilmore Simms used the story as a parable for urban corruption of village manners, through the folly of the feminist movement, in *Charlemont* and *Beauchamp.* Warren's own version borrows all the details offered in the *Confession* without slavishly imitating the man's character as revealed in that document.[21]

There was no need to borrow any one man's private history. Far from being unique, Jereboam was in many ways a representative frontiersman, forced by his own decisions and ikonsmashing migrant ancestors to create the very self on which he daily had to rely. Had he never existed, Jeremiah might still have walked the world, chosen from the company of such men as Sam Houston, whose early life, recorded by Warren in "How Texas Won Her Freedom," seems to paraphrase *World Enough*

and Time. In the wilderness of Tennessee, Sam read Homer
and, reduced to poverty by his father's death, brooded over
his lost heritage until, as a successful lawyer and politician,
he wed an heiress.

He was an actor in the deepest sense—the sense that makes a man see
himself in history. Even in the moment of action such a man sees the
act as a story, fulfilled in the gesture the actor makes. The poor
blundering human being, trapped in life's confusions, is always staring at that grander self-image, outside of Time, which even in the
moment of despair he must discern. Even despair has its drama.[22]

During a "lyric interlude" on a flatboat to Memphis, Sam drifted
into rare peace, "dreaming into nature." More typically he
wrote Jackson, "What am I? an Exile from my home and country. . . ." He fought a duel of honor (using a walking stick) in
Washington; his troops went into battle carrying a white silk
flag that bore a female figure of Liberty and some sweetheart's
glove on the peak of a staff.

In his *Confession* Beauchamp himself wrote with an assurance
that allowed him to abbreviate his thought, within the conventions of early American formal speech. He recorded, he did
not dramatize, his life. The minute analysis of motivation is
Robert Penn Warren's invention. So, too, are the elaborate
histories of minor characters—Wilkie, Skrogg, Lancaster,
Burnham—although hints of their existence appear in the original. The confession is the forthright explanation of a man who
has no doubt that his actions were honorable and imperative,
even indispensable. Warren has transferred to Beauchamp the
theatricality that his wife, Ann Cook, according to her letters,
thought rightfully hers. It was Ann who was easily roused to
acts of violence in her childhood, who yearned for a suitor who
would release the "consuming fire" from her heart's "smoth-
ered volcano," who shot the seducer of her younger sister,
and who found romantic exaltation in her husband's "noble,
heroic, unparalleled deed."[23]

Although the actual Beauchamps died together the day of execution, Warren's concern is with the hardness of admission,
not the ease of condemnation; with possibilities for self-reform,
not with flourishes of legal righteousness or with commemora-
tion of society's habits through judicial opinion. Consequently,
he permits their fictional counterparts, the Beaumonts, to

escape their prison only to discover that they cannot exonerate themselves of their guilt so easily. Their abortive flight, far from being anticlimactic, is crucial. (The contrary assertion of critics becomes doubly ironic if one accepts the possibility that their confusion of the roles in *All the King's Men* required that Warren expand his new narrative in order to demonstrate the extent of Stanton-Beaumont's culpability.) The Arcadia of their wandering is no green garden regained, but a swamp, the backwash of crime and unremembered relic civilization. To prepare this Adam and Eve, driven back to seclusion and a second chance, for the impact of their latter-day choice between animal ignorance and awful knowledge—another recapitulation of the "fortunate fall"—Warren has found it necessary to elaborate their early lives far beyond the few suggestions in his source. Whatever sense of actuality, or its abuse, derives from the "quoted" record of Jerry in the novel is the author's contribution.

Repudiation of "the fathers" (the pretensions as well as the occasional virtues of the past) becomes almost a monotonous pattern in the history of those characters in *World Enough and Time* who think of birth as renunciation of all precedent and consider identity synonymous with detachment and innocence. Ironically, by requiring such identity through separation, they share in the guilt of their own creation. Rachel, Skrogg, Sugg Lancaster, unable to live with the truth of their origins, forecast the oscillating pattern of rejection and embrace that characterizes Jerry (one moment he reassures Rachel's unloved mother with a kiss; the next he betrays her trust, in the typical downstairs seduction scene, while the woman dies deserted). He must kill Fort, who has become his father and therefore his rival. His last rejection of the father image comes with his denial of Burnham's advice that he immerse himself in Immanuel's blood. Instead, wishing frantically to be unborn, he asks for death from the hands of his old tutor.

Jerry's romantic image of himself as knight and deliverer, reinforced by the formalized rhetoric and ostentatious frontier ceremonies, Cavalier vestiges, depends on human perversity, the pharisaical notion that one earns innocence by acting as judge and executioner. Like Perse Munn in *Night Rider* Jerry has made of justice self-justification. His delusions of self-

righteousness, ironically, are dispelled only when he apprehends and convicts himself, finally realizing that he has been
made the unwitting agent of a justice superior to man's. At
last Jerry understands that knowledge is all he needs: "That
is not redemption, but is almost better than redemption." (This
was always the moral position of lawyer Hawgood: truth is superior to innocence and its companion, peace. It is the verdict,
in *All the King's Men*, of Jack Burden; in *Willie Stark*, the last
pronouncement of Willie himself.)

World *Enough and Time* is concerned only incidentally with
a particular crime and the fixing of a murderer's legal guilt.
The graphic, melodramatic quality of such details, unless seen
ironically as glittering appointments of the false knight (become, however, pilgrim unaware, doubling the irony), may
divert attention from the real drama: the tortuous way of the
world in which man must learn to inform against himself. The
political issue, which envelops the personal, is a field of con-
straint lying between two polar concepts: that of law as an absolute moral ruler to which the individual must submit and
that of law as a servant of man's needs. Just as Beaumont
wants to take the law into his own hands to exact justice from
Colonel Fort, so the New Court wants to interpret and exploit
the state constitution at will. (Their archtype is Willie Stark,
man with a meatax, proof that, although the law is what the
Supreme Court makes it, the court is what *he* wants to make
it.) The novel enlists these two forces against each other in
a tournament of endurance so cunning and deceptive that any
victory must seem provisional. Ambiguity, life's doubleness,
is not only the subject but also the method of *World Enough and
Time*.

Irony with a center, which Warren praised in Ransom and
Katherine Anne Porter, interprets his Spenserian epigraph
with its contrast of past virtues and present shortcomings.
The antebellum characters of *World Enough and Time* are as
insecure in their traditions as any modern man. Jerry is more
than an island unto himself, he is an archipelago, fragmented
within. As his own wife becomes inaccessible to him, his loneliness achieves the thoroughness of a living death. Nor, trapped
in life's immediacy and finding even the recent past already
obscure, can he ever be sure of his own motives—man's ageless

quandary. He can only pay for the crime of being man, of being alive.

However, this thematic center recoils periodically, whenever the cross-purposes of Warren's complex "reverberators" make the intricate web of circumstance shudder convulsively. The literal line of action, evaluated introspectively, is recorded by Beaumont in his journal. Then the anonymous historian makes comments (often misleading) on that journal. Not only is Jerry committed throughout most of his twenty-five years to the belief that life follows a fortuitous pattern of delusion and justification, but the historian-narrator himself maintains the attitude that truth about the past always eludes even the most careful study.

Of what use, then, are the quantities of minute details from the history of the most minor characters, result of incredible total recall that analyzes with more than Puritan scruple each compartment of Jerry's motivation? What effect is gained by Mr. Barron's description of simple agrarian life in Virginia or Munn Short's tale of salvation, since neither of these alternatives makes any impression on Jerry? Nor are such token offerings convincing as evidence of a climate of invisible grace that envelops refractory man, because one cannot help wondering how Barron or Short would appear if Warren struck through their defensive calm and divulged their innermost mystery, as he has with Jerry. No testimony to the good life is secure from the author's acute cross-examination. Wherever life obtains, there is risk of major infection.

Certainly the more credible the inchoateness of the characters appears at first, the less credible is any final clarification. Jerry can meet the world only on terms that he has made up as he went along. The dawn of expiation, after his prolonged midnight struggle, seems a gratuitous dispensation of grace rather than an earned reward. Had Jerry not been decapitated, given twenty-four hours and the habits of his life, surely he would have found some new error, some new self-deception with which to torment himself. Is there ever world enough and time for final demonstrations? The demand for such proof is the pragmatic trap; faith has its own affirmation. Faith generated by understanding of sufficient details is all that Warren requests. But an oversufficiency may generate despair instead, if one sees the galactic tangle without apprehending the center of its revolution. Where some particle of faith precedes the experience of fiction and needs only to be quickened again by it, the author's risk is lessened. But no contemporary author can presume the presence of such a common body of belief. Warren's audience, therefore, is partly responsible for the limited success of this novel.

All the King's Men criticizes the neutrality of commonplace history, which can accumulate facts but not judge them. The singular detachment of the narrator in *World Enough and Time* illustrates such neutrality. It is he, not Jerry, who says, "Explanations can only explain explanations, and the self is gratuitous in the end." Here, as in "The Circus in the Attic," Warren satirizes the historian's professional blindness to the truth that surrounds him. The italicized "modern epilogue" is the only portion narrated directly by the author. But the final question, "Was all for naught?" not italicized, suggests the presence of his voice, too, in its community of undertones: Jerry's hopeful anguished outcry; the historian's passionless question of fact; and Warren's challenge—is our common past to escape us because we trust unexceptional historians, self-deprived of insight, to preserve and interpret its documents? Here is more than the South's resentment toward "scholarship" about itself.

This multiplicity of narration, intended to represent the complexity of mass efforts at absolute knowledge, is a risk not always overcome. With too much proximity, the perspectives tend to corrode rather than correct each other. And the author's values, instead of serving as fixed reference from which error can be measured, are always in danger of becoming just another portion of man's general perplexity.

Band of Angels (1955)

In a 1957 *Paris Review* interview, trying to explain changes in images of the Negro from *I'll Take My Stand* to *Band of Angels* and *Segregation*,[24] Warren almost apologetically recalls "the jangle and wrangle" of writing his Agrarian "Briar Patch" essay, drafted at Oxford at the same time as his first novelette. The discomfort of reducing Negroes to the obligatory status of farmhands contrasted with "the holiday sense" of writing "Prime Leaf." Though convinced that in 1929, no one—

South, North, Negro—was ready to end segregation, he recalls that the world of essays encouraged a rhetoric of evasion
more so than fiction. "In the essay I reckon I was trying to
prove something and in the novelette trying to find out something."

Because the biography of John Brown, somewhat later, was
a roundabout defense of the Southern temper, its Negroes became "kinky heads" hardly worth civil disorder or disturbance
of local practices. In other novels, however, they were sympa-
thetic if minor figures, proportioned to the theme at hand,
ready scapegoats for men deluded by their own righteousness.
A Negro is executed for Bunk Trevelyan's crime, and Perse
Munn, defender of the guilty man, nearly kills another Negro
later in a panic of flight; Anse, Murdock's Negro manservant,
is almost lynched after being falsely accused of Sue's murder;
Cass Mastern's thoughtless affair with Mrs. Trice ends when
his witness, her dark-skinned waiting maid, is sold downstream; Jerry Beaumont disguises his face by means of a black
cloth after killing his surrogate-father Fort, so that the slayer
will seem to have been a Negro (a mulatto slave was supposed
to have fathered Rachel's firstborn: Jerry is avenging this
defamation which he believes originated with Fort). In "Blackberry Winter" and "Her Own People," the manner of Negro
suffering illuminates the meaning of the tribulations of all mankind, sometimes better than anyone is prepared to realize.

The Negro as symbolic victim first achieves prominence in
the character of George, the slave boy bullied, quartered,
and mutilated in *Brother to Dragons*. Unresisting and at the
moment of execution almost consenting, George has only three
spoken lines in the whole narrative:

> I was lost in the world and the trees were tall.
> I was lost in the world, and the dark swale reared.
> I was lost in my anguish and did not know the reason.

Yet these were the first lines of *Brother to Dragons* that Warren composed.[25] Living, George is articulate though mute;
dead, his bones speak for him. Neither his suffering nor the
terribleness of the crime is in itself so important as the before
and after of those whose lives interlock with his.

The characterization of George, for all its fierce impact
on our compassion, is not conceived as social protest for its

own sake. This, Warren cautions in his interview at the American Academy in Rome, "denies the textures of life. The problem is to permit the fullest range of life into racial awareness. . . . Race isn't an isolated thing—I mean as it exists in the U.S.—it becomes a total symbolism for every kind of issue." In *Segregation* he argued that racism, by the very act of taking refuge in "antique virtue," denies change, which alone has the capacity to create individual features. By denying the Negro his right to self-definition, Southerners have multiplied divisions existing in all men and have failed to achieve their own moral identity. They have sunk back into the anonymity that accompanies mass emotional reaction and deliberation. Similarly, in *Band of Angels* treatment of the problem of miscegenation makes direct comment on the results of classification by race, yet more important provides a symbol for man's inner self-divisions, his angry, half-impulsive, half-repelled attempts and failures to discover identity.

Like George, Amantha Starr is a victim, but a highly conscious one, articulate even in the shuddering reaches of her inward journey. With extraordinary insight, Warren has made her rebellion against that aging, adolescent self-consciousness the evil source of those cleavages within her that mirror the civil war without. It is Manty's insistent, self-pitying view of herself as victim that victimizes her more than society ever could. (As *Segregation* contends, the problem is not to learn to live with the Negro; it is to learn to live with ourselves.)

The theme of the novel is established by its very first words, the outcry of Manty's heart: "Oh, who am I?" In Warren's long tradition of complaints by the still unborn, Manty's words are akin to Sue Murdock's and Jerry Beaumont's "Oh, what am I?" But now there is the further complication of a refrain, "If I could only be free." Sue also wanted not to belong to anybody, even as she demanded her identity from the person of others. But Manty's own progress toward freedom is more than usually encumbered by her confusion of freedom with non-slavery. Since her story is sensed and described from within the cage of herself, the most difficult problem for the author was to create a woman at once plausible, within the confines of her heritage, and yet increasingly capable of those bitter admissions exacted by life.

Amantha Starr has divided her childhood in Kentucky between two mothers, both dead. She has often played house in
the grassy part of the estate where a vaguely remembered
Renie was buried, and she has played, too, with the lovely
china doll of Miss Eileen, Starr's wife (who for lack of "juice"
had no children of her own). When her father snatches the doll
away, she has only Bu-Bula, a crudely whittled doll; they cling
to each other for confirmation. Shaddy, the grizzled Negro
whose hands had carved Bu-Bula, lays them unblessed on
Manty herself, asking "Yeah, what she?—what she?" Manty
informs on him, and Aaron Pendleton Starr against his own
principles ships the old man away. Manty has the grace to feel
guilty and to realize the quicksand quality of her own life.
Gradually her Negro playmates are granted her company less
and less until in 1852, when she is nearly ten, she is turned
over to Miss Idell, wife of Starr's Cincinnati lawyer, to be
sent among the Abolitionist "whey-faces" at Oberlin.

As her religious sense ripens, Manty often pleads with her
father to end slavery at Starrwood. He asks in honest puzzlement, where could the Negroes go? When Seth Parton, Oberlin's sanctified farmboy, accuses her father of bribing his
slaves with whisky, she defies the young man's uncharitable
arrogance, yet secretly admires him. In 1858, on the occasion
of his first sermon, Seth leads her to the secluded scene of
another woman's seduction, which his continence and Manty's
prayers are to redeem. She tries to be worthy of expected joy,
but later (as disappointed as Anne Stanton must have been with
Jack Burden) weeps in desolation of spirit. Seth's apotheosis
seems planned at the expense of all others. It is almost with
pleasure that he tells Manty one day of her father's death, in
Cincinnati, at the home of adulterous Miss Idell, while her
husband was imprisoned for embezzlement.

At the Starrwood graveyard Manty is deprived of her father
in a more terrible way. She has hurried southward from free
territory, only to be claimed by the sheriff as issue of Renie,
mistress of Starr and now identified as his chattel! In self-
defense, momentarily Manty clings to the belief that she has
not been merely the passing creation of events; does not the
continuity of sensations require the existence of a soul that
can possess them? Yet she is soon impressed with the fact

that chattels have neither souls nor identity. She tries to hang
herself from the hotel window but instinctively saves her own
life. On the boat bound south from Louisville she sees a slave
in the water and hopes that he has jumped; but, when he shouts
for rescue, she feels robbed again of some deep assurance.
She remembers Oberlin sermons, which shame her for calling
her mother "nigger"; she welcomes this sense of participation
in her own punishment, not from contrition but for the feeling
it gives her of being restored as an agent in the travail of
events. Pleasurably, fearfully, she even considers herself
somehow responsible for the obscenity that the New Orleans
slave market has by 1859 become.

Manty is auctioned off to middle-aged Hamish Bond who,
curiously, treats her like a guest in his house. Perversely
resenting his kindness as well as her supposed imprisonment,
still she feels restored at least occasionally to that "deep, redeeming unity in life that makes beauty out of disgust."

Michele, who has charge of Bond's household, is pained
when Manty talks of laws she learned at Oberlin against the
importation of slaves. Bond's kindness, it is said, is so great
that it is like a disease. During the season of yellow fever in
'53, he had even refused to leave the sick, to take refuge on
his Pointe du Loup plantation. And he has always allowed his
k'la, young Rau-Ru, to sit at his table like an heir apparent
or a second self.

One day, having discovered that the watchdog is as tame as
Bond, Manty decides to escape to the riverboat. But she en-
counters Rau-Ru and has to be satisfied with making him carry
home her bags like a servant. Angrily she refuses to eat with
"Massa" Bond any longer and, without being accused, admits
she was running away. That night, during a terrible storm,
almost wordlessly he shuts out the rain from her room; they
cling together like each other's doll.

Who is whose victim? she will some day wonder (the question
of "Circus in the Attic" and *Brother to Dragons*); how is each
small lifetime the epitome of all? What nexus joined that rape
and John Brown at Harpers Ferry? Waking, without wonder,
she kisses the scar on Bond's leg. When he tries to send her
away to Cincinnati she refuses to leave. Together they visit
Pointe du Loup, where among the slaves a kind of ostracism

is substituted for the lash and where the renegade is always welcomed back and after punishment accorded a public "raise-up" (such as Bond feels is Manty's gift to *him*). Other planters are afraid Hamish's easy-going ways might lead to Negro insurrections, and only he is not pleased with the secession that follows Lincoln's election.

One day in Bond's absence Charles Prieur-Denis, an old acquaintance who has forced Bond to help in his "nigger-running," offers more than his companionship to Manty. Rau-Ru intervenes, in spite of her untiring contempt for him. Then, accused of having struck a white man, he knocks Charles down and flees. Bond returns and suggests a suicidal duel. But Charles, who considers any death not in the grand manner gauche, sweatily bows out. Some cold-eyed part of Manty (the "not-you" that spies on her pretenses) rejoices in this new hold she has on Bond. But her guilt at this secret joy is no greater than Bond's when he admits that some part of him had "wanted you to do what you didn't do."

The agony of their contrariness spreads to Rau-Ru, the *k'la,* who fires on Bond in his gig (Charles has proven the fiction of Rau-Ru's role as Bond's "son"; accordingly, Rau-Ru is "free"). It spreads also to restless slaves who become fire-bugs in their discontent, and to petty officials, who in 1861 refuse reinforcement from volunteer regiments of "free colored men."

Farragut's gunboats run the forts, and, while the city burns, Bond recalls his slaver days in Africa, after he was driven from the wharves of Baltimore by his mother's airs. He had stolen both ship and name (his own was Alec Hinks) from the real Hamish Bond, and he was able to forgive himself every atrocity until one day something made him rescue a child from brutal Amazon slave-hunters at the price of a disabled leg. Rau-Ru was that rescued child, now his secret sharer: "That's why he hated me." Bond also admits having bought Manty because he resented the youth of the other buyer. How could this be kindness? When he grinds them both down, seeking refuge in her body, Manty claims that he only wants to make her a "nigger" like the rest. Defeated, Bond gives her her freedom, asking only never to hear from her again.

The irony of John Brown's killing a free Negro at Harpers

Ferry is repeated, in miniature, when Ben Butler's "liberators" treat Manty like a town whore. Luckily she is rescued by Seth Parton and his fellow officer, Tobias Sears of Massachusetts. While hopeful Negroes starve in the streets, Tobias, who supposedly has nobility like a disease, discusses Transcendentalism with Manty and talks himself into marrying her. Seth, already wed to a fat, holy, wholesome woman, threatens to make Manty honest by revealing the defilement of her blood. She assumes that he has already done so when Tobias returns to her. Just before the wedding, Bond appears and himself proposes, saying that he had freed her so that she would not be committed to accept him. But she is sure that Tobias alone has freed her from her old dilemma.

Tobias, however, is himself not free. He is torn between what he thinks is Butler's devotion to emancipation at any price and Emerson's recollected warning "that even if history is the working out of the design of the Great Soul, the redemption of matter is not always complete, that imperfect men must fulfill the perfection of idea. . . ." He is ostracized for leading Negro troops into the campaign of '63, but, when Colonel Morton belittles his success by pointing out that they were freedmen long before the war, he demands a real "blue-gum" commission composed of runaway slaves still not "people" in the liberator's eyes. Meanwhile Manty, working for the Aid Society with runaway slaves, forces herself to kiss a Negro child (just as she had reassuringly kissed Bond's servant, Dollie, before her flight).

Colonel Morton grows rich on confiscated land and cheap Negro labor; Seth, dallying with Miss Idell, now the colonel's wife, refuses to return to his ministry even after Lincoln's assassination. Morton advocates, as Tobias did formerly, limited but progressive black suffrage so that his business with the rebels will prosper. Tobias veers toward total suffrage as his father (who knows little of actual Southern conditions) counsels, but, by deciding impulsively to join the Freedman's Bureau, he spites his father's, and Manty's, wish for his return North. Realizing his loneliness, his need to feel a part of something, Manty forgives the weakness in him that passes for strength. She waits with him among unreconciled planters, soldiers under orders, carpetbaggers, and Rau-Ru, now Lieutenant Oliver Cromwell Jones.

With the passing of the Fourteenth Amendment, Negroes become citizens—without vote, except in rebel states whose congressmen would otherwise not be recognized. When Louisiana resists ratification, the Radicals decide to revive the Unionist Convention of 1864 in order to write a new constitution allowing all Negroes to vote and disfranchising ex-Confederates. Congress refuses support, and General Sheridan refuses protection, but the blood lust of the righteous rises. Tobias draws the anger of all sides by opposing the rump convention (". . . we undertook to do good in the world, but we had not purged our own soul . . ."); but finds some consolation in Manty's admission of her birth. (Seth had revealed only her father's adultery with Miss Idell.) Still, convinced that he would desert her, a "nigger," for his cause, Manty turns to Rau-Ru, whose color she herself has betrayed many times. He is as much an image of guilt for Manty as for Hamish. To her husband she has described almost possessively scars on Rau-Ru's back which she has never seen. Now, alone with Manty, Rau-Ru strikes her each time she asks to see those scars. Outraged by his own pain which he has tried to inflict on her, he urges the riot that follows.

With all officials absenting themselves from responsibility, irrationality is unavoidable. A Negro fires at a policeman for arresting a white boy who has been baiting the Negro procession. The dead and the wounded have to be piled on drays. Taken through swamps to injured Rau-Ru, Manty finds the *k'la* preparing to hang Bond. Fulfilling the promise to his mother that some day he would be "ass-deep in niggers" (he includes Manty), Bond jumps. Rau-Ru puts part of the burden for his act on Manty for having teased him with Bond, as she had teased Charles.

When bushwhackers cut them off, Rau-Ru wearily releases Manty from death beside him by declaring her a white as she insists. Manty returns not to the North but to New Orleans, where Tobias, wounded, does not know she ever fled. (In his own way he, too, had escaped to his "niggers," to solace his conscience.) After withdrawing from time, to heal, they re-

move themselves to St. Louis where Tobias practices law and
their two children are born. In 1877, he exposes the abuses
committed by big business under the aegis of the Fourteenth
Amendment, whose definition of personal rights had been absorbed and abused by corporations. Because she thinks he is
ruled by pity, Manty forgives him an affair with a culturally
undernourished woman. But she discovers later that his poems
are filled neither with anger at the Thingism that has saddled
mankind nor with compassion for its victims. They speak of
self and flight, those poems "dying always into the beauty of
Idea, into the nobility of Truth, dying into the undefiled white-
ness of some self-image." Still, only if she can admit her
own flight from reality, can she renounce his.

They move westward to Kansas, Tobias speculating, inventing, and continually failing; their son dying as if he had
never lived. Seth Parton has died too, bequeathing a school of
theology. Miss Idell has grown so thin and old that her history
as mistress is nearly forgivable.

In Halesburg, Kansas, Manty sees an old Negro beggar whose
scarred back reminds her of Rau-Ru's. Her alms are meant to
purchase absolution and oblivion—or knowledge and identity.
For the first time in years she speaks the word "nigger." The
beggar dies, still anonymous.

Wealthy Josh Lounberry, who has invented a curler to put
kinks in white people's hair, arrives from Chicago to accord
kinship to his father, another Negro, Old Slop the garbage
collector. Josh's forthright offer of honor is a reproach to
the evasiveness of Manty, who suddenly realizes that only she,
and not the New England Abolitionists, can set herself free
and rid herself of the nightmare fears with which she has flag-
ellated herself. At last at the level of sad humanness, she does
not mock Tobias' own descent. Once liberator of Negroes, he
now resents the pitying comradeship offered by Josh. To prove
that he is not a fellow inferior, he fights Josh's battle with his
bare fists and later helps honor Old Slop with a hot scrub bath.
The sidling step is the manner of life's motion, not Tobias'
alone. Having accepted himself, his middling virtue, Tobias
need no longer wear the twisted face of self-satire. He has no
human right to feel ashamed at his failure to relieve divinity
of its role as Redeemer. Now Manty, too, can understand that

her father had refused her manumission papers *because* he loved her, even if no man could appreciate the truth of that love beneath his deception. Amantha Starr is determined never again to let herself be pitied.

The attempt of a few critics to dismiss *Band of Angels* as preconceived Hollywood fare is confuted by the fact that the movie could not even approximate the themes of the novel or suggest the inner contortion of its characters. What the novel provides, for the first time in the Warren effort, is a complete context for credibility, those elements in which the corkscrew motions of the soul can be described without exaggeration as progress. Here are world enough and time, duration—what Perse Munn, Jerry Calhoun, Jack Burden, and Jerry Beaumont were all too young to have in sufficiency. *Band of Angels* gains by being narrated from the point of view of a mature Manty, capable of respecting the anguish of her recollected earlier self. (This technique of retrospection had already been used in *All the King's Men* and, with additions, *World Enough and Time.*) She demands pity or justice no longer, but, like Willie Stark in *Rise and Fall* and Jerry Beaumont, an understanding that surpasseth peace.

It is herself she has been fleeing. Simply by running no more, not because exhausted but because disabused, she stifles the two cries which have shadowed her passage: "Oh, who am I?" and "If only I could be free." Refusing to accept the absolute denial of self imposed by slavery, she retreats in fever to the other extreme, absolute selfishness. She is careless of even those who tried to love her: her father, Hamish Bond, even Rau-Ru, who wanted to give her herself, though he himself was confused. These she rejects after using her sex and youth to incite their pity. They are her dolls, to whom she gives endearments like sweets but secretly clings, needing to be needed. They are her victims, along with Tobias. But she is their victim, too, for thinking to find herself in them, for expecting to make their strength hers.

The characterization is one of Warren's subtlest and truest, though at first glance most puzzling. Manty is so frail and disordered a young woman, so easily denied person and reduced to body by those routines of subjection, passion, and bondage, that she seems to fade in the vicinity of masculine color and mass. But this is precisely her most powerful advantage, the trap that literally kills Hamish Bond and Rau-Ru. No one can really be brutal to her. Manty's suffering is psychological, and largely self-inflicted.

She herself is aware, occasionally, of her hold on Bond. When he offers to shoot Charles in a duel for having insulted her, her pride is caressed. In violent need, Bond himself had earlier raped Manty, as if struggling to repossess his former innocence by violating hers, or in a manner of mutual branding, so that she will never be able to leave him again, nor he ever successfully desert her.

Manty welcomes the rape by Bond (the morning sight of his scarred leg turns her terror to tenderness) and seeks out the cuffs of Rau-Ru as a kind of recognition, decorations from fellow sufferers, to satisfy her own need to be pitiful and to invest herself with the power of forgiveness. But this fault in her defeats itself, almost in mock confirmation of Seth Parton's latter-day edict (years after dispassionately testing his passion by not lusting after her) that "only in vileness may man begin to seek." Her very exaggeration of her role as victim finally forces her to believe that misfortune has sandpapered her down to less than nothing or that her deepest wounds are of her own making. Rather than deny herself identity, she accepts the burden that goes with it and achieves a wavering balance suspended somewhere between solitary confinement and the status of mere chattel, between absolute self and existence as mere statistic in an absolute society.

Such transformation would seem extreme had not Manty been equipped with a certain weakness or strength[26] that manifests itself throughout the book. She has loved Bu-Bula, felt an accessory to the selling of Shaddy, been able to reassure Dollie when the servant felt unloved and to kiss a Negro child who had approached her, sustained Tobias in his need, and forgiven his own nobility turned to selfishness. All these things prepare her for her final quiet and knowledgeable embrace of life. Such rehearsals of grace, intuitive yearnings but with some inner comprehension, preserve Manty from petrifaction through self-concern, at its starkest when a son is born to her in Kansas and dies almost unobserved. At times she is even so scrupulous as to feel burdened with not only all past choices but those not chosen as well:

It was, in a way, as though the thing not done—the flight not made—is always done, too, and never releases you from the grip of the old possibility, and you can only escape from the done, never from the not-done, which in its not-doneness is always there being enacted forever.

But how can the self be found and fulfilled except through "release from that dark realm of undifferentiated possibility," human origins?

Furthermore, although she cannot find herself in others, Manty discovers in their common pattern of illusions why she cannot. Bond, although he often insists that people are only what they are and demands that men face facts, has as much an assumed identity as Manty. In a story within the story he is revealed as Alec Hinks, former slave trader. Alec rejects his mother's pretensions and false memory of slave servants. By acquiring slaves of his own he has made her lie come true, "but true in some shocking not respectable way," as Warren says, "that would violate her need for respectability."[27] Bond, in turn, is rejected by his own "son," Rau-Ru, his *k'la* and secret self, in an attempted denial of the father-son relation. Rau-Ru puts the noose around Bond's neck, although he is not sure that he would actually have killed Bond had the latter not jumped to make sure. By that time Rau-Ru has an assumed identity of his own: Oliver Cromwell Jones, puritan and protector, zealot of his own interpretation of the law. However, cruelty does not fit him well. He saves Manty from the bushwhackers, his motives now obscure even to himself. And it is such fevers of kindness that distinguish Rau-Ru, Bond, and even Tobias (whose nobility is like a disease) from the more permanent and demoniac hypocritical disguises of Charles, Seth Parton, and Miss Idell.

Captive to his own slave-running days,[28] Bond once excused himself with the words: "I didn't make this world and make 'em drink blood, I didn't make myself and I can't help what I am doing." It is Maule's curse in *The House of the Seven Gables* that is summoned by this talk of drinking blood. Hawthorne's novel,[29] in which each member in a family line brings death on himself not through the malignancy of some predestining agency but through his own greed, his own recommission of an original sin, is as relevant here as the epigraph from Housman: "When shall I be dead and rid/ Of the wrong my father did?" (Is it not more than coincidental that "Oliver Cromwell Jones" is a near-rhyme for Oliver Wendell Holmes, Bostonian racist who compiled physiological "proofs" for the heredity of evil?)

Man inherits the conditions of evil, yet is capable of choosing otherwise. Tobias explains, in words that recall Willie Stark, "But it's so hard right in the middle of things to remember that the power of soul must work through matter, that even the filthiness of things is part of what Mr. Emerson calls the perennial miracle the soul worketh, that matter often retains something of its original tarnishment. . . ." Without choice there is no identity. Talk of human helplessness is self-pity in the extreme—which Bond will not allow himself. And so the example is set Manty, who has resented Charles's speaking of Bond as *"pauvre vieux."* In exchange, Bond and Rau-Ru sense in Manty's fragile trust the limits of their own willingness to end pretense. Each becomes at first the accomplice of, then the catalyst for, the others.

Because of this elaborate system of facsimile selves which makes truth shudder through the fabric of disguise, the theme of the novel cannot be diminished even when Manty seems to pale in importance. Indirection is the method not only of the novel but presumably of life. Aaron Starr's attempted kindness to his illegitimate daughter is obstructed by society's manumission laws, but Manty blames only her father. Service of an abstract good can even be a vice, as it is with Seth Parton and as it threatens to be with Tobias, who is rescued by his sense of the incongruous. They are presented as less criminal examples of "Northern justice" than those corrupt reformers, heavy-handed General Butler and light-fingered Colonel Morton, for whom fairness is equated with force. Manty's rebellion against her growing consciousness of a self that displeases her devises scapegoats out of those around her, just as the North purged itself of all guilt by transferring the sins of Yankee slave-traders to the Southern planters' already burdened conscience. But the countermovement of the novel has its own triumphs. Good also works by indirection.

Manty, in reconstructing her past, tries to link her rape with Harpers Ferry and all other simultaneous events of which her own life is the "summing up." In the lives most closely associated with hers, those of lovers and enemies, she discovers the same doubts and delusions, the same struggle against entrapment. The more the wounds are reopened and exhibited for the sake of sympathy, the less chance there is of healing. But the struggle against bondage of whatever kind is sanctified, becomes a bond of glory, provided it is accompanied by recognition that the worst form of human subjugation is self-abasement, assuming the role of pure victim.

Manty in her frailty sometimes believes herself only "an expression of History," as if a lifetime were one enormous livelong rape. "You do not live your life, but somehow, your life lives you, and you are, therefore, only what History does to you," she says. In time, however, she admits that such thoughts are a tactic of evasion. As often as she sidesteps responsibility to be free of all guilt, she is surrendering her right to be herself. The drama enveloping her impersonates and reveals her inner conflict: the Civil War, the whole social fretwork based on the myths of miscegenation—these are projections of her own self-division. The Northern reformers, armed with righteousness and bayonets, do not constitute a band of angels. Reform is a matter for the individual soul, whose health or disease society merely reflects. It cannot be imposed, any more than freedom can be absolutely given or denied, or even defined absolutely from without.

By indirection Manty's western flight becomes pursuit. In the images of Halesburg's beggar and of Old Slop being embraced by a son to whom self-respect is more important than commonplace pride she contemplates herself. Her stumbling, tremulous progress toward self-realization coincides with the progressive suffrage Tobias Sears advocates until, rebelling against his father by carrying the old man's beliefs to their absurd conclusion, he demands immediate and full extension of privilege.

In *Segregation* Warren has made the same point more bluntly: "Gradualism is all you'll get. History, like nature, knows no jumps. Except the jump backward, maybe." In the *Paris Review* he has complained of ineffectual do-gooders and levelers

intent on creating a superconformity in the name of equality:
"I feel pretty strongly about attempts to legislate undifference.
That is just as much tyranny as trying to legislate difference.
. . . Furthermore, you can't legislate virtue." And in his address on "Knowledge and the Image of Man" Warren has described as a congenital part of the Christian ethic "the right
to define oneself," despite a continuous "osmosis of being,"
to distinguish oneself from the world and from other men and
to make one's own way toward salvation or damnation. Even
well-intentioned concern for the common man, the special
form of condescension that New Dealers sometimes promoted,
is therefore objectionable.

In the crucible of flesh which a novel such as *Band of Angels*
provides, such perceptions are tested under a fire that sets in
motion the shuddering ripples of Manty's life, her shriveling
contraction and slow magnification. The central figure, usually
an executioner or apocalyptic knight, has now become victim,
but what is revealed to Manty is neither the perfection of her
grief nor its legitimacy. Through the long welter of circumstance this outcast learns more than endurance, more than
disguise for the sake of survival. She learns that only through
separateness is identity earned; only through identity is personal and social fulfillment possible. Between two absolutes,
rejection and subjection, she achieves her station.

PART III

CHECKPOINT ON THE GANTLET

7

THE RUNNING GAMBLE

American literature in his time has profited from Warren's independence, the relentless claim of his work to the right of self-determination and his refusal to be subject to the professional whims of chronic uncritics beyond their depths in supposed main currents. This is not to say that Warren has remained aloof from his times. Rather, he has avoided readymade images, formulas for liberals. His dialectic, for example, has always been essentially more Socratic than Marxian. When the thirties required "proletarian novels" Warren was writing of the Ku Klux tactics employed by farmers' unions in the South's tobacco wars, as well as the damage done a whole society by the venality of finance capitalism. When public depravity, spurred by depression, brought statism to the outlying parishes, Warren rang brazen bell warnings in *All the King's Men*. When Guernica and the Guaderramas, Buchen-

wald and Anzio flashed in the headlines, Warren was not immune. To the proving grounds of the world he dedicated "Letter
from a Coward to a Hero," "Terror," and "Circus in the Attic," not with the "sense of urgency" used by propagandists
to justify those galvanic reflexes that pass for first thoughts,
but with consideration for the abiding truth which alone, however unflattering, sanctifies the journey into man's interior.
During the days of roaring employment in the fifties he wrote
Promises to the future—a caveat, not a canticle. For he had
also written:

> May we not, however, in some chill hour between dark and dawn,
> have the thought that our own age may—just possibly—have its own
> frauds and deceits, deeper and more ambiguous than those anatomized
> in *The Great Gatsby*, that though this is not the age of provincial self-
> satisfaction, it may be the age of national self-righteousness and re-
> quire a sharper scalpel than even *Main Street*, and that Divine Provi-
> dence has given no written guarantee that It will not rebuke the smug-
> gery of the Great Boom?[1]

His whole effort as author has been to deny the existence of
any "literature to specification."

Private scruple—nourished by the understanding that sometimes comes to Southerners after a century of acting the official
accused, as well as by the New Critics' propensity for keeping
literature in reserve as a mode of meditation—has prevented
Warren's dependence on the axioms of society. As a result
even anti-Marxist critics have chastised him for not being
more useful to their causes. Regardless, Warren continued to
respect individual natures more than those cared to permit
who followed the allegedly fixed course of social forces.

The dialectical configuration in Warren's works does not
derive from undiscerning adherence to the romantic Hegelian
formula for irresistible progress, peculiar forms of which survive in the supposedly realistic twentieth century. As he explained in his American Academy in Rome interview, when he
was a child he was impressed by Buckle's *History of Civilization,* which offered

> . . . the one big answer to everything: *geography.* History is all ex-
> plained by geography. I read Buckle and then I could explain every-
> thing. It gave me quite a hold over the other kids, they hadn't read
> Buckle. . . . Buckle was my Marx. . . . After I had had my session

with Buckle and the one-answer system at the age of 13, or whatever it was, I was inoculated against Marx and his one-answer system when he and the depression hit me when I was about twenty-five.[2]

Warren finds the dialectic valuable as a dramatic device because it suggests that any movement upward, toward a superior realization and state of being, is possible only as struggling evolution, fetal uncoiling, emergence not despite but through the rub of outer and inner circumstance. Sudden mutations, like unprepared intuitions, are rare. Nor is ascent inevitable. The dialectic is also valuable, therefore, as an equivalent to the implacable sifting and winnowing of the self, inasmuch as progress toward the apocalypse has to be earned by the individual rather than by throngs and masses. Or its erratic motion is comparable to multiple vision in painting, to Picasso's only apparent distortions in time and volumetric displacement, composed with insight rather than the oversight of mirror realism. It is a predication of experience, a technique for elaborating the complex exertions of any man to be both human and himself.

However externally motivated certain of Warren's characters may seem to be, the clearly moral center of his work argues that their author is not himself victim of a deterministic philosophy. He has made clear time after time that the darkest compulsions are subconscious, and public motives mere rationalization of these private desires. His interpretation of Coleridge, with whose views he is in sympathy—that "original sin is not hereditary sin; it is original with the sinner and is of his will"—coincides with the admission that Hamish Bond finally makes, after previously absolving himself because he did not make the world. Although the diseased dictates of every character are not exposed to the sunlight on the forum steps, the consensus is that man is a condition in his own conditioning. The cause of any action, therefore, has to be sought in the self as well as in society or in transcendent doom.

If there is no simple division of classes in *Night Rider* or *At Heaven's Gate;* if no ready-made judgment of the "American dictator" in *All the King's Men* can satisfy the novel's purpose; if "Terror" questions the pointless enthusiasm of the "liberal" soldier scurrying after death around the compass; if *Brother to Dragons* questions even Jefferson, compadre with John Tay-

lor of American agrarian theory; if *Band of Angels* is in all
honesty critical of the average plantation holder (Bond is exceptional) as well as of Yankee slave traders and fumbling "do-
gooders, " the critic restricted to the expected and to epigram-
matic expression objects. Neither "proletarian" nor "liberal"
in his work, Warren slips through the major categories of such
a mind, nor is he sufficiently obscure to be treated with half
envious scorn. Consequently, *World Enough and Time* is simply
demoted to the rank of "costume novel, " romanticized historical fiction. In other works, violence and yeoman farmer set-
tings are dismissed as "typically Southern, typically naturalistic. "

Warren's choice of formidable structures (his willingness,
for example, to risk an anticlimax by refusing Beaumont his
historic execution) and of thorny textures (his habit of total
recall even of seemingly insignificant details, because all life
interlocks) has not catered to popularity. The canon itself has
been too unorthodox to win quick admiration or even agreement.
Furthermore, his critical essays have from the start ad-
monished facile prejudgment of intent and achievement in literature. He has long admired not only Tudor and Jacobean
drama, but also the "kitchen criticism" of the period, its con-
noisseur interest in "how to make the cake, "[3] as he has called
it. Not finding ready at hand the judicious kind of readers required by his work, he has had to help train them.

Even if Warren had used crude experience classifiable as
"proletarian" or "liberal, " he would not have felt that subject
alone, without art and craft, had already decided the issue
of values. The priority assigned a writer's concerns was
confirmed by Warren during the Vanderbilt reunion in 1956.
Throughout two sessions he had hardly spoken while other ex-
Fugitives lamented their failure to write a culture epic or at
least poems resonant with political pronouncements. Finally
he interrupted, saying that

> . . . it seems to me greatness is not a criterion—a profitable cri-
> terion—of poetry; that what you are concerned with is a sense of con-
> tact with reality. And it's maybe a pinpoint touch or a whole palm of
> a hand laid . . . but the important thing is the shock of this contact.
> . . . And when you get around to talking about the scale, it's not the
> most important topic . . . it's something that comes in very late in

the game. . . . It's that stab of some kind, early; that's the important thing for me in the sense of an image that makes that thing available to you indefinitely, so you can go back to it, can always find that
peephole on the other world. . . .

Later he quoted with approval Wordsworth's reply to a clergy-
man who had admired his poems "for their fine morality."
Wordsworth had answered, "I don't value them for that. I value
them for the new view they gave of the world." That is, meaning is never pre-experiential but processive. [4]

The writer has to accept responsibility for his work just as
certainly as his characters must be made responsible for their
actions. His signature is his risk, and sometimes his glory.
Because Warren has respected his characters, refined in the
fires of dramatic irony, whatever they wear or say or touch
becomes a memorable part and projection of them, and they
live with an authentic intensity far beyond the anesthetic average. Life is true to *them*.

However, if Warren's works have refused to snuggle up cozi-
ly in the day's categories, if they have voted themselves the
right to self-determination, have they also achieved in any
sense self-sufficiency? There is much in his textbooks to suggest that such a condition is possible and desirable. Repelled
by the abuse of literature as a means to paltry ends, the New
Critics at first spoke of literature as an end in itself (just as
the Agrarians argued that labor, through fulfillment of the
worker, could be its own best reward). Fortunately, Warren
has been enabled to enjoy the undeniable advantages of the New
Critics' procedures for literary investigation, while still avoiding their earliest confusion of self-possession with self-indul-
gence, through the sacramental vision of life which he has un-
covered in others and, in turn, verified in his own poetry and
fiction.

In "Causerie," Allen Tate has discountenanced Warren and
others for reluctance to be doctrinaire ("Warren thirsty in
Kentucky, his hair in the rain, asleep . . ."). Yet Warren's
example has encouraged the survival in American letters of
the thinking and moral man, as well as the economic and political man. His characters struggle to appropriate their own unconscious will, to know themselves completed—a more ex-
hausting and perplexing task than even that set by the true

courtier, the Elizabethan "complete man, " a model Warren
has admired only less than the seventeenth-century metaphysical visionary. Why does man feel that he inhabits an alien
world? Because birth is separation; because identity is division as well as classification; because some compulsion,
half-comprehended, drives him to repudiate his past, makes
him want to rinse his mouth of the taste of his father's failures and, instead, fulfill to its farthest corner his own sense
of self and his importance, in new circumstances.

This is the first stage in the life of Willie Stark, Jerry Calhoun, Dr. Charles Lewis, and the young boys in "Eidolon"
and "Blackberry Winter." A wind comes out of the West, and
the young man yearns for more flesh, just as anyone might
wonder if he is man yet or still a bobbing plug in a booming
tiderace, or might long to play renegade from old wounds in
a newfound land. From God or the fathers, those founts of
generic traditions, he leaves so abruptly that he crystallizes
his incompletion. There is temporary buoyancy in the motionless waters of the moment. There is trial innocence, the attempt to be untouchable, the sanitary silence of the hospital.
But selfhood is more than being; it involves hazards of engagement. There can be no secession from grandeur. Although
each man may distinguish himself from unaspiring nature,
once begun to emerge, self asks for justification to prevent
itself and its actions from appearing gratuitous. There is admission of a continuum of selves. Anything short of that would
be mutilation, denial of cycles of dreams and seasons of memories. But the momentum of these same mechanisms for self-
assurance reaches back, acknowledging the past; reaches out,
covering human multitudes under the beatitude of one common
skin; reaches up, for assumption into the Mystical Body and
the higher innocence that more than compensates for the confession of sin, price of belief in God. Thus analogies are can-
tilevered outward from the literary concept of indivisible form
and the unified sensibility.

Warren once said that John Milton's writings have a single
continuous theme, developed through a variety of subjects.[5]
This has become true of his own world of fiction, with its exploration of unbroken years of homesickness.[6] Some men feel
satisfactorily cured in the world, finding secular salvation

through human community and living undisturbed in nature, like the grackles in *Night Rider*. Others are convinced that present agony is meant to be a rehearsal of future glory, that to avoid assimilation by matter they must finally accede to divine absorption. For these, violence can become the pangs of birth rather than death spasms; there can be a splendor of wounds, changed to stigmata by religious discipline. Stoicism, the Hemingway acceptance of disability without self-pity, is not enough: even the mountains erode. Because ignorance is not true innocence, endurance in darkness is also not enough, for the darkness festers and after a little time flesh rots. In the canon of Robert Penn Warren, people live with the knowledge of abortion and miscarriage as well as with assassinations and fatal duels, symbols of death and the end of man, but also directives for mortification.

Ashby Wyndham lives by a vision. So do Cass Mastern, the Scholarly Attorney, Munn Short, Jerry Beaumont in his last moments, and others. Each fashions his myth, that body of symbols which stimulates awareness of human possibility (through trial self-images) not in response to wish-fulfillment but through immersion in the destructive element itself. Jerry Beaumont's hope is in immortality, his faith as strong as foreknowledge; he is content to die because life is contamination. For others the fact of guilt and the desire for innocence are never stilled but between them attenuate the human form like the figures of El Greco, living currents of worried light.

Such characters, suffering from the daily failure of their dream, not because it is false but because it is too demandingly true, act as a corrective to the easy optimism that science occasionally adopts as a result of small successes. Warren is not alone in objecting to the extreme tendency of scientism to predict the growing adequacy of man in his universe only by reducing the dimensions of both man and that universe. The doctors in *Proud Flesh* and *All the King's Men* belong to the society of surgeons who, confronted by the soul, cry first for amputation. Warren's characters discover that self-assertion, in its elementary stages an act of pride, matures paradoxically through the humbling effect of understanding (Perse Munn, who does not quite understand, is only humiliated and baffled), through comprehension of one's station in the gossamer cos-

mic web. Like Amantha Starr they earn their right to themselves by accepting the necessity of pain and error as natural
elements in their definition. They try to meet life on their own
terms, but these are terms informed by life itself. There is a
mutual roil of verification between introspective man and the
tumble of events. It requires consummate imagination to measure accurately the motion of a system in which the calculator
himself is moving. This, too, is cause for humility and caution
though not for the indulgence of despair.

In Warren, the artist's instinct for amplification has checked
the critic's tendency to circumscribe. Attempting to place judgment of literary value beyond the reach of clinical pragmatism,
which accepts only what it can test and therefore rejects metaphysical problems, Warren helped promote the New Critical
concern for assessing inner relationships of literature considered as literature-in-itself (in the jargon of the early days:
intransitive, autotelic, autonomous). At times his views have
seemed indistinguishable from John Crowe Ransom's (literature affords a means of realizing the world, not of improving
it) and from Cleanth Brooks's or early Allen Tate's (the work
of fiction is its own best scholar and lover). Permission for
fiction to live in the world has been granted reluctantly, lest
it be corrupted again. But if love is not lust, mere possession
and use, neither need it be the mutual contemplation of navels.
It should be consummated.

T. S. Eliot was not sure that he had not departed from the
domain of literary demands when he became the first New
Critic to admit the "principle of importance" into his evalu-
ations *(The Sacred Wood,* 1928, expresses a preference for
the poetry of Dante to that of Shakespeare "because it seems
to me to illustrate a saner attitude toward the mystery of life").
By 1936, in "Religion and Literature," after some initial hedg-
ing ("The 'greatness' of literature cannot be determined solely
by literary standards; though we must remember that whether
it is literature or not can be determined only by literary standards . . .") the eventual coalescence of esthetic, ethical, and
theological judgments is considered desirable.

A more complicated development is conspicuous in the criticism of Robert Penn Warren. Although his introduction to *A
Southern Harvest* (1937) warned against equating the importance

of literature with the temporary relevance of journalism, he did accept some degree of social responsibility for fiction when he described how it had helped the South in "a process of self-scrutiny and self-definition." If the stories included in the anthology "quicken our comprehension of general human nature and of a particular heritage, then they have fulfilled their 'social' function for all possible readers except the fanatic."

A more constricted concept of fiction, however, rules the Brooks and Warren textbooks in the name of teaching closer reading. Through the clinical isolation and microscopic examination of the *corpus* etherized, they have sometimes inclined dangerously toward the very scientific methodolatry which the New Critics sprang into existence to prevent. When such isolation as a means for narrowing temporarily the fields of concentration passes for affirmation of the final and fixed nature of the work itself, the critic is borrowing again the premature contentment of scientism over minuscule achievements. Literature presents forms of awareness valid for more than exploration of self. A heightened sense of reality is surely conducive to the discovery of issues humanly vital. Fortunately, Warren's virtuosity has delivered him time and again from the error of the overspecialist. If his critical esthetic has sometimes impaired his fiction, nevertheless that fiction in turn, obliged to reconcile the two worlds of idea and action, has served to correct his esthetic.

With Warren, formal analysis has not diminished in importance; on the contrary, into the enlarging concept of form has gravitated a "principle of importance" not unlike Eliot's. Especially in his discussions of Coleridge, Eudora Welty, and Katherine Anne Porter, Warren has argued that the immediacy and complexity of the literary experience should be of sufficient order to alter the reader's sense of the world. What that sense of the world might become is suggested by his own fiction and poetry, as well as by his remarks on Hemingway, Faulkner, and that most "philosophical novelist," Conrad. Only Coleridge, however, has committed himself as completely as Warren to the theological translation of those terms in which man's hunger for peace and for community must ultimately be defined.

Brother to Dragons stands as a special station along the cir-

cuitous route of Warren's canon. "R.P.W.," speaking of a
ballad he once planned on the subject of the Lewis brothers'
crime, is reminded:

> No, the action is not self-contained, but contains
> Us too, and is contained by us, and is
> Only an image of the issue of our most distressful
>   self-definition.

Later, the centrifugal force of literature as one of the major
modes of knowledge is conceded:

> I reckon knowing is,
> Maybe, a kind of being, and if you know,
> Can really know, a thing in all its fullness,
> Then you are different, and if you are different,
> Then everything is different, somehow, too.
> And that means things will happen differently.

The artist's symbolic imagination could not have it otherwise. The pathological privacy of his characters' lives in novel
after novel clearly has been not a predetermined condition but
one to which their own selfishness and incapacity for love has
contributed. Life has never rigidly defined the self as an in-
sular entity deprived of others, like an immaculate Imagistic
poem. Furthermore, Warren has challenged the concept of
"good-in-itself," particularly in *Proud Flesh* and *All the King's
Men*, as he has also rejected comparable notions of the gratuitous act, the (historian's) neutral attitude, and the sentimental
approach to innocence. Throughout his work, from the "Kentucky Mountain Farm" sequence on, Warren has valued understanding far above peace ("The end of man is to know," Burden
says). The difficulties of arriving at truth have justified the
complication of his method, the erratic progress of his fugitives. Could the author who has commended his characters to
their various ordained responsibilities escape his own? For
them there is no discernible place to hide, no permanent private cell for unvisited contemplation. Always they must return to the world and to time. Soo, too, must the work of art.
  There was that other conjugation, once, of esthetic and social concerns: the New Agrarianism. But after the 1930's such
interests seemed dormant or metamorphosed, the debaters
excused by allowing that they were not professional sociolo-
gists after all. Nevertheless, they have let drop startlingly

pertinent observations about philosophy, history, science, and society in the course of their "silence." Unfortunately, the limits of their critical method have correspondingly circumscribed the seriousness they and their disciples have been able to attribute to literature. At times it has been in danger of being classified with the nonobjective arts.

How critical interests can broaden respectably is shown by T. S. Eliot's *The Idea of a Christian Society* (1939)—on some points reminiscent of Agrarianism—and *Notes towards the Definition of Culture* (1948). When Monroe Spears assumed editorship of the *Sewanee Review,* he invited criticism "consciously impure" in the sense that its concern would no longer have to be intramural, since preliminary formal analyses could now be taken for granted. Cleanth Brooks skeptically dissented. Nevertheless, Allen Tate as recently as 1956 complained about perfectors of apparatuses for explication "in a kind of prelapsarian innocence of the permanently larger ends of criticism."[7] Especially those New Critics who enjoy their own tempers too much to accept meekly being classified with others have considered these divergencies symptoms of health.

Warren's special version of consubstantial being has found corroboration in his use of protean forms of public testimony. In both off-Broadway loge and Main Street drugstore booth he has sought an active audience to match his own prodigious range. Art for him could never play the stay-at-home long, nor should it be asked to, out of consideration for the consequence of his views. In 1924, when Warren was still a newcomer at Vanderbilt, Tate could mock his naïveté in "To a Romantic," proclaiming, "And because your clamorous blood/ Beats an impermanent rest/ You think the dead arise/ Westward and fabulous. . . ."[8] An uncle of Warren's had run away as a boy, first to the West and then to Mexico, ending as a miner in exotic parts. But, when Warren himself arrived in Berkeley to study at the age of twenty, he was mature enough to subtract contemporary fact from imagined history and to call the difference a mirage. (Or did he feel more strongly, not just disappointment but the disgust of a Jerry Beaumont awakened to his hag's embrace? Years later he would say flatly that "any man needs a good sousing in the Blood of the Lamb worse than he needs a paid vacation in California.")[9]

The death of the western dream, for him, was made more
dismal by a progressive recognition that the kindred Jeffersonian myth of humankind was incongruous in the world he beheld.
His disenchantment, fortunately, was not complete. The art
of fiction provided forms for discriminating between sentimentality and more usable remnants of faith. It furnished procedures for "putting the question to human nature." The fact
that one man, Jefferson, in one night had had to formulate a
governing image, an identity, an ideal that Americans were
enjoined to make actual has given this country, according to
Warren, "a curious kind of abstraction." These beliefs inherited from the Enlightenment have not always been successfully reconciled with the daily problems of getting ahead, opening world markets, or simply raising children.

The image of man in Warren's fiction, on the contrary, is
joined with the Minotaur. Rationality, in excess, becomes the
instrument of rationalization or the symptom of irrationalism.
There is the constant melodrama of the self-deceived, the John
Browns, agents of justice whose every accusation may be
transmogrified in a moment into an excuse. Warren's characters, like Faulkner's, require meticulous examination according to their polarities, oppositions, paradoxes, inversions of
roles. The indirection of Warren's method, the constant dramatic irony, indicates the devious track of man's crablike
progress.

To other Jeffersonianisms, however, Warren is the satisfied heir. As a young man, he admired the Founding Father's
decision to let North and South develop each according to its
own nature. In *Segregation* Warren still finds himself explaining that the South wants to be understood, not treated as if it
had no personality of its own, no pieties to observe but those
imposed by the "plug uglies of virtue." Even salvation is still
largely an individual matter, indifferent to legislation.

Nor has he declined to replace the myths found inadequate
but has constantly urged formulation of new definitions, believing with Conrad in the necessity of myths, personal and
public, when they are projects of the creative, not the destructive, will. Although he is forced by this faith to under-
take the difficult reconciliation of individual freedom and one's
responsibility to his fellow men (as well as their esthetic coun-

terparts, the autotelic principle and the unified sensibility), even such a daily hazard, for what it attempts, is preferable to the professional detachment of scientism from moral problems.

The novelist-poet's obstinacy in requiring some kind of accountability from all men has not been completely ineffectual in humanizing social engineers of the machine-city and in converting fellow critics to a fuller awareness of the philosophical consequences of literature. The shatterers of the world on occasion act conscience-stricken, although this fact does not prevent the risk of annihilation. And former Agrarians, embarrassed by their exaggerated suspicion of applied science when that suspicion is turned against the scientific method indiscriminately (after all, is not the physical grounding of fiction a kind of empiricism?), have pressed for a truce lest they aggravate the very divisions they have always distrusted. With each meeting of minds—made in the name of truth, not of unanimity for its own sake—the closed view of literature has opened a little more. There is a growing willingness to interpret earlier stands not as permanent denial but as temporary suspension of secondary considerations, so that first things could be accomplished first.

Twenty years have passed since Ransom noticed resemblances between the views of T. S. Eliot and John Dewey on matters of literature, morals, and religion; twenty years since professional pragmatist Charles W. Morris became his favorite critic for having developed a terminology to relieve art (for reasons of its particularity, and therefore unpredictability) of the workaday burdens of scientific proof. Moreover, nonliterary perspectives have often dealt with problems crucial to Warren's fiction. I. A. Richards long ago showed the absurdity of the notion of "emotions-in-themselves," unrelated to people or objects. American pragmatism has challenged the concept of "good-in-itself." John Dewey has described the self not as an inborn essence but as the sum of unpredetermined self-stages; and George H. Mead has followed the growth of that self in the context of society through language, either spoken or internalized as symbol.

In their own way, the trials of such men have paralleled what Warren, as a critic, long ago decided was his first ob-

jective: to heal the division between content and form. And
in Warren's fiction there has always been a clamor for definition (in *Proud Flesh* Adam cries, "There's a tooth that gnaws,
and gnaws our definitions . . .") through reconciliation of apparent opposites, negation of the negation. In *World Enough
and Time* Jerry Beaumont tells himself, "There must be a
way whereby the word becomes flesh. There must be a way
whereby the flesh becomes word. Whereby loneliness becomes
communion without contamination. Whereby contamination becomes purity without exile." In *Brother to Dragons*, "R.P.W."
declares:

> The recognition of complicity is the beginning
>   of innocence.
> The recognition of necessity is the beginning
>   of freedom.
> The recognition of the direction of fulfillment
>   is the death of the self
> And the death of the self is the beginning of
>   selfhood.

Warren has attempted to resolve paradoxes by redefining their
terms at a level superior to semantics.

It would be difficult to determine how much the static view
of literature has tampered with the fiction and poetry of Robert
Penn Warren. *(Band of Angels,* however, affords sufficient
duration for its disclosures to mature, so that the climax is
no antidramatic summing up of the issues or mere program
for the future; and *Promises* is a motion made toward the future, an act of testament offering the past for ratification by
the next generation. These are reassuring signs.) Perhaps
the early New Critics' assumption that belief without action
is possible, like the doctrine of the efficacy of faith without
works, accounts in part for the fact that so many of Warren's
major characters have died at the moment of revelation or
disappeared with their intention to change not yet put to the
test of action. Perse Munn dies still a stranger to his life processes; Jerry Calhoun lies abed, accusing himself of contributing to the death of his fiancée, but no act of amendment proves
his contrition; Jack Burden sits down to write a book before
re-entering time; penitent Jerry Beaumont is overtaken and

slain, a welcome end to the misery he has caused in his confusion.

Rather, it is the minor characters from the *exempla*—Willie Proudfit, Ashby Wyndham, Cass Mastern, and Munn Short—who, having survived their spiritual crises, painstakingly tend their own gardens. However, with the possible exception of Cass Mastern, none of these men has suffered the nagging agony of the tormented, self-flagellating mind of the major characters. In terms of the canon they are too extraordinary to serve adequately as models of conduct. Furthermore, the *exempla* are short and are narrated by the subjects themselves. The stories of the central characters are long, compiled in detail, not in summary, and are generally related by an additional narrator whose analysis adds to their complexity. Before Amantha Starr, there was never quite space enough and ripening time to demonstrate convincingly an idea in action.

Still, if the hermetic view of literature can threaten art, so too can the web philosophy of multiple relations. The cry "nothing is lost, ever lost" properly magnifies the implication of "Crime" that conscience is a stern judge and constant warden. But, when total recall is practiced as a technique in the novels to such an extent that the texture of things weighs down and muffles the introspective parts (even when this is intended to represent man's struggle to throw off the saddle of Thingism), any advance of the characters toward enlightenment may seem to arrive suddenly, preparations meanwhile having become indistinct. Total recall jeopardizes *All the King's Men* on several occasions: Cass Mastern's unjustifiably itemized search for Mrs. Trice's slave is one. It is a recurrent distraction throughout *World Enough and Time*. The physical particulars do not demonstrably bear constant witness to each other, as the philosophy might suggest, and it is well that they do not, or officious fate would seem to be managing each character each agitated instant. Even such friendly critics as William Van O'Connor and John Crowe Ransom have at one time or another overemphasized the naturalistic elements in Robert Penn Warren, as a result of this reproduction of minutiae.

Fortunately, these tendencies resist each other. The ascetic recluse and the lover with the world-wide embrace are counter-

forces. The problem of their reconciliation, the fumbling for
mutual respect of self and society, ego and superego is not the
artist's alone. A risk more personally Warren's is his concept
of the gropings of history as magnification of the individual's
dark grasp of his own life span. If the past is part of every
man's identity, but history is obscure, how can he ever know
himself? How can he ever be sure of his motives? And, without
such certainty, what confidence can he have in his moral standards? Although Warren has cautioned against rash judgment
of others, he has never advised suspension of the conscience.
But which inner voice shall a man trust?

Such inarticulateness is descriptive of a common flaw in the
characters, not of deliberate perversity in their author. The
struggle for self-knowledge *is* the act of definition and therefore *is* the line of resistance in Warren's novels, the pattern
for figurative elaboration. *Exempla* have been relied on because, the vision of each major character being afflicted in
some degree, clarification has to come in part from outside.
For the character trying to understand himself, language and
action are useless, worn thin through too much handling as the
currency for self-delusion. "The Mango on the Mango Tree"
and "End of Season" imply the need for communion but do not
specify any path for the pilgrim. If each has his own path, his
own truth, is this not a return to the nominalism and personal
relativism of romanticism? God's eye watches; but what is his
will? Warren's canon justifies the existence of evil, but the
questions asked incidentally in *All the King's Men*—What is
good? Where does value come from?—go unanswered. If evil
helps define man, what defines evil? Does a thin line, or only
thin air, separate Willie Stark's definition of good from pragmatism? Is the darkened judgment of the individual satisfactorily differentiated from the descriptive morality of science?
Colonel Cassius Fort, who has a plan to resolve the questions,
What is law? Is it absolute or man-made? is killed before it
can be announced.

Spiritual truth in Warren is never given into the custody of
the ministry, as a whole cast of characters prove: hypocritical
Seth Parton in *Band of Angels*, the saturnalian revivalist in
World Enough and Time, the perjured preacher of "The Confession of Brother Grimes" or *At Heaven's Gate* (Sweetwater's

father), the slothful shepherd from "The Circus in the Attic."
It is the dogmatic and the doctrinaire whom Warren has satirized most.[10] Rejection of formal authority places the problem
back in the world where it must be solved in perilous, and
therefore more meritorious, fashion.

Because the preliminary stages of man's way are confused
and misdirected, any clarity at the culmination of his journey
may seem to come with the suddenness of grace bestowed gra-
tuitously, a providential act, like the sorting out of damned
and elect by the Puritan God. Warren, however, is suspicious
of gifts since they weaken the beneficiary's self-reliance and
self-respect. But a reward is different, a reward is honorable.
Salvation can be earned by subscribing to responsibility. It
must be earned in the world and in time. This requirement is
one of the few human constants: to define oneself in motion,
under reversible circumstances; to know some unity in the varieties of change; to treasure that knowledge more than peace.

From his early poems through *World Enough and Time* and
Brother to Dragons, Warren's imagery has recognized an au-
tumnal time, given a legend of meaning in "Knowledge and the
Image of Man":

Man can return to his lost unity, and if that return is fitful and precarious, if the foliage and flower of the innocent garden are now somewhat
browned by a late season, all is the more precious for the fact, for
what is now achieved has been achieved by a growth of moral awareness. . . . Man eats of the Tree of Knowledge, and falls. But if he
takes another bite, he may get at least a sort of redemption.[11]

In the same address Warren speaks of literary form as a
"vision of experience, but of experience fulfilled and redeemed
in knowledge. It is not a thing detached from the world but a
thing springing from the deep engagement of spirit with the
world." Literature is a mode of knowledge, the "evocation,
confrontation, and definition of our deepest life," but not a
program for inducing a trance: "No, that gazing prepares for
the moment of action, of creation, in our world of contingen-
cy." Therefore literature is not tidy or genteel, prissy or im-
potent. It is a living gamble, an act of faith meant to redeem
the demand of those finally born: *Was all for naught?* But the
terms of the gamble turn with the game and change again with
the player. A man who has written as he willed and who has

respected the individual voice of his characters would not be consistent if he failed to regard the experience of others, and to trust it.

To the growing child in *Promises*, Robert Penn Warren wrote:

You will live your own life, and continue
The language of your own heart, but let that conversation
In the last analysis, be always of whatever truth you would live.

Each man bears the responsibility for remembering and foreseeing, for redefining truths if possible beyond the need of his generation. This is the price of admission to manhood, as the burden of choice is the glory of being.

NOTES

Foreword

1. Ralph Ellison and Eugene Walter, "The Art of Fiction, XVIII: Robert Penn Warren, " *Paris Review*, IV (Spring-Summer, 1957), 124-25.

2. Nicholas Joost, "'Was All for Naught?': Robert Penn Warren and New Directions in the Novel, " in *Fifty Years of the American Novel—A Christian Appraisal*, ed. Harold C. Gardiner, S. J. (New York: Scribner's, 1952), p. 274.

3. Edward Wagenknecht, *Cavalcade of the American Novel* (New York: Henry Holt and Co., 1952), p. 457.

4. Frederick J. Hoffman, *The Modern Novel in America, 1900-1950* (Chicago: Henry Regnery, 1951), p. 200.

5. Ray B. West, Jr., *The Short Story in America, 1900-1950* (Chicago: Henry Regnery, 1952), p. 79.

6. Louise Bogan, *Achievement in American Poetry, 1900-1950* (Chicago: Henry Regnery, 1951), p. 108.

7. John McCormick, "White Does and Dragons, " *Western Review*, XVIII (Winter, 1954), 165.

8. Hamilton Basso, "The Huey Long Legend, " *Life*, XXI (December 9, 1946), 116.

Chapter 1, "A Symposium of Voices"

1. "Knowledge and the Image of Man, " *Sewanee Review*, LXIII (Winter, 1955), 189.

2. "The Frontier Hypothesis and the Myth of the West, " *American Quarterly*, II, (Spring, 1950), 8-9.

3. *Segregation: The Inner Conflict in the South* (New York: Random House, 1956), p. 55.

4. *Ibid.*, p. 43.

5. *Ibid.*, p. 63.

6. Ralph Ellison and Eugene Walter, "The Art of Fiction, XVIII: Robert Penn Warren, " *Paris Review*, IV (Spring-Summer, 1957), 123.

7. "Remember the Alamo!" *Holiday*, February, 1958, p. 52.

8. "How Texas Won Her Freedom, " *Holiday*, March, 1958, p. 72.

9. In 1920, when Warren was fifteen, his family moved from Guthrie, Kentucky, to Clarksville, Tennessee. After graduation from Vanderbilt University in nearby Nashville, Warren lived in every quarter of of the country—California, Louisiana, Minnesota, Connecticut—as well as, seasonally, in the hills of Italy. Perhaps the very impermanence of these other residences made him consider Tennessee his home during all those years.

Chapter 2, "The New Criticism"

1. Allen Tate, *"The Fugitive:* 1922-1925, " *Princeton University Chronicles*, III (April, 1942), 81-82.

2. In her authoritative study, *The Fugitive Group: A Literary History* (Baton Rouge: Louisiana State University Press, 1959), Louise Cowan documents two prolonged controversies among the early Fugitives. One concerned the question of editorship of their magazine; the other, irreconcilable preferences for poems traditional in form or "futuristic, " classically allusive or politically topical, epic and social or lyric and personal.

Even among the four Fugitives who became Agrarians there were grievous disagreements over the title of *I'll Take My Stand* and over Warren's essay, "The Briar Patch" (1930). Davidson particularly objected to the sociologically "progressive" ideas of Warren (although the essay fixed the Negro's destiny forever as fieldhand or tenant farmer!). When the Agrarians could not agree on a manifesto, Ransom drafted a set of principles to which they subscribed in order to prevent cancellation of the whole project.

Similarly, on their return to Vanderbilt in 1956, the ex-Fugitives continued their lively disagreement. *Fugitives' Reunion: Conversations at Vanderbilt*, edited by Rob Roy Purdy (Nashville: Vanderbilt University Press, 1959), records what is best described as unprogramed pluralism, the divergent remarks of a confederacy of presumed equals. Far from being outraged with one another's inflexibility, the participants seemed to enjoy their companions' remarks as valuable occasions for self-formulation. Such mutual provocation may well have influenced Brooks's concept of form through tension and Warren's consistent view of progress through struggle.

3. S. I. Hayakawa, "Semantics, " *Etc.: A Review of General Semantics*, IX (Summer, 1952), 245.

4. Nathan A. Scott, Jr., *Rehearsals of Discomposure* (New York: King's Crown Press, 1952).

5. An example of latter-day extraliterary criticism is Robert Gorham Davis' review of *All the King's Men*, which follows its implicit

charge of collaboration between fascist governor and hired apologist with these words: "Warren does not ask—the question apparently has no imaginative appeal for him—whether American tradition does not demand that we fight men like Long with the utmost resolution and with all the democratic means at our disposal, in order to preserve in this country and in the world free, open, pluralistic societies in which individual rights are protected by law and in which ultimate control is invested below in the people and not above in Willie Stark." *New York Times Book Review,* August 18, 1946, p. 3.

6. "The Agrarians Today, " *Shenandoah,* III (Summer, 1952), 29.

7. "Reflections on American Poetry: 1900-1950, " *Sewanee Review,* LXIV (Winter, 1956), 61.

8. Communication, *Shenandoah,* III (Autumn, 1952), 44-47.

Chapter 3, "The New Agrarianism"

1. Charles W. Ramsdell, "The Southern Heritage, " in *Culture in the South,* ed. W. T. Couch (Chapel Hill: University of North Carolina Press, 1935), p. 14. See also "The Farmers' Revolt" in Ina Woestemeyer Van Noppen, *The South: A Documentary History* (Princeton, N.J.: D. Van Nostrand Co., 1958), pp. 404-34; and Frank Lawrence Owsley, *Plain Folk of the Old South* (Baton Rouge: Louisiana State University Press, 1949).

2. *"I'll Take My Stand:* A History, " *American Review,* V (Summer, 1935), 304.

3. "Autobiographical Notes, " *Wilson's Bulletin,* XIII (June, 1939), 652.

4. In *Poems 1922-1947* (New York: Scribners, 1948), p. 79.

Chapter 4, "Approach to Literature"

1. Quoted by Harvey Breit in "Talk with Mr. Warren, " *New York Times Book Review,* June 25, 1950, p. 20.

2. "The Love and the Separateness in Miss Welty, " *Kenyon Review,* VI (Spring, 1944), 249.

3. *Ibid.,* p. 256.

4. "Melville the Poet, " *Kenyon Review,* VIII (Spring, 1946), 214.

5. *Ibid.,* p. 215.

6. "Cowley's Faulkner, Part I, " *New Republic,* CXV (August 12, 1946), 177.

7. *Ibid.,* p. 178.

8. "Cowley's Faulkner, Part II, " *New Republic,* CXV (August 26, 1946), 237.

9. "Nostromo, " *Sewanee Review,* LIX (September, 1951), 377.

10. "The Themes of Robert Frost, " in *The Writer and His Craft,* ed. Roy Cowden (Ann Arbor: University of Michigan Press, 1954), p. 230.

11. "Nostromo, " p. 391.

86   Notes

Chapter 5, "Poetry: The Golden Eye"
   1. "The Phoenix in the World, " *Furioso,* III (Spring, 1948), 45.
   2. Quoted in *Modern Poetry, American and British,* ed. Kimon Friar
and John Malcolm Brinnin (New York: Appleton-Century-Crofts, 1951),
p. 542.
   3. *Ibid.*
   4. "The Inklings of 'Original Sin, '" *Saturday Review of Literature,*
XXVII (May 20, 1944), 11.
   5. Robert Penn Warren, "The Way It Was Written, " *New York Times
Book Review,* August 23, 1953, pp. 6, 25.
   6. Correspondence, Warren to author, August 13, 1957.

Chapter 6, "Fiction and Biography: The Ornate Web"
   1. Correspondence, Warren to author, January 14, 1957.
   2. Robert Penn Warren, "Paul Rosenfeld: Prompter of Fiction, "
Commonweal, XLVI (August 15, 1947), 425; also correspondence, Warren to author, November 13, 1952, and September 1, 1958.
   3. The dilemma of the honest historian is illustrated by Warren in
"How Texas Won Her Freedom, " *Holiday,* XXIII (March 1958), p. 72:
"Sam Houston and the Battle of San Jacinto are twin halves of one event.
We cannot think of one without the other, but we do not know, precisely,
how to think of them. Did Houston make San Jacinto, or did San Jacinto
make Houston? Hagridden by ambition and pestered by a dark, mysterious, suicidal sense of guilt, he came to Texas to seek in greatness the
peace he had never known. Houston found the greatness, but in finding
it was he simply the victim of events, stumbling upon victory in a blind
campaign? Or did he plan that victory and create his destiny?"
   4. The victor-victim motif provides still another link with *Brother
to Dragons,* as Bolton's father is described growing "aware of the powerful, vibrating, multitudinous web of life which binds the woman and child
together, victor and victim (but which is which? he asks himself: is the
present the victim of the past, or the past victim of the present?). . . ."
The downstairs seduction scene in "Circus" seems a foreshadowing,
too, of Jerry Beaumont's gratification of Rachel on the night of her mother's death.
   5. Correspondence, Warren to author, March 13, 1953.
   6. J. Létargeez, in "Robert Penn Warren's View of History, " *Revue
des langues vivantes,* XII (1956), 533-43, traces in detail parallels between the novel and the actual tobacco trust whose curtailment of com-
petitive warehouse sales, in the early 1900's, led to organization of a
"Possum Hunters Organization" under a Dr. David A. Amoss. After
a dynamite raid on Hopkinsville, Kentucky (during which a man was
killed from ambush), Amoss was tried but found not guilty. Warren has
foreshortened the duration of events, used the external disorders as a
correlative for inner displacements in Munn, and tightened the run of
circumstance to near-coincidence.

7. Correspondence, Warren to author, August 13, 1957.

8. Correspondence, Warren to author, March 13, 1953.

9. "A Note to *All the King's Men, " Sewanee Review,* LXI (Summer 1953), 478.

10. Shakespeare's "compensation sonnet" (XXIX) whose agonist, self-pitying and covetous but at last rescued from narcissism through remembrance of love, "sings hymns at heaven's gate, " would serve as appropriately ironic source for Warren's devourers of one another's flesh. However, the novel's title derives from no Shakespearean source exclusively (correspondence, Warren to author, March 15, 1958). Bird of dawn at heaven's gate in Elizabethan verse, the lark often was companion to the ravished nightingale. "Jug, jug, jug, jug, tereu, " the latter weeps in Lyly's *Campaspe;* and her song of transfigured pain finds melodic notation in Eliot's *Waste Land.* The lark's song, less consequential, is perhaps more appropriate to the false dawn heralded by the Murdocks and so like the night of Perse Munn.

11. In the prefatory note to Wyndham's story, as anthologized in *Spearhead,* Warren suggests a double function for the confession: "First, the story provides one of the various views which are contrasted in the novel, the naïve religious view at one end of the scale. Second, the story serves a purpose in the over-all organization of the plot. Ashby is driven out on his pilgrimage by two forces: by the effect, even in his remote corner of the world, of the financial speculation and corruption in the city, and by his own repentance and vision. When he finally reaches the city, he, in his innocence, brings down the house of cards which is Bogan Murdock's empire." *Spearhead* (New York: New Directions, 1947), p. 415.

12. "A Note to *All the King's Men, " Sewanee Review,* LXI (Summer, 1953), 476-80.

13. "The Old and the New of It, " program notes to *Willie Stark: His Rise and Fall,* Margo Jones Theater, Dallas, November 25, 1958, p. 7.

14. Correspondence, Warren to author, August 13, 1957.

15. "A Note to *All the King's Men,"* p. 480.

16. Correspondence, Warren to author, August 13, 1957.

17. Correspondence, Warren to author, March 15, 1958.

18. To prevent confusion with the Erwin Piscator version of *All the King's Men* (1947), the very different play as directed by Aaron Frankel in Dallas (1958) and by Mark Schoenberg in New York (1959) will continue to be referred to here as *Willie Stark: His Rise and Fall.*

19. Aaron Frankel explains the device, reminiscent of Brecht's, thus: "Given the cue, they [the actors] step outside the action of the story to observe, comment on and justify themselves to the audience. The illusion on the stage, while still sought after, is important only so long as the characters, like a chorus, may argue about its meaning, making not merely the stage but audience and whole theater into a tribunal, a forum." From the program notes to *Willie Stark: His Rise and Fall,* Margo

Jones Theater, Dallas, November 25, 1958, p. 3.

20. R. G., "Biographical Sketch, " *Saturday Review of Literature,* XXXIII (June 24, 1950), 12.

21. A more extended exploration of source documents, chronicles, and newspaper accounts is available in Calvin M. Lane's Narrative Art and History in Robert Penn Warren's World Enough and Time (Ph. D. dissertation, University of Michigan, 1956). Unfortunately, arguing that the flight into the canebrakes is "anti-climatic at best, " Lane is forced to conclude that Jerry could more credibly have achieved complete self-knowledge while awaiting execution than while recovering from the "grand guignol" dénouement. Supposedly the melodrama of his sources overwhelmed Warren—despite the fact that the whole section in question has no source in the Beauchamp affair !

22. *Holiday,* XXIII (March, 1958), 72.

23. Compare *Jereboam O. Beauchamp's Confession* (Bloomfield, Ky. : Gervis S. Hammond, 1826) and *The Letters of Ann Cook, Late Mrs. Beauchamp,* ed. W--R--n (Washington, D.C., 1826).

24. The research and writing of *Segregation* were occasioned, in part, by a neighborly discussion with a *Life* magazine editor about integration in Southern schools; and in part by earnest questioning earlier of the misrepresentation of various novels like *Band of Angels.* Correspondence, Warren to author, September 1, 1958).

25. Reported in the original uncut transcript for the *Paris Review* but omitted from the published interview (Spring-Summer, 1957). Used with permission of Robert Penn Warren and interviewer Ralph Ellison, and verified by correspondence from Warren, July 25, 1959.

26. Even full-grown in wisdom, Manty is never quite sure: "Is it our need that makes us lean toward and wish to succor need, or is it our strength? . . . Do we give love in order to receive love, and even in the transport or endearment carry the usurer's tight-lipped and secret calculation, unacknowledged even by ourselves? . . . Or do we simply want a hand, any hand, a human object, to clutch in the dark on the blanket, and fear lies behind everything?"

27. Reported in the original uncut transcript of Warren's interview with the *Paris Review.*

28. The meticulous factuality of *Band of Angels* had its inception not only in Winston Coleman's *Slavery Days in Kentucky* and Canot's autobiography, but also in memoirs of officers on slave patrol, hearings in the British Parliament, and other documents from the Brown University and Yale collections. Correspondence, Warren to author, September 1, 1958.

29. There are strong similarities, as well, between Hawthorne's concept of intellectual detachment, the Unpardonable Sin, and the overweening pride of Warren's Avengers who invent their own codes while in motion, in the best vigilante tradition.

Chapter 7, "The Running Gamble"

1. "A Lesson Read in American Books, " *New York Times Book Review,* December 11, 1955, p. 1.

2. Ralph Ellison and Eugene Walter, "The Art of Fiction, XVIII: Robert Penn Warren, " *Paris Review,* IV (Spring-Summer, 1957), 115-16.

3. Ellison and Walter, "Robert Penn Warren, " p. 130.

4. *Fugitives' Reunion: Conversations at Vanderbilt,* ed. Rob Roy Purdy (Nashville: Vanderbilt University Press, 1959), pp. 142-43, 162.

5. "Some Recent Novels, " *Southern Review,* I (Winter, 1936), 627-28.

6. Warren has suggested that "Blackberry Winter, " *All the King's Men,* and his reading of Coleridge's *The Ancient Mariner* share a common realization, discoverable elsewhere in his work as well, that "out of change and loss a human recognition may be redeemed, more precious for being no longer innocent. " "Writer at Work: How a Story Was Born and How, Bit by Bit, It Grew, " *New York Times Book Review,* March 1, 1959, p. 5.

7. Allen Tate, "Reflections on American Poetry: 1900-1950, " *Sewanee Review,* LXIV (Winter, 1956), 61.

8. Allen Tate, *Poems 1922-1947* (New York: Scribners, 1948), p. 139.

9. Correspondence, Warren to author, August 13, 1957.

10. Logically, therefore, even Warren's firmest conviction and vision must be free to develop and to be verified by subtler, broader experience. When Ralph Ellison in Rome asked him if a sense of righteousness in an author was not fatal to the seriousness of his work, Warren agreed: "Once you start illustrating virtue as such you had better stop writing fiction. Do something else, like Y-work. Or join a committee. Your business as a writer is not to illustrate virtue but to show how a fellow may move toward it—or away from it. " Ellison and Walter, "Robert Penn Warren, " p. 138. What fiction communicates is fundamentally the experience of a discovery.

11. "Knowledge and the Image of Man, " *Sewanee Review,* LXIII (Winter, 1955), 187.

THE WORKS OF

ROBERT PENN WARREN:

A CHRONOLOGICAL CHECKLIST

Books

John Brown: The Making of a Martyr. New York: Payson and Clarke, 1929.
Thirty-six Poems. New York: Alcestis Press, 1935.
Night Rider. Boston: Houghton Mifflin, 1939.
Proud Flesh. Unpublished, 1939. First performance, 1946.
Eleven Poems on the Same Theme. Norfolk, Conn. : New Directions, 1942.
At Heaven's Gate. New York: Harcourt, Brace and Co., 1943.
Selected Poems, 1923-1943. New York: Harcourt, Brace and Co., 1944.
All the King's Men. New York: Harcourt, Brace and Co., 1946.
Blackberry Winter. Cummington, Mass. : Cummington Press, 1946.
All the King's Men (stageplay). Unpublished, 1947. Performance of Piscator version, 1947.
Circus in the Attic and Other Stories. New York: Harcourt, Brace and Co., 1948.
World Enough and Time: A Romantic Novel. New York: Random House, 1950.
Brother to Dragons: A Tale in Verse and Voices. New York: Random House, 1953.
Band of Angels. New York: Random House, 1955.
Segregation: The Inner Conflict in the South. New York: Random House, 1956.
Promises: Poems 1954-1956. New York: Random House, 1957.
Selected Essays. New York: Random House, 1958.
Remember the Alamo! New York: Random House, 1958. "Landmark" children's book.
The Cave. New York: Random House, 1959.
The Gods of Mount Olympus. New York: Random House, 1959. "Legacy"

children's book.

All the King's Men (stageplay). New York: Random House, 1960. Premiere as Willie Stark: His Rise and Fall, 1958, Dallas.

Textbooks and Anthologies

An Approach to Literature, ed. Cleanth Brooks, R. P. Warren, and John T. Purser. 1st ed., Baton Rouge: Louisiana State University Press, 1936; 2nd ed., New York: F. S. Crofts and Co., 1944; 3rd ed., New York: Appleton-Century-Crofts, Inc., 1952.

A Southern Harvest: Short Stories by Southern Writers, ed. R. P. Warren. Boston: Houghton Mifflin Co., 1937.

Understanding Poetry, ed. Cleanth Brooks and R. P. Warren. 1st ed., New York: Henry Holt and Co., 1938; 2nd ed., 1951.

Understanding Fiction, ed. Cleanth Brooks and R. P. Warren. New York: Appleton-Century-Crofts, Inc., 1943; 3rd ed., 1960.

Modern Rhetoric, ed. Cleanth Brooks and R. P. Warren. 1st ed., New York: Harcourt, Brace and Co., 1949 (published also without readings, as *Fundamentals of Good Writing*, 1949); 2nd ed., 1958.

The Southern Review (anthology), ed. Cleanth Brooks and R. P. Warren. Baton Rouge: Louisiana State University Press, 1953.

Short Story Masterpieces, ed. R. P. Warren and Albert Erskine. New York: Dell, 1954; 2nd ed., 1958.

Six Centuries of Great Poetry, ed. R. P. Warren and Albert Erskine. New York: Dell, 1955.

A New Southern Harvest, ed. R. P. Warren and Albert Erskine. New York: Bantam, 1957.

Short Fiction and Excerpts

"Prime Leaf," *American Caravan* IV, ed. Van Wyck Brooks *et al.* New York: Macaulay Co., 1931. Pp. 3-61.

"Her Own People," *Virginia Quarterly Review*, XI (April, 1935), 289-304.

"Testament of Flood," *The Magazine*, April, 1935, pp. 230-34.

"When the Light Gets Green," *Southern Review*, I (Spring, 1936), 799-806.

"Christmas Gift," *Virginia Quarterly Review*, XIII (Winter, 1937), 73-85.

"How Willie Proudfit Came Home," *Southern Review*, IV (Autumn, 1938), 299-321.

"Goodwood Comes Back," *Southern Review*, VI (Winter, 1941), 526-36.

"The Life and Work of Professor Roy Millen," *Mademoiselle*, XVI (February, 1943), 88, 145-49.

"Statement of Ashby Wyndham," *Sewanee Review*, LI (Spring, 1943), 183-236. Reprinted in *Spearhead*. New York: New Directions, 1947.

Pp. 415-57.

"Cass Mastern's Wedding Ring, " *Partisan Review*, XI (Fall, 1944), 375-407.

"A Christian Education, " *Mademoiselle*, XX (January, 1945), 96-97, 155-57.

"The Love of Elsie Barton: A Chronicle, " *Mademoiselle*, XXII (February, 1946), 161, 282-90.

"The Patented Gate and the Mean Hamburger, " *Mademoiselle*, XXIV (January, 1947), 188-89, 242-43, 245-46.

"The Circus in the Attic, " *Cosmopolitan*, CXXIII (September, 1947), 67-70, 73-74, 76, 78, 80, 83-84, 86, 88.

"The Confession of Brother Grimes, " *Cronos*, I (Fall, 1947), 29-30.

"Portrait of La Grand' Bosse, " *Kenyon Review*, XII (Winter, 1950), 41-50.

"The Destiny of Hamish Bond, " *Sewanee Review*, LXIV (Summer, 1955), 349-81.

"The Natural History of Ikey Sumpter, Formerly of Johnstown, Tenn., " *Sewanee Review*, LXVII (Summer, 1959), 347-400.

Reviews and Articles

Voices, IV (November, 1924), 24-25. Review of John Crowe Ransom's *Chills and Fever*.

Voices, IV (January, 1925), 89-90. Review of Roy Campbell's *The Flaming Terrapin*.

Fugitive, IV (March, 1925), 29-30. Review of Joseph Auslander's *Sunrise Trumpets*.

"The Romantic Strain, " *New Republic*, LIII (November 23, 1927), 23-24. Review of Edith Sitwell's *Rustic Elegies*.

"Sacheverell Sitwell's Poems, " *New Republic*, L (February 29, 1928), 76. Review of *Cyder Feast and Other Poems*.

"The Bright Doom, " *New Republic*, LIV (April 4, 1928), 227. Review of John Hall Wheelock's *The Bright Doom*.

"Guinea-Fowl, " *New Republic*, LIV (May 2, 1928), 330-31. Review of Leonard Bacon's *Guinea-Fowl and Other Poultry*.

"Hawthorne, Anderson and Frost, " *New Republic*, LIV (May 16, 1928), 399-401. Review of Herbert Gorman's *Nathaniel Hawthorne*; Gorham Munson's *Robert Frost*; N. Bryllion Fagin's *The Phenomenon of Sherwood Anderson*.

"The Gentle Buccaneer, " *New Republic*, LVI (September 5, 1928), 81. Review of Lowell Thomas' *Count Luckner, the Sea Devil*.

"Merrill Moore's Sonnets, " *New Republic*, LXI (January 29, 1930), 280. Review of *The Noise That Time Makes*.

"A French View of Jefferson, " *New Republic*, LXII (April 2, 1930), 196-97. Review of Gilbert Chinard's *Thomas Jefferson: The Apostle of Americanism*.

"The Briar Patch, " *I'll Take My Stand: The South and the Agrarian Tradition.* New York and London: Harper and Brothers, 1930. Pp. 246-64.

"The Gamecock, " *New Republic,* LXVI (March 25, 1931), 158-59. Review of Robert W. Winston's *High Stakes and Hair Trigger* and Elizabeth Cutting's *Jefferson Davis.*

"The Second American Revolution, " *Virginia Quarterly Review,* VII (April, 1931), 282-88. Review of Howard K. Beale's *The Critical Year* and George F. Milton's *The Age of Hate.*

"Lavender and Old Ladies, " *New Republic,* LXVII (August 5, 1931), 321. Review of John Peale Bishop's *Many Thousands Gone.*

"Not Local Color, " *Virginia Quarterly Review,* VIII (January, 1932), 153-60. Review of Elizabeth Madox Roberts' *A Buried Treasure;* Caroline Gordon's *Penhally;* Evelyn Scott's *A Calendar of Sin;* William Faulkner's *These Thirteen,* etc.

"Two Poets, " *New Republic,* LXX (February 24, 1932), 51-52. Review of Alan Porter's *The Signature of Pain and Other Poems* and Eda Lou Walton's *Jane Matthew and Other Poems.*

"A Georgian Laureate, " *Poetry,* XL (April, 1932), 47-50. Review of *The Poems of Lascelles Abercrombie.*

"A Note on Three Southern Poets, " *Poetry,* XL (May, 1932), 103-13.

"James Stephens Again, " *Poetry,* XL (July, 1932), 229-32. Review of *Strict Joy and Other Poems.*

"Sight Unseen, " *Poetry,* XLII (August, 1933), 292-94. Review of Thomas C. Chubb's *Ships and Lovers.*

"Old Words, " *Poetry,* XLII (September, 1933), 342-45. Review of Cale Young Rice's *High Perils.*

"The Blind Poet: Sidney Lanier, " *American Review,* II (November, 1933), 27-45.

"T. S. Stribling: A Paragraph in the History of Critical Realism, " *American Review,* II (February, 1934), 463-86.

"Georgian Middle Life, " *Poetry,* XLIII (February, 1934), 287-90. Review of Edmund Blunden's *Halfway House.*

"Working Toward Freedom, " *Poetry,* XLIII (March, 1934), 342-46. Review of John Peale Bishop's *Now With His Love.*

"Twelve Poets, " *American Review,* III (May, 1934), 212-27. Review of Archibald MacLeish's *Poems, 1924-1933;* William Faulkner's *Green Bough;* W. H. Auden's *The Orators,* etc.

Poetry, XLIV (September, 1934), 334-37. Review of R. T. Coffin's *Ballads of Square-Toed Americans* and *Yoke of Thunder.*

"John Crowe Ransom: A Study in Irony, " *Virginia Quarterly Review,* XI (January, 1935), 93-112.

"The Middle Flight, " *Poetry,* XLV (January, 1935), 226-28. Review of Haniel Long's *Atlantides.*

"The Fiction of Caroline Gordon, " *Southwest Review,* Book Supplement, XX (January, 1935), 5-10. Review of *Aleck Maury, Sportsman.*

"A Note on the Hamlet of Thomas Wolfe, " *American Review,* V (May,

1935), I91-208.

"Set in a Silver Sea, " *Poetry,* XLVI (September, 1935), 346-49. Review of Victoria Sackville-West's *Collected Poems.*

"Some Recent Novels, " *Southern Review,* I (Winter, 1936), 624-49. Review of Marjorie Kinnan Rawlings' *Golden Apples;* H. L. Davis' *Honey in the Horn,* etc. Reprinted as "Literature as a Symptom, " in *Who Owns America: A New Declaration of Independence,* ed. Herbert Agar and Allen Tate. New York: Houghton Mifflin, 1936. Pp. 264-79.

"Dixie Looks at Mrs. Gerould, " *American Review,* VI (March, 1936), 585-95. (With Cleanth Brooks, Jr.)

"Straws in the Wind, " *Poetry,* XLVIII (June, 1936), 172-75. Review of Ann Winslow's *Trial Balances.*

"Some Don'ts for Literary Regionalists, " *American Review,* VIII (December, 1936), 142-50.

"The Reading of Modern Poetry, " *American Review,* VIII (February, 1937), 435-49. (With Cleanth Brooks, Jr.)

"Jeffers on the Age, " *Poetry,* XLIX (February, 1937), 279-82. Review of *Solstice and Other Poems.*

"Homage to T. S. Eliot, " *Harvard Advocate,* CXXV (December, 1938), 46.

"Arnold vs. the 19th Century, " *Kenyon Review,* I (Spring, 1939), 217-26. Review of Lionel Trilling's *Matthew Arnold.*

"Autobiographical Notes, " *Wilson's Bulletin,* XIII (June, 1939), 652.

"The Situation in American Writing, Part II, " *Partisan Review,* VI (Fall, 1939), 112-13.

"The Present State of Poetry: In the United States, " *Kenyon Review,* I (Fall, 1939), 384-98.

"Statement Concerning Wallace Stevens' *Harmonium, " Harvard Advocate,* CXVII (December, 1940), 32.

"The Snopes World, " *Kenyon Review,* III (Spring, 1941), 253-57. Review of William Faulkner's *The Hamlet.*

"Editorial, " *Southern Review,* VII (Autumn, 1941), iv, vi, viii, ix, xii. (With Cleanth Brooks, Jr.)

"Katherine Anne Porter (Irony with a Center), " *Kenyon Review,* IV (Winter, 1942), 29-42.

"Poor White, " *Nation,* CLIV (February 28, 1942), 261-62. Review of Robert Ramsey's *Fire in the Summer.*

"Homage to Oliver Allston, " *Kenyon Review,* IV (Spring, 1942), 259-63. Review of Van Wyck Brooks's *Opinions of Oliver Allston.*

American Prefaces, VII (Spring, 1942), 195-209. Critique of Ernest Hemingway's "The Killers." (With Cleanth Brooks.)

"Editorial Announcement, " *Southern Review,* VII (Spring, 1942), iv. (With Cleanth Brooks, Jr.)

"Principle and Poet, " *Nation,* CLIV (April 11, 1942), 438-39. Review of Rolfe Humphries' *Out of the Jewel.*

"The Lady of Lourdes, " *Nation,* CLIV (May 30, 1942), 635-36. Review of Franz Werfel's *The Song of Bernadette*.

"Poems by Kenneth Patchen, " *Nation,* CLV (July 4, 1942), 17. Review of *The Dark Kingdom*.

"Poets and Scholars, " *Nation,* CLV (August 15, 1942), 137. Review of Allen Tate's *Princeton Verse between Two Wars*.

"Asides and Diversions, " *Nation,* CLV (December 5, 1942), 625. Review of Edmund Wilson's *Note Books of Night*.

"Button, Button, " *Partisan Review,* IX (December, 1942), 537-40. Review of Mary McCarthy's *The Company She Keeps*.

"The Poetry of Mark Van Doren, " *Nation,* CLVI (February 6, 1943), 209-11. Review of *Our Lady Peace and Other War Poems*.

"Pure and Impure Poetry, " *Kenyon Review,* V (Spring, 1943), 228-54.

"Our Literary Harvest, " *New York Times Book Review,* June 13, 1943, pp. 5, 18. Review of Edmund Wilson's *The Shock of Recognition*.

"The Love and the Separateness in Miss Welty, " *Kenyon Review,* VI (Spring, 1944), 246-59.

Accent, IV (Summer, 1944), 251-53. Review of E. E. Cummings' *lxl*.

"The War and the National Monuments, " *Library of Congress Quarterly Journal of Current Acquisitions,* II (September, 1944), 64-75.

"A Sheaf of Novels, " *American Scholar,* XIV (Winter, 1945), 115-22. Review of Aldous Huxley's *Time Must Have a Stop,* Howard Fast's *Freedom Road,* Harry Brown's *A Walk in the Sun,* Joseph S. Pennell's *History of Rome Hanks,* etc.

"Melville the Poet, " *Kenyon Review,* VII (Spring, 1946), 208-23.

"A Poem of Pure Imagination (Reconsiderations VI)" *Kenyon Review,* VIII (Summer, 1946), 391-427.

"Cowley's Faulkner, Part I, " *New Republic,* CXV (August 12, 1946), 176-80.

"Cowley's Faulkner, Part II, " *New Republic,* CXV (August 26, 1946), 234-37.

"Hemingway, " *Kenyon Review,* IX (Winter, 1947), 1-28. Reprinted as introduction to *A Farewell to Arms*. New York: Scribner's, 1949.

"Paul Rosenfeld: Prompter of Fiction, " *Commonweal,* XLVI (August 15, 1947), 424-26.

"From the Underground, " *Nation,* CLXIX (December 3, 1949), 547-48. Review of Elio Vittorini's *In Sicily*.

"Nostromo, " *Sewanee Review,* LIX (September, 1951), 363-91. Reprinted as introduction to Joseph Conrad's *Nostromo*. New York: Modern Library, 1951.

"The Redemption of Temple Drake, " *New York Times Book Review,* September 30, 1951, pp. 1, 31. Review of William Faulkner's *Requiem for a Nun*.

"Notes, " *Modern Poetry, American and British,* ed. Kimon Friar and John Malcolm Brinnin. New York: Appleton-Century-Crofts, 1951. Pp. 541-43.

"A Note to *All the King's Men,* " *Sewanee Review,* LXI (Summer, 1953),

476-80.
"The Way It Was Written *(Brother to Dragons), " New York Times Book Review,* August 23, 1953, pp. 6, 25.
"The Themes of Robert Frost, " *The Writer and His Craft,* ed. Roy Cowden. Ann Arbor: University of Michigan Press, 1954. Pp. 218-33. Delivered as Hopwood Award presentation speech, 1947.
"Knowledge and the Image of Man, " *Sewanee Review,* LXII (Winter, 1955), 182-92.
"A Lesson Read in American Books, " *New York Times Book Review,* December 11, 1955, pp. 1, 33.
"Divided South Searches Its Soul, " *Life,* July 9, 1956, pp. 98-99, 101-2, 105-6, 108, 111-12, 114. Portions of *Segregation.*
"A First Novel, " *Sewanee Review,* LXV (Spring, 1957), 347-52. Review of Madison Jones's *The Innocent.*
"Remember the Alamo!" *Holiday,* XXIII (February, 1958), 52-55, 106, 108-10, 112-13.
"How Texas Won Her Freedom, " *Holiday,* XXIII (March, 1958), 72-73, 160, 162-67.
"Writer at Work: How a Story Was Born and How, Bit by Bit, It Grew (Blackberry Winter), " *New York Times Book Review,* March 1, 1959, pp. 4-5, 36.

Poetry

"Vision, " *American Poetry Magazine,* V (December, 1922), 23.
"Crusade, " *Fugitive,* II (June, 1923), 90-91.
"After Teacups, " *Fugitive,* II (August, 1923), 106.
"Midnight, " *Fugitive,* II (October, 1923), 142.
"Three Poems": "Beyond this bitter shore, " "So many are the things that she had learned, " "I knew not down what windy nights I fled, " *Fugitive,* III (April, 1924), 54-55.
"Death Mask of a Young Man: 1. The Mouse. 2. The Moon, " "Nocturne, " *Fugitive,* III (June, 1924), 69-70.
"Sonnets of Two Summers: Sonnet of a Rainy Summer, Sonnet of August Drouth, " "Praises for Mrs. Dodd, " *Fugitive,* III (August, 1924), 117-18.
"Portraits of Three Ladies, " *Double Dealer,* VII (August, 1924), 191-92.
"Autumn Twilight Piece, " "Admonition to the Dead, " *Double Dealer,* VII (October, 1924), 2.
"Alf Burt, Tenant Farmer, " "Admonition to Those Who Mourn, " *Fugitive,* III (December, 1924), 154-55.
"Iron Beach, " "The Mirror, " *Fugitive,* IV (March, 1925), 15-16.
"Easter Morning: Crosby Junction, " "Mr. Dodds' Son, " "To a Face in the Crowd, " "The Wrestling Match, " *Fugitive,* IV (June, 1925), 33-37.
"August Revival: Crosby Junction, " *Sewanee Review,* XXXIII (December,

1925), 439.

"Images on the Tomb. 1. Dawn: The Gorgon's Head. 2. Day: Lazarus. 3. Evening: The Motors. 4. Night: But a Sultry Wind, " *Fugitive,* IV (September, 1925), 89-92.

"Pro Sua Vita, " *New Republic,* L (May 11, 1927), 333.

"Croesus in Autumn, " *New Republic,* LII (November 2, 1927), 290.

"At the Hour of the Breaking of the Rocks, " *American Caravan,* ed. Van Wyck Brooks *et al.* New York: Literary Guild of America, 1927. P. 803.

"Letter of a Mother, " *New Republic,* LIII (January 11, 1928), 212.

"Rebuke of the Rocks, " *Nation,* CXXVI (January 11, 1928), 47.

"Garden Waters, " *New Republic,* LIV (March 7, 1928), 99.

"To One Awake, " *New Republic,* LV (May 30, 1928), 47.

"History among the Rocks, " *New Republic,* LVII (December 5, 1928), 63.

"Pondy Woods, " "(Genealogy) Grandfather Gabriel, " *Second American Caravan,* ed. Van Wyck Brooks *et al.* New York: Macaulay Co., 1928. Pp. 120-22.

"For a Self-Possessed Friend, " *New Republic,* LXI (November 27, 1929), 14.

"The Return, " *New Republic,* LXI (January 15, 1930), 215.

"Tryst on Vinegar Hill, " *This Quarter,* II (March, 1930), 503-4.

"Empire, " *This Quarter,* III (August, 1930), 168-69.

"Blue Cuirassier (The Jay), " *Saturday Review of Literature,* VII (July 11, 1931), 953.

"The Last Metaphor, " *New Republic,* LXIX (December 9, 1931), 105.

"Kentucky Mountain Farm: The Cardinal, The Watershed, The Owl, " *Poetry,* XL (May, 1932), 59-61.

"The Limited, " *Poetry,* XLI (January, 1933), 200.

"The Problem of Knowledge, " *Southwest Review,* XVIII (July, 1933), 47.

"Two Poems on Truth: Aged Man Surveys the Past Time, Toward Rationality, " "Letter to a Friend, " "Aubade for Hope, " "Eidolon, " *American Review,* III (May, 1934), 236-39.

"So Frost Astounds, " *Poetry,* XLIV (July, 1934), 196.

"The Return: an Elegy, " *Poetry,* XLV (November, 1934), 85-89.

"For a Friend Parting, " *New Republic,* LXXXI (December 26, 1934), 186.

"Ransom, " "Letter from a Coward to a Hero, " *Southern Review,* I (July, 1935), 92-94.

"Two Poems on Time: History, Resolution, " *Virginia Quarterly Review,* XI (July, 1935), 352-56.

"Picnic Remembered, " *Scribner's,* XCIX (March, 1936), 185.

"Monologue at Midnight, " *Virginia Quarterly Review,* XII (July, 1936), 395.

"Athenian Death, " *Nation,* CXLIII (October 31, 1936), 523.

"Bearded Oaks, " *Poetry,* LI (October, 1937), 10-11.

"Love's Parable, " *Kenyon Review,* II (Spring, 1940), 186-88.

"Crime, " *Nation,* CL (May 25, 1940), 655.

"Goodbye, " *American Prefaces,* VI (Winter, 1941), 113-14.

"Terror, " "Question and Answer, " *Poetry,* LVII (February, 1941), 288-89.

"Revelation, " *Poetry,* LIX (January, 1942), 202-3. Reprinted in *Angry Penguins* (Australia), September, 1943.

"Pursuit, " *Virginia Quarterly Review,* XVIII (Winter, 1942), 57-59.

"End of Season, " *Nation,* CLIV (March 7, 1942), 286.

"Original Sin: a Short Story, " *Kenyon Review,* IV (Spring, 1942), 179-80.

"Mexico is a Foreign Country, " *Poetry,* LXII (June, 1943), 121-27.

"The Ballad of Billie Potts, " *Partisan Review,* XI (Winter, 1944), 56-70.

Brother to Dragons (first half), *Kenyon Review,* XV (Winter, 1953), 1-103.

"The Lie" (Meriwether Lewis, from *Brother to Dragons),* *Poetry,* LXXXII (June, 1953), 125-32.

"To a Little Girl One Year Old, In Ruined Fortress, " "Sirocco, " "Gull's Cry, " "The Child Next Door, " "The Flower, " "Colder Fire, " *Partisan Review,* XXII (Spring, 1955), 171-78.

"Courtmartial, " "School Lesson Based on Word of Tragic Death of Entire Gillum Family, " "Walk by Moonlight in Small Town, " "Lullaby in Moonlight, " "Mad Young Aristocrat on Beach, " "Foreign Shore, Old Woman, Slaughter of Octopus, " "Dragon Country: to Jacob Boehme, " "Lullaby: A Motion Like Sleep, " "Necessity for Belief" (selections from *Promises),* *Yale Review,* XLVI (Spring, 1957), 321-40.

"Ballad of a Sweet Dream of Peace, " "And Don't Forget Your Corset-Cover, Either, " "Keepsakes, " "Go It, Granny—Go It, Hog!" "Friend of the Family, Or Bowling a Sticky Cricket, " "You Never Knew Her Either, Though You Thought You Did, Inside Out, " "I Guess You Ought to Know Who You Are, " "Rumor Unverified Stop Can You Confirm Stop" (selections from *Promises),* *Kenyon Review,* XIX (Winter, 1957), 31-36.

"Promises, to Gabriel (born, July 19th, 1955)": "What Was the Promise That Smiled from the Maples At Evening?" "Gold Glade, " "Dark Night Of, " "Country Burying: 1919, " "Summer Storm (Circa 1916) and God's Grace, " "Dark Woods, " "Founding Fathers, 19th Century Style, South-East U.S.A., " "Infant Boy at Midcentury, " "Lullaby, " *Encounter,* VIII (May, 1957), 3-14.

"Boy's Will, Joyful Labor Without Pay, and Harvest Home (1918)" (from *Promises),* *Botteghe Oscure,* XIX (Spring, 1957), 203-6.

"Two Pieces After Suetonius: Apology for Domitian, Tiberius on Capri, " *Partisan Review,* XXV (Spring, 1958), 223-25.

"Prognosis, " "And Oh—, " "What the Sand Said, " "What the Joree Said, " *Sewanee Review,* LXVI (Spring, 1958), 252-55.

"From *You, Emperors, and Others:* Garland for You: Poem, Three Nursery Rhymes: Knockety-Knockety-Knock, Little Boy Blue, Mother

Makes the Biscuits, Debate: Question, Quarry, Dream," *Yale Review*, XLVII (Summer, 1958), 494-99.

"Some Quiet, Plain Poems: 1. Ornithology in a World of Flux. 2. Holly and Hickory. 3. The Well-House. 4. In Moonlight, Somewhere, They Are Singing," *Saturday Review*, XLI (November 22, 1958), 37.

"Garland for You: 1. A Real Question Calling for Solution. 2. Lullaby: Exercise in Human Charity and Self-Knowledge. 3. The Letter About Money, Love, Or Other Comfort, if Any. 4. The Self that Stares," *Virginia Quarterly Review*, XXXV (Spring, 1959), 248-57.

"Nocturne: Traveling Salesman in Hotel Bedroom," *American Scholar*, XXVIII (Summer, 1959), 306-7.

"Two Poems: Nursery Rhyme, In Italian They Call the Bird *Civetta*," *Prairie Schooner*, XXXIV (Autumn, 1959), 244-45.

SELECTED BIBLIOGRAPHY

Aldridge, John.W. *In Search of Heresy*. New York: McGraw-Hill, 1956.

Allen,. Charles A. "Robert Penn Warren: the Psychology of Self-Knowledge," *Literature and Psychology*, VIII (Spring, 1958), 21-25.

Anderson, Charles R. "Violence and Order in the Novels of Robert Penn Warren," *Hopkins Review*, VI (Winter, 1953), 88-105. Reprinted in *Southern Renascence: The Literature of the Modern South*, ed. Louis D. Rubin, Jr. and Robert D. Jacobs. Baltimore: Johns Hopkins Press, 1953. Pp. 207-24.

Antonini, Giacomo. "Il mito della dignità umana. Penn Warren: Nostalgia per il vecchio Sud," *La fiera letteraria*, January 22, 1956, pp. 1-2.

--------. "Penn Warren e il primato dello stile," *La fiera letteraria*, January 12, 1955, pp. 5-6.

Baker, Joseph E. "Irony in Fiction: *All the King's Men*," *College English*, IX (December, 1947), 122-30.

Basso, Hamilton. "The Huey Long Legend," *Life*, XXI (December 9, 1946), 106-8, 110, 112, 115-16, 118, 121.

Bennett, John. The Iron Beach: A Study of the Poetry of Robert Penn Warren. M.A. Thesis, Vanderbilt University, 1948.

Bentley, Eric. *"All the King's Men,"* *Theatre Arts*, XXXI (November, 1947), 72-73.

--------. "The Meaning of Robert Penn Warren's Novels," *Kenyon Review*, X (Summer, 1948), 407-24.

Blonski, Jan. "Robert Penn Warren," *Tworczosc* (Warsaw) (March, 1956), pp. 164-67.

Blum, Morgan. "Promises as Fulfillment," *Kenyon Review*, XXI (Winter, 1959), 97-120. Review of *Promises*.

Bradbury, John M. *The Fugitives: A Critical Account*. Chapel Hill: University of North Carolina Press, 1958.

--------. "Robert Penn Warren's Novels: The Symbolic and Textural Patterns," *Accent*, XIII (Spring, 1953), 77-89.

Brantley, Frederick. "The Achievement of Robert Penn Warren, " in
    Modern American Poetry, ed. B. Rajan. London: Dennis Dobson Ltd.,
    1950. Pp. 66-80.
Breit, Harvey. "Talk with Mr. Warren, " *New York Times Book Re-
    view*, June 25, 1950, p. 20. Reprinted in *The Writer Observed*. New
    York: World Publishing Co., 1956. Pp. 131-33.
Brooks, Cleanth. *Modern Poetry and the Tradition*. Chapel Hill: Uni-
    versity of North Carolina Press, 1939.
Byrne, Clifford M. "The Philosophical Development in Four of Robert
    Penn Warren's Novels, " *McNeese Review*, IX (Winter, 1957), 56-58.
Campbell, Harry Modean. "Warren as Philosopher in *World Enough and
    Time*, " *Hopkins Review*, VI (Winter, 1953), 106-16. Reprinted in *South-
    ern Renascence: the Literature of the Modern South*, ed. Louis D.
    Rubin, Jr. and Robert D. Jacobs. Baltimore: Johns Hopkins Press,
    1953. Pp. 225-35.
Cargill, Oscar. "Anatomist of Monsters, " *College English*, IX (Octo-
    ber, 1947), 1-8.
Casper, Leonard. "The Founding Fathers, " *Western Review*, XXII (Au-
    tumn, 1957), 69-71. Review of *Promises*.
-------. Loss of the Sense of Community and the Role of the Artist in
    Robert Penn Warren. Ph. D. dissertation, University of Wisconsin,
    1953.
-------. "The New Criticism and Southern Agrarianism, " *Diliman Re-
    view* (Philippines), II (April, 1954), 136-49.
-------. "Robert Penn Warren: an Assessment, " *Diliman Review*, II
    (October, 1954), 400-24.
-------. "Robert Penn Warren: Method and Canon, " *Diliman Review*,
    II (July, 1954), 263-92.
Clark, Marden J. Symbolic Structure in the Novels of Robert Penn War-
    ren. Ph. D. dissertation, University of Washington, 1957.
Coleman, Thomas Emmett, Jr. Form as Function in the Novels of Robert
    Penn Warren. M. A. thesis, University of Louisville, 1950.
Cottrell, Beekman W. "Cass Mastern and the Awful Responsibility of
    Time, " in *All the King's Men: A Symposium*, ed. A. Fred Sochatoff
    et al. Pittsburgh: Carnegie Press, 1957. Pp. 39-49.
Cowan, Louise. *The Fugitive Group: A Literary History*. Baton Rouge:
    Louisiana State University Press, 1959.
Cowley, Malcolm. "Luke Lea's Empire, " *New Republic*, CIX (August
    23, 1943), 258. Review of *At Heaven's Gate*.
Craib, Roderick. "A Novel on Freedom, " *New Leader*, XXXVIII (Sep-
    tember 26, 1955), 24-25. Review of *Band of Angels*.
Curtiss, Mina. "Tragedy of a Liberal, " *Nation*, CXLVIII (April 29,
    1939), 507-8. Review of *Night Rider*.
Daniels, Jonathan. "Scraping the Bottom of Southern Life, " *Saturday
    Review of Literature*, XXVI (August 21, 1943), 6. Review of *At Heav-
    en's Gate*.

Davidson, Donald. "The Thankless Muse and Her Fugitive Poets," *Sewanee Review*, LXVI (Spring, 1958), 201-28.

Davis, Robert Gorham. "Dr. Stanton's Dilemma," *New York Times Book Review*, August 18, 1946, pp. 3, 24. Review of *All the King's Men*.

Deutsch, Babette. "Poetry Chronicle," *Yale Review*, XLIII (Winter, 1954), pp. 277-78. Review of *Brother to Dragons*.

-------. "Robert Penn Warren's Savage Poem: Old Murder, Modern Overtones," *New York Herald Tribune Book Review*, August 23, 1953, p. 3. Review of *Brother to Dragons*.

Dickey, James. "In the Presence of Anthologies," *Sewanee Review*, LXVI (Spring, 1958), 307-9. Review of *Promises*.

Dupee, F. W. "Robert Penn Warren and Others," *Nation*, CLIX (November 25, 1944), 660, 662. Review of *Selected Poems: 1923-1943*.

Ellison, Ralph, and Eugene Walter. "The Art of Fiction XVIII: Robert Penn Warren," *Paris Review*, IV (Spring-Summer, 1957), 112-40. Reprinted in *Writers at Work: The Paris Review Interviews*, ed. Malcolm Cowley. New York: Viking, 1958, pp. 183-207.

Fergusson, Francis. "Three Novels," *Perspectives U.S.A.*, VI (Winter, 1954), pp. 30-44. Review of *All the King's Men*.

Fiedler, Leslie A. "On Two Frontiers," *Partisan Review*, XVII (September-October, 1950), 739-43.

-------. "Romance in the Operatic Manner," *New Republic*, CXXXIII (September 26, 1955), 28-30. Review of *Band of Angels*.

-------. "Seneca in the Meat House," *Partisan Review*, XXI (March-April, 1954), 208-12. Review of *Brother to Dragons*.

Fitts, Dudley. "Of Tragic Stature," *Poetry*, LXV (November, 1944), 94-101. Review of *Selected Poems*.

-------. "A Power Reaffirmed," *New York Times Book Review*, August 18, 1957, pp. 6, 20. Review of *Promises*.

Fjelde, Rolf. "The Ruined Stone and the Sea-Reaches," *Poetry*, XCII (April, 1958), 49-52. Review of *Promises*.

Flint, F. Cudworth. "Five Poets," *Southern Review*, I (Winter, 1936), 650-74. Review of *Thirty-six Poems*.

-------. "Mr. Warren and the Reviewers," *Sewanee Review*, LXIV (Autumn, 1956), 632-45.

-------. "Poetic Accomplishment and Expectation," *Virginia Quarterly Review*, XXXIV (Winter, 1958), 118-19. Review of *Promises*.

-------. "Robert Penn Warren," *American Oxonian*, XXXIV (April, 1947), 67-79.

-------. "Search for a Meaning," *Virginia Quarterly Review*, XXX (Winter, 1954), 143-48. Review of *Brother to Dragons*.

Ford, Newell F. "Kenneth Burke and Robert Penn Warren: Criticism by Obsessive Metaphor," *Journal of English and Germanic Philology*, LIII (April, 1954), 172-77.

Forgotson, E. S. "The Poetic Method of Robert Penn Warren," *Ameri-*

can Prefaces, VI (Winter, 1941), 130-46.

Frank, Joseph. "Romanticism and Reality in Robert Penn Warren," *Hudson Review*, IV (Summer, 1951), 248-58.

Frank, William. "Warren's Achievement," *College English*, XIX (May, 1958), 365-66.

Frohock, W. M. "Mr. Warren's Albatross," *Southwest Review*, XXXVI (Winter, 1951), 48-59. Reprinted in *The Novel of Violence in America*. 2nd ed. Dallas: Southern Methodist University Press, 1957. Pp. 86-105.

Garrett, George Palmer. *The Georgia Review*, XII (Spring, 1958), 106-8. Review of *Promises*.

--------. "The Function of the Pasiphae Myth in *Brother to Dragons*," *Modern Language Notes*, LXXIV (April, 1959), 311-13.

Garrigue, Jean. "Many Ways of Evil," *Kenyon Review*, VI (Winter, 1944), 135-38. Review of *At Heaven's Gate*.

Geismar, Maxwell. "Agile Pen and Dry Mind," *Nation*, CLXXXI (October 1, 1955), 287. Review of *Band of Angels*.

Gerhard, George. *"All the King's Men*: A Symposium," *Folio*, XV (May, 1950), 4-11.

Girault, Norton R. "The Narrator's Mind as Symbol: an Analysis of *All the King's Men*," *Accent*, VII (Summer, 1947), 220-34.

Gordon, Clifford M. "Original Sin: A Short Story," *Explicator*, IX (December, 1950), 21.

Gregory, Horace. "Of Vitality, Regionalism, and Satire in Recent American Poetry," *Sewanee Review*, LII (Autumn, 1944), 572-93. Review of *Selected Poems*.

Gross, Seymour L. "The Achievement of Robert Penn Warren," *College English*, XIX (May, 1958), 361-65.

--------. "Conrad and *All the King's Men*," *Twentieth Century Literature*, III (April, 1957), 27-32.

--------. "Laurence Sterne and Eliot's 'Prufrock': an Object Lesson in Explication," *College English*, XIX (November, 1957), 72-73.

Hart, John A. "Some Major Images in *All the King's Men*," in *All the King's Men: A Symposium*, ed. A. Fred Sochatoff *et al*. Pittsburgh: Carnegie Press, 1957. Pp. 63-74.

Heilman, Robert B. "Melpomene as Wallflower; or, The Reading of Tragedy," *Sewanee Review*, LV (January-March 1947), 154-66.

--------. "The Tangled Web," *Sewanee Review*, LIX (Summer, 1951), 107-19.

Hendry, Irene. "The Regional Novel: the Example of Robert Penn Warren," *Sewanee Review*, LIII (Winter, 1945), 84-102.

Herschberger, Ruth. "Poised between the two alarms . . ." *Accent*, IV (Summer, 1944), 240-46. Review of *Selected Poems*.

Hoffman, Frederick J. *The Modern Novel in America, 1900-1950*. Chicago: Henry Regnery, 1951.

Hudson, Richard B. *"All the King's Men*: A Symposium," *Folio*, XV (May, 1950), 11-13.

Humboldt, Charles. "The Lost Cause of Robert Penn Warren," *Masses and Mainstream*, I (July, 1948), 8-20.

Hynes, Sam. The Poet as Dramatist: Robert Penn Warren and Some Predecessors. M.A. thesis, Columbia University, 1948.

-------. "Robert Penn Warren: The Symbolic Journey," *University of Kansas City Review*, XVII (Summer, 1951), 279-85.

Isherwood, Christopher. "Tragic Liberal," *New Republic*, LXXXXIX (May 31, 1939), 108. Review of *Night Rider*.

Janeway, Elizabeth. "Man in Conflict, Mind in Torment," *New York Times Book Review*, June 25, 1950, pp. 1, 22. Review of *World Enough and Time*.

Jarrell, Randall. "On the Underside of the Stone," *New York Times Book Review*, August 23, 1953, p. 6. Review of *Brother to Dragons*.

Jones, Ernest. "Through a Glass, Darkly," *Nation*, CLXXI (July 8, 1950), 42. Review of *World Enough and Time*.

Joost, Nicholas. "The Movement toward Fulfillment," *Commonweal*, LIX (December 4, 1953), 231-32. Review of *Brother to Dragons*.

-------. "'Was All For Naught?': Robert Penn Warren and New Directions in the Novel," in *Fifty Years of the American Novel—a Christian Appraisal*, ed. Harold C. Gardiner, S. J. New York: Scribner's, 1951. Pp. 273-91.

Kelvin, Norman. "The Failure of Robert Penn Warren," *College English*, XVIII (April, 1957), 355-64.

Kenner, Hugh. Omnibus review of poetry textbooks, *Poetry*, LXXXIV (April, 1954), 43-53. Review of *Understanding Poetry*.

-------. "Something Nasty in the Meat-House," *Hudson Review*, VI (Winter, 1954), 605-10. Review of *Brother to Dragons*.

King, Roma A., Jr. "Time and Structure in the Early Novels of Robert Penn Warren," *South Atlantic Quarterly*, LVI (Autumn, 1957), 486-93.

Kristol, Irving. "American Ghosts," *Encounter*, III (July, 1954), 73-75. Review of *Brother to Dragons*.

Lane, Calvin M. Narrative Art and History in Robert Penn Warren's *World Enough and Time*. Ph.D. dissertation, University of Michigan, 1956.

Létargeez, J. "Robert Penn Warren's Views of History," *Revue des langues vivantes*, XXII (1956), 533-43.

Linenthal, Mark, Jr. Robert Penn Warren and the Southern Agrarians. Ph.D. dissertation, Stanford University, 1957.

Lowell, Robert. "Prose Genius in Verse," *Kenyon Review*, XV (Autumn, 1953), 619-25. Review of *Brother to Dragons*.

MacDonald, William. *Nation*, CXXXI (July 2, 1930), 22-23. Review of *John Brown: Making of a Martyr*.

Magmer, James, S. J. "Robert Penn Warren's Quest for an Angel," *Catholic World*, CLXXXIII (June, 1956), 179-83.

Martin, Terence. "*Band of Angels:* The Definition of Self-Definition," *Folio*, XXI (Winter, 1956), 31-37.

Matthiessen, F. O. "American Poetry Now, " *Kenyon Review,* VI (Autumn, 1944), 683-96.

McCormick, John. "White Does and Dragons, " *Western Review,* XVIII (Winter, 1954), 163-67. Review of *Brother to Dragons.*

McDowell, Frederick P. W. "Psychology and Theme in *Brother to Dragons,* " *PMLA,* LXX (September, 1955), 565-86.

-------. "Robert Penn Warren's Criticism, " *Accent,* XV (Summer, 1955), 173-96.

-------. "The Romantic Tragedy of Self in *World Enough and Time,* " *Critique: Studies in Modern Fiction,* I (Summer, 1957), 34-49.

Mizener, Arthur. "Amphibium in Old Kentucky, " *Kenyon Review,* XII (Autumn, 1950), 697-701.

-------. "A Nature Divided Against Itself, " *New York Times Book Review,* August 21, 1955, pp. 1, 18. Review of *Band of Angels.*

Mohrt, Michel. "Robert Penn Warren and the Myth of the Outlaw, " *Yale French Studies,* No. 10 (1953), pp. 70-84, translation by Beth Brombert of "Robert Penn Warren ou le mythe du hors-la-loi, " *Le nouveau roman américain.* Paris: Gallimard, 1955. Pp. 207-23.

Nemerov, Howard. *"All the King's Men, " Furioso,* II (Fall, 1946), 69-71.

-------. "The Phoenix in the World, " *Furioso,* III (Spring, 1948), 36-46.

O'Connor, William Van. *An Age of Criticism: 1900-1950.* Chicago: Henry Regnery, 1951.

-------. "Robert Penn Warren: 'Provincial' Poet, " in *A Southern Vanguard: the John Peale Bishop Memorial Volume,* ed. Allen Tate. New York: Prentice-Hall, 1947. Pp. 92-99.

-------. "Robert Penn Warren's Short Fiction, " *Western Review,* XII (Summer, 1948), 251-53.

Olson, Elder. "A Symbolic Reading of the *Ancient Mariner,"* in *Critics and Criticism: Ancient and Modern,* ed. R. S. Crane. Chicago: University of Chicago Press, 1952. Pp. 138-44.

Phillips, William. "Coils of the Past, " *Nation,* CLVII (August 28, 1943), 243-44. Review of *At Heaven's Gate.*

Pulos, C. E. "Warren as Critic, " *Prairie Schooner,* XXXIII (Spring, 1959), 1-2. Review of *Selected Essays.*

Purdy, Rob Roy, ed. *Fugitives' Reunion: Conversations at Vanderbilt.* Nashville, Tenn.: Vanderbilt University Press, 1959.

Raben, Joseph. *"All the King's Men:* A Symposium, " *Folio,* XV (May, 1950), 14-18.

Raiziss, Sona. *The Metaphysical Passion: Seven Modern American Poets and the Seventeenth Century Tradition.* Philadelphia: University of Pennsylvania Press, 1952.

Ransom, John Crowe. *"All the King's Men:* A Symposium, " *Folio,* XV (May, 1950), 2-3.

-------. "The Inklings of 'Original Sin, '" *Saturday Review of Literature,*

XXVII (May 20, 1944), 10-11.

R. G. "Biographical Sketch, " *Saturday Review of Literature*, XXXIII (June 24, 1950), 12.

Ridgely, Joseph V. "Tragedy in Kentucky," *Hopkins Review*, IV (Autumn, 1950), 61-63. Review of *World Enough and Time*.

Rubin, Louis D., Jr. "All the King's Meanings," *Georgia Review*, VIII (Winter, 1954), 422-34.

————. "The Eye of Time: Religious Themes in Robert Penn Warren's Poetry," *Diliman Review*, IV (July, 1958), 215-37.

Ruoff, James. "Humpty Dumpty and *All the King's Men*: A Note on Robert Penn Warren's Teleology," *Twentieth Century Literature*, III (October, 1957), 128-34.

Satterwhite, Joseph N. "Robert Penn Warren and Emily Dickinson," *Modern Language Notes*, LXXI (May, 1956), 347-49.

Schutte, William M. "The Dramatic Versions of the Willie Stark Story," in *All the King's Men: A Symposium*, ed. A. Fred Sochatoff *et al*. Pittsburgh: Carnegie Press, 1957. Pp. 75-90.

Schwartz, Delmore. "The Dragon of Guilt," *New Republic*, CXXIX (September 14, 1953), 17-18. Review of *Brother to Dragons*.

Sillars, Malcolm O. "Warren's *All the King's Men*: A Study in Populism," *American Quarterly*, IX (Autumn, 1957), 345-53.

Skillin, Edward, Jr. "Mighty Like Despair," *Commonweal*, XXXVIII (August 6, 1943), 398.

Slack, Robert C. "The Telemachus Theme," in *All the King's Men: A Symposium*, ed. A. Fred Sochatoff *et al*. Pittsburgh: Carnegie Press, 1957. Pp. 29-38.

Sochatoff, A. Fred. "Some Treatments of the Huey Long Theme," in *All the King's Men: A Symposium*, ed. A. Fred Sochatoff *et al*. Pittsburgh: Carnegie Press, 1957. Pp. 3-15.

Southard, W. P. "The Religious Poetry of Robert Penn Warren," *Kenyon Review*, VII (Autumn, 1945), 653-76.

Southworth, James G. *More Modern American Poets*. Oxford: Basil Blackwell, 1954.

Stallknecht, Newton P. "*All the King's Men*: A Symposium," *Folio*, XV (May, 1950), 18-22.

Stallman, Robert. "Robert Penn Warren: A Checklist of His Critical Writings," *University of Kansas City Review*, XIV (Autumn, 1947), 78-83.

Steinberg, Erwin R. "The Enigma of Willie Stark," in *All the King's Men: A Symposium*, ed. A. Fred Sochatoff *et al*. Pittsburgh: Carnegie Press, 1957. Pp. 17-28.

Stewart, James T. "Two Uses of Maupassant," *Modern Language Notes*, LXX (April, 1955), 279-80.

Stewart, John L. "The Achievement of Robert Penn Warren," *South Atlantic Quarterly*, XLVII (October, 1948), 562-79.

————. The Fugitive-Agrarian Writers: A History and a Criticism.

Ph. D. dissertation, Ohio State University, 1947.

-------. "Robert Penn Warren and the Knot of History," *ELH*, XXVI (March, 1959), 102-36.

Tate, Allen. *"The Fugitive*, 1922-1925, " *Princeton University Library Chronicles*, III (April, 1942), 75-84.

Thale, Jerome. "The Narrator as Hero, " *Twentieth Century Literature*, III (July, 1957), 69-73.

Trilling, Diana. *Nation*, CLXIII (August 24, 1946), 220. Review of *All the King's Men*.

Tyler, Parker. "The Ambiguous Axe, " *Poetry*, LXXXIII (December, 1953), 169-71. Review of *Brother to Dragons*.

-------. "Novel into Film: *All the King's Men, " Kenyon Review*, XII (Spring, 1950), 369-76.

Virtanen, Reino. "Camus' *Le Malentendu* and Some Analogues, " *Comparative Literature*, X (Summer, 1958), 232-40.

Wagenknecht, Edward. *Cavalcade of the American Novel*. New York: Henry Holt and Co., 1952.

Wasserstrom, William. "Robert Penn Warren: From Paleface to Redskin, " *Prairie Schooner*, XXXI (Winter, 1957), 323-33.

-------. "Warren's New Poems, " *Prairie Schooner*, XXXII (Spring, 1958), 67-69. Review of *Promises*.

Watkins, Floyd C. "Billie Potts at the Fall of Time, " *Mississippi Quarterly*, XI (Winter, 1958), 19-29.

-------. "Thomas Wolfe and the Nashville Agrarians, " *Georgia Review*, VII (Winter, 1953), 410-23.

Welker, Robert. The Underlying Philosophy of Robert Penn Warren: A Study in the Poetic Attitude. M.A. Thesis, Vanderbilt University, 1952.

White, Robert. "Robert Penn Warren and the Myth of the Garden, " *Faulkner Studies*, III (Winter, 1954), 59-67.

Whittemore, Reed. "Five Old Masters and Their Sensibilities, " *Yale Review*, XLVII (Winter, 1958), 281-88. Review of *Promises*.

Wilson, Angus. "The Fires of Violence, " *Encounter*, IV (May, 1955), 75-78. Review of *Night Rider*.

Woodruff, Neal, Jr. "The Technique of *All the King's Men, "* in *All the King's Men: A Symposium*, ed. A. Fred Sochatoff *et al*. Pittsburgh: Carnegie Press, 1957. Pp. 51-62.

Zabel, Morton D. "Problems of Knowledge, " *Poetry*, XLVIII (April, 1936), 37-41. Review of *Thirty-six Poems*.

INDEX

Agrarianism, xi, 6, 21-22, 24-
32, 36-37, 45, 53, 78, 93-94,
148, 168-69, 174-75, 177, 184n
Aldridge, John W., viii, xi
American Review, 30, 43-44,
46, 54
Anderson, Charles, x
Anderson, Sherwood, 40-41, 100
Arnold, Matthew, 37, 42
Avant garde, 15-16

Barr, Stringfellow, 26
Basso, Hamilton, viii, xiii, 132
Beach, Joseph Warren, viii
Belloc, Hilaire, 26, 29, 43
Bentley, Eric, xvi, 116
Bogan, Louise, ix
Bowie, Jim, 11, 80
Bradbury, John M., ix
Brantley, Frederick, xi-xii
Brooks, Cleanth, ix, 14, 22-23,
29-31, 36, 38, 46, 172-73,
175, 184n

Campbell, Harry Modean, x
Christianity, xi, 19, 21, 23, 30,
50, 96, 129, 162
Coleridge, Samuel Taylor, ix,
20, 22, 49-50, 53, 75, 121,
167, 173, 189n
Communism, 26, 40, 43-44
Conrad, Joseph, xiii, 9, 52-53,
55, 80-81, 104, 127, 137, 173,
176
Cowie, Alexander, viii
Cowley, Malcolm, 50, 113
Crane, Hart, 6, 57

Dante, 107, 128, 172
Davidson, Donald, 14, 27-28, 31,
41, 56, 184n
Davis, Robert Gorham, 184n
Dewey, John, 5, 20, 22, 27, 40,
177
Distributism, 26, 29, 43

Eliot, T. S., ix, xii, 13, 16, 18,
20-22, 46-47, 61, 172, 175, 177,
187n

Fascism, 5, 43-44, 68, 101, 104,
116, 133, 185n
Faulkner, William, viii, xi-xii,
xiv, 6, 32, 39, 42, 50-51, 53,
64, 173, 176
Fergusson, Francis, xii
Fitts, Dudley, xii
Fletcher, John Gould, 41
Flint, F. Cudworth, xvi
Forgotson, E. S., xii
Frohock, W. M., ix
Frost, Robert, 52-53
Fugitives, xi, 13-14, 16, 19, 24-
26, 40, 56-58, 84, 86, 184n

Garrett, George P., xi
Geismar, Maxwell, viii
Girault, Norton, xvi
Gordon, Caroline, 6, 39, 93
Gregory, Horace, xi
Gross, Seymour L., xiii

Hamlet, xii, 140
Hawthorne, Nathaniel, 40, 159,
188n